NEWS AND CIVIL SOCIETY

T0361862

News and Civil Society
The Contested Space of Civil Society in UK Media

JEN BIRKS
University of Nottingham, UK

Routledge
Taylor & Francis Group

LONDON AND NEW YORK

First published 2014 by Ashgate Publishing

2 Park Square, Milton Park, Abingdon, Oxfordshire OX14 4RN
52 Vanderbilt Avenue, New York, NY 10017

Routledge is an imprint of the Taylor & Francis Group, an informa business

First issued in paperback 2020

Copyright © 2014 Jen Birks

Jen Birks has asserted her right under the Copyright, Designs and Patents Act, 1988, to be identified as the author of this work.

All rights reserved. No part of this book may be reprinted or reproduced or utilised in any form or by any electronic, mechanical, or other means, now known or hereafter invented, including photocopying and recording, or in any information storage or retrieval system, without permission in writing from the publishers.

Notice:
Product or corporate names may be trademarks or registered trademarks, and are used only for identification and explanation without intent to infringe.

British Library Cataloguing in Publication Data
A catalogue record for this book is available from the British Library

The Library of Congress has cataloged the printed edition as follows:
Birks, Jen.
  News and civil society : the contested space of civil society in UK media / by Jen Birks.
    pages cm
  Includes bibliographical references and index.
  ISBN   978-1-4094-3615-7   (hardback)
  1. Civil society—Great Britain. 2. Mass media—Great Britain. 3. Law enforcement—Great Britain. I. Title.
  JC337.B57 2013
  300.941—dc23
                                                                          2013011975

ISBN 978-1-4094-3615-7 (hbk)
ISBN 978-0-367-60099-0 (pbk)

Contents

List of Tables

Acknowledgments

I am indebted to the Leverhulme Trust for their generous funding of this project, and to colleagues at the University of Stirling for their support throughout – not least to Neil Blain for sage advice, unstinting encouragement, and coffee meetings that always turn into boozy lunches. I am also grateful to my editor, Neil Jordan, for invaluable guidance and patience with missed deadlines.

There are very many people to whom I owe thanks, and apologies to those not mentioned here. For erudite feedback on work in progress and stimulating debate at various conferences, I must thank Michael Higgins, Stuart Price, Mick Temple, Heather Savigny, Alec Charles, and John Downey. My friends in Glasgow got me through some very tough times over the course of writing this book, and I can't thank them enough for their kindness and fabulous company, especially Natasha Augustus, Sarah Neely, Kirsteen Paton, Alanna Burns, Campbell Mitchell, Craig Whitehill, Martin Cloonan, and David Archibald. In Nottingham, special thanks go to Eva Giraud for keeping me sane, and by no means least, Seb Roshlau for keeping me going through the final stages with the very finest kedgeree and pancakes. My deepest thanks of course go to my parents, Gill and Alan Birks, and my siblings Kate and Ste, whose support I have always been able to rely on.

Chapter 1

Introduction

Civil society is a term that has enjoyed periodic renaissance, often at times of significant social change. John Keane published his key defining text (in two volumes) in 1988, on the cusp of the revolutions in Eastern Europe that precipitated the fall of Communism. Mary Kaldor wrote her examination of *Global Civil Society* as "an answer to war" (2003) in the aftermath of 9/11. Following the events of Tahir Square and the 'Arab Spring', the Indignados of the Spanish 15M movement, and the global Occupy movement, and also the anti-austerity riots in Greece and elsewhere, theorists such as Hardt and Negri (2011), Badiou (2012), and Castells (2012) have already put forward their analyses. But Keane (1998) asserted that his interest in the topic was motivated by a concern for how the concept could be useful in mature democracies, not only emerging ones.

And so to less dramatic beginnings. During campaigning for the 2010 UK general election, the Liberal Democrats included civil liberties in their manifesto, whilst the Conservative Party launched their Big Society idea. The two seemed to reflect different understandings of civil society – the first about the freedom to dissent and the power to hold politicians to account, and the second about the responsibility of communities for their own welfare. After the coalition was formed between the two parties, the Liberal Democrat leader tried to argue that there was no ideological difference:

> What I'm discovering – I'm sure the Prime Minister will feel the same – is that we've been using different words for a long time and actually mean the same thing. 'Liberalism': 'Big Society'. 'Empowerment': 'Responsibility'. It means the same thing. (Nick Clegg, speaking at Big Society launch, 18 May 2010[1])

Together the two aspects recalled Blair's 'rights and responsibilities' discourse, inspired by the 'new' or 'responsive' communitarianism of Amitai Eztioni, which seeks to instil civic virtue through social expectation rather than democratic agreement. In any case, the public response to austerity measures that were in neither manifesto has not been to pitch in to the space vacated by the retreating state, by volunteering to keep the library open or running the local school, but to strike, march, protest and occupy.

Meanwhile, among the few concrete examples of autonomous organisations providing public services, the Catholic Church has faced legal challenges to its

---

1   Available from: http://www.dpm.cabinetoffice.gov.uk/news/pm-and-deputy-pm%E2%80%99s-speeches-big-society-launch.

public exercise of religious values. Equality legislation that required adoption agencies to consider same-sex couples as prospective parents resulted in the closure of Catholic agencies that could not countenance going against the teaching of the church. The precise definition of tolerance – as the central value of civil society – has thus been contested over the ground of identity politics, and especially the competing rights claims of religious and LGBT groups. This prompts questions about how we distinguish between public and private, and how we understand the role of values in democracy in general and contested politics in particular, including the notion that political debate is in itself uncivil due to this often fierce contestation.

Academic theorising offers a range of definitions, normative models, and determinations of legitimacy, some of which filter through to some extent into public consciousness, especially through the news media. So, of interest here is how the models of civil society promoted by political leaders and other figures of authority are reproduced, debated, and challenged, with particular attention to the sources of dissent from civil society itself.

Research questions

This book is, centrally, an enquiry into the popular definition of civil society in news reporting, and in particular how legitimacy is determined. This includes the various boundaries of inclusion and exclusion (of associations and activities) between the realm of civil society and the business of the political system and the market, and the paths of influence between them. It also encompasses the distinctions drawn between public and private, and how civil society straddles the two realms; for instance to bring privately experienced problems to public attention, to argue for private interests as related to the public interest, to argue that the private is political.

The principal aim of exploring these definitions is to examine the associated criteria of legitimacy across various legitimating structures in legal, moral, political, social and cultural terms. The research will explore the extent to which news media reporting on civil society reflects the contested nature of the concept, and whether some normative understandings of civil society are excluded or delegitimised.

Structure of the book

The various dimensions of legitimacy in civil society in the different normative models will be set out in the next chapter, starting with definitions and boundaries, and then outlining the ways in which civil society is theorised under four headings that correspond with the four analytical chapters.

The first of these is 'the good society' – the values that are promoted or appealed to as defining a shared notion of the common good, and that underpin publicly-minded social and political participation. These values are understood to originate in various different sources, including traditional moral authority (such as the church), national attachments and sentiments, democratically-agreed statutes (such as human rights), and personal conscience. Although virtues and vices are clearly distinguished, and most would agree on virtues in the abstract (kindness, honesty, courage, fortitude), with a few exceptions (greed is good, equality is disincentivising), there is far less agreement on their interpretation and application. For instance, an appeal to fairness will rarely straightforwardly resolve a dispute, simply because the parties will have a different interpretation of what is fair.

We are not given to offering reasons for our values, which are often inherited or learned and held intuitively, but in as far as this is possible at all, it comes down to different conceptions of liberty, and in particular, an emphasis on negative or positive liberties as most defining the human condition. Chapter 4 therefore analyses the news-framing of various claims that locate civic virtue or moral sentiment in either religious instruction or individual pursuit of utility (both claiming freedom from state regulation of virtue) and in democratically agreed standards of justice (enforced via state regulation).

Secondly, these freedoms, rights and responsibilities are encoded into law, including that which circumscribes legitimate behaviour and action in civil society. Repertoires of dissent and protest are legally constrained and delegitimised in various ways, especially 'disorder' and 'violence', including property damage and behaviour that could be perceived as unruly or threatening. The activities of trade unions are also subject to industrial law, and civil action is increasingly used to end, prevent or deter action such as occupation. Public order policing, however, once framed as uncontroversially legitimate as the force of law and order against destabilising elements, is increasingly subject to scrutiny, not least in the wake of the death of Ian Tomlinson at the 2009 G20 protest in London. However, the most controversial ground in the policing of protest is the increasing use of surveillance to monitor peaceful protest. Chapter 5 explores the ways in which the boundaries between legitimate protest and legitimate public order policing are represented, including the use of civil disobedience as a moral justification for law-breaking.

Thirdly, in as far as civil society is understood to have a political role, the legitimacy of organisations, associations and movements is judged in terms of both their internal democracy and their external communication. The decision-making structures within civil society vary, with trade unions obliged to reproduce the mechanisms of representative democracy, and more peripheral movements challenging the legitimacy of that model and experimenting with radical forms of direct, participatory and deliberative democracy. Whilst communicative legitimacy is most commonly defined in terms of rational argumentation and deliberation, the ways in which that is understood in practical terms, in relation to advocacy, rhetoric, values, and interests, is more complex and contradictory. For those who see the deliberative public sphere as an unattainable ideal, the imperative is to find forms of communication that can cut through the ubiquitous commercial messages of the screen age, requiring more spectacular and performative strategies. Chapter 6 addresses the inconsistent and strategic invocation of these legitimating criteria, especially as regards the connection between the private and public spheres.

Finally, legitimacy is accorded by the broader society in the form of public opinion, and judged in relation to mainstream norms and expectations. Judgements are attributed to the public, not only on the legal and political legitimacy discussed in previous chapters, but also on participants' acceptability as individuals in relation to an expected level of social conformity, including personal appearance, manners, and fulfilment of social duties. Individuals' personal legitimacy is also judged on the basis of their political sincerity and emotional authenticity. Chapter 7, then, examines the construction of public opinion via polls, vox pop interviews with bystanders, letters to the editor, and in unsubstantiated claims about the public, analyses the legitimacy of emotion in personal and political terms, and interrogates the extent to which public space is understood as social rather than a political arena.

Chapter 2

Theorising Legitimacy in Civil Society and the Media

Civil society is a normative project; a shared aspiration; a set of liberties, principles, and practices; and a site variously of self-interested exchange, altruistic cooperation, rational deliberation, radical dissent and symbolic performance. It implies a range of conflicting values and criteria of legitimacy that are circulated, reinforced and contested in news media. This chapter will set out the four themes addressed in the book: the good society, dissent and civil rights, democratic participation, and civility and offence, and will explore the debates around the legal, moral, political, and social legitimacy of civil society according to different models of society. The following chapters will then examine the range of and comparative emphasis on these understandings in coverage of key news stories about civil society organisations, associations, and movements. First the lines of dispute around the definition of the concept will be outlined.

Defining civil society

The one point of agreement within the literature on civil society is that there is no agreement on a definition of civil society. All that could be universally agreed is perhaps *the autonomous realm between private life and system(s) of power*, which is rather limited in its descriptive power and throws up more questions than answers. If it is not private in terms of the domestic sphere, is it public? How is systemic power defined – as the state or the market, or both? What is the role of civil society, and what form does it take?

In descriptive terms, civil society is generally taken to mean social, voluntary, and political associations, although different models place emphasis on certain of those specific categories of association, and exclude others. To complicate matters further, the term is also used more broadly to refer to the moral/ethical aspirations of society (the 'good') and accepted mechanisms for reaching agreement (institutions and procedures, including the public sphere). These aspects are often distinguished as separate, but are also interrelated.

Civil society is related to citizenship, especially in terms of the cultivation of civility or civic virtues such as trust, open-mindedness and cooperation. However, citizenship refers to individuals' relationship with the state, whilst civil society includes the agency of groups, associations and even, for some, corporations (Perez-Diaz 1995, Whitehouse 2005). Furthermore, citizenship includes individuals' duties to the state in return for the rights conferred by membership of the nation-state (such as payment of taxes, abiding by the rule of law, and to some extent voting), whilst civil society doesn't (necessarily) have such an instrumental relationship to the state, and needn't involve political participation in this formal sense. In fact, civil society is such a highly contested term that there is no agreement on whether it is a political entity at all, whether it makes demands on the state or defends against them, what values it needs or produces, and in short how its legitimacy is defined.

Models of civil society

The various different ways of understanding civil society have been most clearly delineated by Mary Kaldor (2003), who outlined five models of civil society, all "both normative and descriptive" (2003: 11), though the 'real world' description may not live up to the normative ideal. Two are historical versions: *societas civilis* and *Bürgerliche Gesellschaft,* and three are contemporary: neo-liberal, activist, and postmodern.

Societas civilis is the earliest notion of civil society, and the source of the notion of civil society as a goal, with 'civil' used as a normative descriptor – a society that *is* civil. A civil society is one characterised by peaceful stability as distinct from violent unrest, regardless of how democratic that stability is; indeed, Elias (1969) connected the civilising process with clientalism, deference, and etiquette as instruments of prestige and power (see also Silver 1997: 51). In particular, this rests on the rule of law in governing relations between individuals, requiring the state to hold the public monopoly on legitimate violence. This definition is akin to the contemporary notion of the 'good society', though it is a more limited ideal than the range of values now asserted as 'civilised' (democracy, equality, tolerance, and so on), and this is now considered only one aspect of civil society.

Bürgerliche Gesellschaft, or bourgeois society, emerged with the rise of the modern nation as a mass society, democratic governance, and capitalist economic relations. This model was theoretically informed by the philosophers of the Scottish Enlightenment, for whom individual freedom was exercised through the market, which operated as a limit on state power. Civil society was therefore defined as including the market, but distinct from the state, and concerned with the balance between the two. Marx also understood civil society in these terms and therefore rejected it as expressive of bourgeois individualism and the exercise of capitalist power, whilst Gramsci argued that civil society was not intrinsically connected to hegemonic power and could be the site of challenge to state domination as a form of counter-hegemony (Powell 2007). Jürgen Habermas' (1989 [1963]) view of *Bürgerliche Gesellschaft* focused instead on individuals' freedom in relation to the democratic process – as the freedom to form a political will and hold state authorities accountable – an arguably idealised view of the fruits of modernity (Curran 1993, Keane 1998) that he argued had since been lost through the refeudalisation of this bourgeois public sphere.

Of the contemporary versions, the neo-liberal model has the clearest inheritance from the bourgeois society, defining individual freedom in terms of voluntary relations in the free market. However, it is a more emphatically libertarian approach that focuses on negative liberty, the absence of constraint – it "might be described as 'laissez-faire politics', a kind of market in politics" (Kaldor 2003: 9) – although the coherence of 'neo-liberalism' as a term used to describe a political (as opposed to purely economic) perspective has been questioned (Thorsen and Lie 2010). In this model, civil society is descriptively limited to 'third sector' organisations – charitable and not-for-profit organisations – as a substitute for the state, in particular state welfare, but also public services. This is often characterised as a 'neo-Tocquevillian' approach (Powell 2007: vii), as for Tocqueville civil society included the pursuit of individuals' "private economic interests" ('civil association'), as well as the cooperative projects of groups ('political association'), with both being oriented toward self-sufficiency (Bryant 1995: 143). For Tocqueville and his inheritors, virtue in society is generated by the very activity of association, especially by breeding trust and a cooperative disposition. However, critics argue that this is not borne out by the evidence, given that not all associations display these values, and it also ignores power disparities that may be exacerbated by blindly or indiscriminately trusting relationships (Edwards 2009). The neo-liberal model is, however, unconcerned with inequalities in power and resources, and their implications for the inclusiveness of quasi-market regulated pluralism.

The activist model, in contrast, focuses on what could be termed the 'public autonomy' of political access, engagement and participation – collective self-determination, over and above the 'private autonomy' of negative liberties (Baynes 2002: 20), building on Habermas' interpretation of the *Bürgerliche Gesellschaft* in terms of an emerging public sphere. The central participants in this model of civil society are those that engage in political participation outside of the formal political system, such as advocacy and protest groups and social movements, and also, for some proponents of the model, interest and identity groups, but only those who are "civic-minded or public-spirited" (Kaldor 2003: 10). It involves demands for a redistribution of power to accommodate political self-organisation and pressure, as opposed to, in the neo-liberal model, a redistribution to markets and consumer. More particularly, political demands should ideally emerge through the deliberative ideal of disinterested rational debate (Habermas 1996), advancing "subordinated needs" (Kenny 2004: 70) through emancipatory networks of social engagement (Cohen and Arato 1992) that employ public reason (Rawls 2001). For Powell (2007), this includes securing and maintaining humanistic goals associated with welfare and human rights. However, this model struggles to account convincingly for a democratically legitimate consensus on the values and goals of society. In particular, it is difficult to see how this can be achieved through detached and rational debate (Baynes 2002).

The postmodern model of civil society is defined more clearly in terms of what it is *not* than what it *is*. In particular, it opposes the liberal universalism of the neo-liberal and activist versions, and the illusion of value consensus. Instead it conceives of civil society as a more antagonistic domain "of pluralism and contestation, a source of incivility as well as civility" (Kaldor 2003: 9). Kaldor argues that postmodernists accommodate nationalists and religious fundamentalists among the multiple identities that are "a precondition for civil society" (2003: 10), although postmodernism itself rejects the nation-state as a modernist project and religions as grand narratives, and, as she acknowledges, the only theorist identified as a proponent of this model, John Keane, rejects cultural relativism and mandates tolerance as a universal (1998). Powell argues that since civil society is a product of modernity, postmodernity poses challenges, especially to the nation and connectedly to the welfare state and the very idea of progress (Powell 2007: vii–1). In particular, he argues that it effectively "represents a triumphant neo-liberalism" as it heralds the end of the subject as "a moral and political actor" (Powell 2007: 19). The main defining characteristic of the postmodern model, however, is its inclusion of other non-liberal models of society such as multiculturalism and communalism or communitarianism.

Multiculturalism and the politics of identity are often interpreted as a threat to liberal principles, and contemporary politics as a battleground between hubristic liberalism and militant pluralism, but some liberal scholars such as Michael Kenny (2004) make a less polarised distinction. He sees strong continuities between the traditional politics of interests and ideologies and the politics of identity, and certainly there are apparent overlaps between identity politics and Kaldor's activist model of civil society, in particular, emancipatory movements such as women's and gay liberation. However, feminist perspectives do present a challenge to liberal definitions of the public/private divide, and identity-based militancy is matched by a neo-conservative backlash against their claims for both recognition and rights, increasingly through the counter-assertion of competing rights claims for traditional (dominant) culture. Nonetheless, liberal theories increasingly try to accommodate the less insular and defensive forms of identity politics, and acknowledge the validity of moral controversies in public debate. However, even those liberals willing to incorporate voluntary identifications exclude ascribed and oppressive communal identities (Kenny 2004).

Communal and communitarian forms of society prioritise the community over the individual, which liberals criticise as undemocratic and potentially oppressive. However, Etzioni (2004) distinguishes his 'new' or 'responsive' communitarianism as advocating community moral codes in the context of contemporary Western societies characterised by voluntary attachment, and argues that decisions ultimately rest with the individual. In fact, he argues that social pressure is less coercive than state control, though he fails to recognise that legislation is democratically agreed, unlike community expressions of a republican 'general will'.

It is apparent that the different models propose different roles for civil society. In the activist model, civil society takes a political role in holding power to account, engaging in debate to forge and communicate public opinion. The neo-liberal model emphasises an economic role in terms of charity and social enterprise replacing the state provision of services. Both include a moral-social element in terms of virtuous dispositions to cooperation (whether through political debate and deliberation or reciprocal market relations), but it is communitarian thought that really prioritises this role for (civil) society. These differences are particularly apparent in the ways that the different models conceptualise civil society in relation to the decision-making and governance of the political system, market-based relations and the private realm of the domestic, intimate, or particularistic.

Contested boundaries between civil society and the state, market, and private realm

The Scottish Enlightenment notion of civil society focused on market relations as enabling the autonomous self-organisation of individuals without the need for central control, which was limited to securing negative liberties and private property rights. The emergence of social liberalism and social democracy, culminating in the welfare state and civil rights movements, shifted the emphasis toward *positive* freedoms that took more account of the effects of inequalities in resources on the ability to exercise personal autonomy, and changed the relationship of civil society to the state to one of making demands on political society in the interests of social justice. More recently, the globalisation of capital and the parallel development of global civil society have challenged the notion of civil society and the public sphere as connected to the nation-state (Kaldor 2003, Fraser 2007), and on the other hand, the growth of the politics of identity and recognition have introduced the personal into the public sphere. Not only is there disagreement on the inclusion or otherwise of the market and private realm, and the nature of the relationship with the state, but there are also grey areas between the various realms.

The boundary with the state
The grey area between civil society and the state includes parliament, political parties, QUANGOs (quasi-autonomous non-governmental organisations), and political organisations. From an activist perspective, Cohen and Arato (1992) argue that 'political society' – parties and parliament – mediates between civil society and the state, but is rooted in the former. Habermas' (1996) account of public sphere deliberation similarly defines political society as the more accessible part of the core of decision-making, with civil society close to the periphery. The emphasis is therefore on the influence brought to bear on legislative processes by autonomous actors in civil society via deliberative political participation.

> What is meant by "civil society" today, in contrast to its usage in the Marxist tradition, no longer includes the economy as constituted by private law and steered through markets in labor, capital and commodities. Rather, its institutional core comprises those nongovernmental and non-economic connections and voluntary associations that anchor the communication structures of the public

sphere in the society component of the lifeworld. Civil society is composed of those more or less spontaneously emergent associations, organisations, and movements that, attuned to how societal problems resonate in the private life spheres, distil and transmit such reactions in amplified form to the public sphere. (Habermas 1996: 366–7)

However, is it notable that the role of civil society is one of raising problems, not advocating or debating solutions, which occurs in the more 'prominent' elements of the public sphere, principally the media, which might be regarded as a rather limited scope for political engagement. Others suggest a more actively political role: Powell (2007) argues that civil society represents "'strong' (participatory) democracy in contrast to the 'thin' (representative) democracy that characterises the age we live in" (2007: 4), but he defines this in Rousseauian civic republicanism terms rather than deliberative democracy as favoured by and Cohen and Arato (1992).

In contrast, the neo-liberal model regards the political system as a corrupting influence on the independence of associations. In the US especially, this is seen in Kantian terms as endangering their non-partisan character and orientation to the common good or public interest (Edwards 2009), but that is to assume an uncontroversial understanding of the goals of the good society. The neo-liberal conception of the good is defined in economic and instrumental terms, with faith in Adam Smith's 'invisible hand' – of market efficiency producing wealth and consumer choice directing it toward useful outcomes. Therefore political representations that press other claims are associated with state interference in the functioning of this mechanism of consumer autonomy.

Well-meant, sensible governmental attempts at policies to reduce suffering and social misery have regularly been put to the service of building up extraordinary concentrations of political and economic power which, in turn, have distorted the functioning of the markets and abused governments' regulatory and administrative powers under cover of pursuing (though in fact at the expense of) the common welfare. (Perez-Diaz 1995: 84)

Perez-Diaz asserts that the welfare state has shifted the character of civil society from "civil association" (drawing on Tocqueville's definition), where associations do not have collective goals but impose some order on individuals' pursuit of their personal goals, toward "association as enterprise", where associations require members to contribute to and make sacrifices for common goals. Instead of allowing people to determine their own local needs and cooperate freely to achieve them, state intervention is argued to underestimate and undermine individuals' agency (Perez-Diaz 1995: 99).

Of course this rhetoric conceals an underlying ideology of individualism and lack of concern with power and social justice. Nonetheless, it could be argued that there is a danger of state 'capture' of certain associations by government departments, especially through reliance for funding (Edwards 2009), for instance some Islamic groups are co-opted, others maligned or proscribed, and still others ignored. Conversely, the state could be excessively influenced by more powerful associations through private lobbying. This can be exacerbated by formal procedures of political engagement with civil society such as consultation and civic forums, even if the intention is rather to compensate for inequalities in power, partly because some groups *choose* to be outsider groups and appeal to public support rather than conform to the strictures of being an insider group (Grant 2000, Schlesinger et al. 2001).

Communitarians concur with the neo-liberal argument that the coercive power of the state cannot impose virtue. Etzioni equates politics with a "state related or mitigated" existence (2004: 148) that undermines agency in society, as opposed to with democratic participation and dissent. When he argues that communitarianism is consistent with liberal principles, it is the negative freedom emphasised by neo-liberalism that he appeals to, on the basis that the "basically voluntaristic nature of the moral voice is the reason the good society can, to a large extent, be reconciled with liberty, while a state that fosters good on a wide front cannot" (2004: 154). However, Etzioni makes little mention of the market, and understands 'natural' cooperation in society as social and moral rather than *either* political or through market exchange. He is critical of "libertarians" and "neoclassical economics" for their atomising individualism, but rather than seeing positive rights as entailing duties that *constrain* that self-interested individualism, he argues that dominant discourse focuses on rights *without* emphasising responsibilities, which breeds a culture of instrumentalism and entitlement.[1]

Powell (2007) offers a response to the neo-liberal and communitarian critique of state interventionism as authoritarian. He distinguishes between the "socialisation of the state" and the "statisation of society" – the former being welfare and social reform, whilst the latter is the authoritarian intervention of the state into the private or social domain. Neo-conservatives or social conservatives, conversely, see the former as the 'nanny state' and the latter as legitimate law and order, for example, anti-social or criminal behaviour orders. Bryant argues that the sociological definition of civil society seeks "to find a middle way between 'unbridled individualism' and 'the atomisation of competitive market society' on the one hand, and 'a state-dominated existence' on the other" (1995: 144). There is a balance to be struck between on the one hand state governance of interactions to support equal relations within pluralistic civil society, and on the other negative liberty securing free self-expression and pursuit of personal goals. Keane (1998: 9) similarly argues that we must steer between "state-without-society" and "society-without-state", but adds that there is no zero-sum relationship between state and society, so an increase in state intervention does not necessarily harm the autonomy of civil society.

---

1   Etzioni was the inspiration behind Tony Blair's mantra of 'rights and responsibilities' as part of his respect agenda whilst Prime Minister (Etzioni 2000).

The boundary with the market

The 'not-for-profit' sector of the economy is the principal grey area between civil society and the market. This includes cooperatives and mutuals such as credit unions, social enterprise such as the Big Issue or Jamie Oliver's restaurant Fifteen, and the more egoistic and less democratic philanthrocapitalism, such as the Bill and Melinda Gates Foundation. Powell praises the "social economy" of credit unions and cooperatives as part of a tradition of mutualism that originated in utopian thinkers of the 18th century (2007: 43), and Victorian "social reformers" who laid the groundwork for the welfare state (2007: 50), but he is more critical of philanthropy as "domestic colonialism" (2007: 49) and contemporary US voluntarism (2007: 54) as egoistic and a mere safety net for unfettered capitalism.

However, for Perez-Diaz (1995), charity and voluntary work illustrate that instrumental self-interest is not inimical to market-based civil society, and associations can be "egoistical" or "altruistic" or a combination of the two. He defines associational life in market terms, as "the morals of economic markets, and of the quasi-markets of voluntary associations and conversational communities", distorted by the state (as discussed above). The market is advanced by neo-liberals as the most effective way of limiting the state to its (Kantian) liberal democratic role as a neutral mechanism for achieving uncoercive agreement between free, self-interested individuals, with no role for public virtue, which is associated instead with illiberal communitarianism. However, critics have noted that this is in itself a value position, favouring individualism, tolerance and associated rights over other notions of 'the good'. Essentially, market logics crowd out other virtues such as justice and equality.

The activist model of civil society challenges the neo-liberal assumption that the market neutrally facilitates reciprocal exchange between free agents and introduces a concern with power, resource, and opportunity. However, it is not necessarily an anti-capitalist position, and broadly socially progressive scholars are often ambivalent about the wealth creation role of markets. For Edwards (2009) and Keane (1998) there is a co-dependence between civil society and economic power – business is dependent on civil society for trust, and civil society is dependent on "the surplus that market economies create" (Edwards 2009: 59) to fund the social demands of progressive movements. However, Edwards does argue that unregulated corporate power serves its own interests rather than the public interest, necessitating corporate social responsibility and accountability. Whether this social responsibility implies the inclusion of the market in the definition of civil society is also, however, a matter of debate.

Keane (1998: 17) argues that excluding the economic realm would make civil society a passive concept, as it would be lacking the resources that bring power. He argues that this would imply that trade unions should be excluded from a definition of civil society, even where their activities are aimed at broad civil liberties such as anti-racism (rather than sectional economic interests). This seems to suggest that exclusion of the market from the definition of civil society means the exclusion of all arguments over resources, which confuses the inclusion of the market *in* civil society with demands placed *on* the market *by* civil society. Whitehouse (2005) takes a slightly different approach, arguing that global corporations should be brought into the realm of global civil society because their power as global actors has a greater influence over conditions than any other. Rather than merely demanding corporate social responsibility, this would develop "corporate citizenship" by encouraging them to reject the systemic logic of neo-liberal capitalism. On the whole, the *relationship* between market forces and the social needs expressed through civil society is more important than the definition of the precise *boundary* between them, though the boundary is used to legitimise approaches to that relationship.

Civil society and the public/private divide
The different understandings of the boundaries between civil society, state and market also imply different interpretations of the public/private divide and the location of civil society in either the private or public sphere, or straddling both. Again, this is related to the advent of modernity, as under feudalism there was, arguably, no meaningful distinction between public and private since personal relationships were bound up with formal obligations (Weintraub 1997: 13). Whilst Keane (1998) points out that Elias (1969) identified a pre-modern notion of privacy, it was limited to courtly behaviour – civility, in terms of codes of proper conduct, included the social expectation that some behaviour would be conducted only in private. This is the distinction of *sociatas civilis* – the rules of peaceful and respectful coexistence, and associated notions of etiquette and shame.

The *liberal* distinction between public and private, traced back to the 18th century and especially to the Scottish Enlightenment, is regarded as central to the liberation of the 'private' individual from 'public' expectations of virtue, with individual moral psychology taking over from the community as the basis of the good society (Seligman 1995). However, Weintraub (1997) points out that, although it stands as a "grand dichotomy", the public/private divide is used in different, overlapping, and contradictory ways. In general terms, it can be understood as private or sectional interests as opposed to 'the public interest' (where publicity is understood as 'collectivity' and related to the designation of issues as either political or non-political) or as privacy as opposed to *in* public (where public is understood as visibility). More specifically Weintraub identifies uses of the public/private binary to refer to public sector (state) versus private sector (market); public sphere or realm (which he describes in republican terms of self-governance, rather than a Habermasian deliberative democracy) versus state and market; private domestic domain versus public order of politics and market (a feminist account that is alone in focusing on the private over the public); and public life of sociability (of non-political intersubjectivity) versus intimate domestic life and individualistic, impersonal society.

The neo-liberal version regards civil society as private in the sense of the private sector (non-governmental) and as an aggregate of private (self-interested) individuals, whilst for proponents of the activist model, civil society is public in the political sense – as operating in the public sphere – as opposed to an understanding of the political as referring to the state. However, within the neo-Marxist perspective, there are disagreements over whether this necessarily means the exclusion of personal concerns. The liberal tradition holds that, whilst concerns may arise from private concerns and particularistic value systems (such as religious belief), those interests and attachments should be put aside in the rational and disinterested public sphere. This is essentially Habermas' view, but other proponents of the public sphere do include private life in their definition of civil society (Kaldor 2003, Cohen and Arato 1994), especially in terms of personal judgement.

The communitarian notion of society is as a network of community attachments, so whilst Etzioni does not dismiss public universalism, he argues for a role for particularistic attachment as the basis of a 'good society' underpinned by moral values and cooperation that is not "merely civil" (2004: 154). However, he understands this as social rather than either private or political, which can be understood as a different form of public (Weintraub 1997) or as a realm between public and private, with some characteristics of both (Wolfe 1997). Particularistic identity groups – especially from a feminist perspective – challenge the public/private divide in terms of delineating the political. The personal concerns of domestic relations, sexuality, and particularistic values, including religious convictions, are variously claimed as political or as having a legitimate place in the public sphere. However, there is also a concern that if the private/personal is political, then the authority of society stretches into the private sphere, with potentially authoritarian or oppressive consequences (Elshtain 1997). The postmodern model also includes particularistic attachments, but it doesn't include a theory of political cooperation between those conflicting value systems.

Summary

The activist model emphasises the political role of civil society, which is independent of both market and state but may make demands on government in terms of redistribution or regulation of society in the interests of social justice (positive rights), including intervention into market mechanisms. They may be ambivalent or conflicted about grey area associations such as NGOs and social enterprise. The neo-liberal model, in contrast, defines civil society in market terms, as part of that principal mechanism that facilitates the autonomous life of individuals, free from state control or intervention, with a focus on community self-sufficiency, voluntary and charitable work. This economic role is framed as apolitical, assuming its individualistic notion of the good society to be merely pragmatic, with politics equated with a state-mediated life of constraint.

In this it has much in common with the (new or responsive) communitarian perspective, since it does depend on individual altruism without state coercion, but where neo-liberalism fails to provide a convincing explanation for such behaviour, communitarianism steps in with the imposition of moral obligation through social expectation and moral pressure. This is the most emphatic assertion of the social role of civil society. Unlike Kantian liberal perspectives (including neo-liberalism), communitarianism rejects the notion of a value-neutral state, and views state coercion through law as functioning to back up existing dominant morality, whilst allowing people to serve particularistic obligations related to families or community attachments related to personal identity. The postmodern model deals differently with multiculturalism, identity politics and conflicting value systems – whilst it also supports a pluralism of particularistic moral value system, it opposes any notion of or ambition for value consensus, defining politics as an arena of permanent and irresolvable contestation.

The next section will pick up on the claims made for consensus on the values of the good society, such as liberty, justice and equality, and debates over where virtue comes from, whether individual moral conscience, traditional moral authority, or sentiments of national or community belonging. The rest of the chapter will then turn to the practices of civil society in relation to these conceptions of the good.

The good society: Virtues defining the common good or public interest

Despite what Powell (2007) refers to as "endisms" – the end of ideology, the end of history – politics has not been reduced to managerial decisions over the most effective means to universally agreed ends. The post-war consensus and the apparent triumph of capitalist democracy after the end of the Cold War turned out to be no such thing, and politics continues to be overwhelmingly related, at heart, to values that continue to be contested. Civil society is both the terrain on which these disputes can be exercised and the basis of cooperation; characterised by both pluralism and solidarity. This section will set out the themes and debates that underpin the analysis in Chapter 4. Firstly it will address theoretical approaches to virtue in civil society, exploring the role of traditional community values, moral authority, and personal conscience; national identity and cultural cohesion; and the role of the state in the regulation of virtue. Secondly, it will examine various theories of justice – as liberty, fairness, equality, and recognition.

The origin of virtue: Authority, conscience, sentiment and governance

Peaceful cooperation requires, even in the more neo-liberal interpretations, virtues such as trust, respect, and tolerance, and also, for the activist version, other forms of other-orientation such as an open-minded and rational approach to public deliberation. These values could be regarded as ends in themselves (the good society as peaceful cooperation) and as means to agreeing the goals toward which cooperation is oriented (the good society as – for instance – prosperous, equal, or God-fearing). However, if liberal democracy is understood in Kantian terms of value neutrality, the question arises as to how we are to understand these values as emerging or justified in political deliberation without resorting to communitarian social pressure or other oppressive forms of moral authority.

Civility and civic virtue – traditional values, moral authority and personal conscience

Civic virtue and civility are different ways of understanding or negotiating the relationship between the individual and society, although the terms are often used interchangeably. Civic virtue requires the subjugation the self to the community, so that the private conscience is subsumed by the public (collective) definition of virtue, to produce a republican Rousseauian conscience collective or communitarian notion of the common good. Civility is a liberal theorisation of the moral individual, whereby the personal conscience is informed by private moral sentiments such as kindness, sympathy, and so on. However, these other-oriented dispositions do presume a social context, especially in terms of individuals' regulation of their own behaviour through the imagined judgements of others. The precise theoretical differences between these concepts rests in the interpretation of individuals' 'natural' private inclinations, the extent to which these should be subject to public scrutiny (visibility) and expectation (collectivity), and the distinction between the 'social' and the 'political' within the 'public'.

Both communitarian and republican proponents of civic virtue assume that the private individual is primarily selfish and define morality as public, but for communitarians the public is understood as *collective* but not *governmental*, whilst republicans locate expression of the general will through institutions of popular government. Etzioni argues that a shared notion of the common good is essential to provide a goal or "vision" (2004: 2) to inspire altruism, and to and refer to in the adjudication of disputes. He is critical of both 1960s expressive individualism and 1980s instrumental individualism as creating a culture of entitlement that has led to contemporary litigiousness, where each claims their rights without being willing to acknowledge any duty to others, which can only be corrected through social expectation and pressure. Liberals reject this as oppressive, undermining individual liberty and autonomous moral judgement.

The Scottish Enlightenment philosophers – sometimes referred to as the 'Scottish moralists' – were concerned about atomisation of an individualistic society, but argued that individual psychology facilitated a reflexive personal morality. Ferguson termed it "moral sentiment" seeing virtue as a particular emotion, which Bryant (1995: 207–8) criticised as naïve, though Aristotle also argued that emotions contributed to virtuous (or vicious) dispositions (Sokolon 2006). Smith's version, a principle of "sympathy and approbation" is based on the imagined judgement of another, defined as a reflexive "constitution of the self through that higher morality" (Bryant 1995: 209). Etzioni counters that whilst people do naturally seek the approval of others, "without continual external reinforcement, the conscience tends to deteriorate" (2004: 152). In contrast, Gellner (1995) argues that humans are *not* naturally social or communal, and therefore can't be bound by a (republican) social contract, but instead contribute to a variety of associations and institutions in a more 'modular' way through a variety of contingent and flexible personal commitments. This modular network of attachments updates Durkheim's theory of organic solidarity through functional interdependence in modern society, using modern furniture as a metaphor, rather than a biological organism, to indicate a more individualistic and flexible conception of cooperation.

The more neo-liberally inclined tend to be less concerned with how socially useful the individual's values are. Perez-Diaz (1995: 82) defines moral sentiment in terms of utility – "associated with the pursuit of interest or happiness" – though he does include social bonds as useful or desirable to individuals, among other incentives:

> [...] the salvation of the soul, a sense of community, the search for truth, employment in active exertions or in sensual gratifications, beauty, the possession of wealth, power or status, or whatever. Nothing, however, in the nature of these moral preferences predetermines their contents in so far as they can be either 'egotistical' or 'altruistic' or any combination of the two, depending on how interest or happiness is defined. (1995: 82)

This is rather more ambivalent about the source or content of values, including particularistic attachments such as religion, just as long as they are satisfying to the individual, and therefore most likely to the aggregate population of individuals. Perez-Diaz therefore subscribes to a consequentialist form of neo-liberalism, where the legitimacy of market mechanisms over state intervention (and political processes more generally) is justified in term of useful outcomes.

Generally, neo-liberalism is associated with economic liberalism – a belief that the market is the most efficient way to organise resources in a society – and not with an overtly moral or political philosophy. However, Blomgren (1997, cited in Thorsen and Lie 2010: 12–13) analysed the work of Milton Friedman, Friedrich von Hayek and Robert Nozick and discovered a range of philosophical underpinning, with Friedman and Hayek offering a mixture of consequentialist utility and natural law that defines autonomy as the essence of human existence, and Nozick taking a more deontological approach to natural rights without concern for consequences. Thorsen and Lie argue that neo-liberalism has been poorly defined, with the term primarily used as a criticism, and offer a definition that is "better able to function within the framework of a disinterested analysis" (2010: 14), which includes a peripheral moral component.

> Neoliberalism could also include a perspective on moral virtue: the good and virtuous person is one who is able to access the relevant markets and function as a competent actor in these markets [...] Individuals are also seen as being solely responsible for the consequences of the choices and decisions they freely make: instances of inequality and glaring social injustice are morally acceptable, at least to the degree in which they could be seen as the result of freely made decisions. (Thorsen and Lie 2010: 15)

Whilst in their own analysis Thorsen and Lie avoid making generalisations about the theoretical grounding of neo-liberalism, this moral perspective does seem to support Blomgren's conclusions, since the implication is that the good is connected to utility – to competence within the mechanisms of rational utility-maximisation – and that the most significant right is personal autonomy – so that the greatest good is produced by the greatest liberty, regardless of the distribution of the resources that make that negative liberty (from interference) meaningful.

Both Perez-Diaz and Etzioni employ a goal-based form of moral reasoning, in which the 'good' is determined by beneficial outcomes – for Perez-Diaz maximum utility for the maximum number of people is secured by allowing individuals to pursue their own goals, whilst Etzioni argues that individuals need external pressure to ensure that their choices are 'pro-social', but neither are concerned with conflicting or marginalised interests. An interest-based moral theory would consider positive rights on the basis of their "moral strength" (Rowan 1999: 7), which entail moral duties from others. This is Powell's (2007) broadly republican position when he argues that citizens are "made capable of common purpose and mutual action by virtue of their civic attitudes and participatory institutions rather than their altruism or their good nature" (2007: 4). He asserts that other-oriented virtues do not come from personal conscience and need to be actively developed through the public institutions of social democracy through which the state adjudicates on morally-justifiable needs, which may to some extent include cultural recognition where this relates to power and resource inequalities. Perez-Diaz's account is sanguine about the morality of un-coerced *private* individuals, whilst Powell's approach to *public* morality interprets state involvement as moral leadership rather than coercion, and Eztioni's relies on a neither public nor private, but rather *social* source of morality, with Smith combining a little of both the neo-liberal and the communitarian.

National identity, nationalism and multiculturalism
The relationship between individual and mass society is related to the nation, both as modernist project and 'imagined community'. Whilst the former is associated with the emergence of an impersonal mass society, the latter argues that some aspects of personal attachment in small-scale communities are reproduced in the concept of nation. Anderson's (1983) account of the modern nation as an 'imagined community', attempts to explain how it is that national attachments are deep enough to inspire sacrifices such as military service and dying for one's country, and ascribes a significant role to the national circulation of knowledge and culture via the mass media (though the media landscape has since fragmented). Similarly, Weber argued that a nation is based on shared culture, experience, and sentiment in the organic *gemeinschaften* sense, and has a co-dependent relationship with the *gesellschaftlich* state.

The role of emotion in communal attachment and solidarity is important but problematic, especially as emotional bonds are understood to be particularistic, and therefore based on a distinction of insiders from outsiders. Particularistic orientations are associated with 'hot' emotions, such as love of one's own, but also hatred of the other, whilst liberal tolerance is supposed to be based in rational and dispassionate virtuous disposition, but which could be seen as precarious without emotional reinforcement. For Nash (2005) the distinction between 'hot' and 'cool' national emotions centres on the relationship between emotion and action, and whether a rational reflexivity intervenes between the two (in Aristotlean terms). However, Billig (1995) points out that nationalism is often so culturally-embedded as to be barely recognised – it is a 'banal nationalism' of everyday routines and assumptions.

The extension of *gemeinshaften* community to mass society is associated with exclusivistic nationalism by some liberal scholars (Bryant 1995, Gellner 1995), whilst more tolerant and pluralistic forms of national identity are associated with the more *gesellschaftlich* liberal civil society, and with civility rather than civic virtue. Gellner (1995) argues that modern nationalism's *rhetoric* of community is contradicted by its *ideology* of the homogenous nation, with no tolerance for diverse local cultures and traditions.

> Notwithstanding the fact that its real social roots lay in the emergence of a mass standardized culture, it adopted the pretence (held in all sincerity by its protagonists) that it was defending and perpetuating a folk culture. Rooted in *Gesellschaft*, it preached *Gemeinschaft*. (Gellner 1995: 46)

Nonetheless, he argues that cooperation in contemporary society depends on a certain amount of homogeneity and therefore nationalism (as a necessary evil) in order to facilitate the essential flexibility of association. Most civil society theorists, however, regard nationalism as a threat to civil society, though that does not mean that they reject national identity altogether, but instead limit its importance as just one of many sources of identity, including a cosmopolitanism that extends beyond national borders (Kaldor 2003, Keane 1998).

Whilst Keane (1998: 96) agrees that nationalism is an ideology that essentialises the nation, with an exclusive notion of 'us' against an othered 'them', he also argues that national confidence facilitates tolerance of diversity and disagreement, rather than requiring homogeneity and involving an impulsive response to difference. Bryant is more cautious, acknowledging that civility is a "cool concept" (1995: 145), requiring citizens to treat others with respect regardless of whether they *like* them, but he argues that it is possible to instil a sense of moral sentiment in the nation without resorting to communitarianism or nationalism, through a sense of 'civil religion'. He associates nationa*lism* with an 'ethnic' conception of the nation in terms of the genetic inheritance of domestic nationals, as opposed to a 'civic' understanding of nation and national identity based on territory and association. Part of the cultural construction and reinforcement of civic nationhood is through the rituals of 'civil religion', such as national flags and anthems, national monuments, and national holidays and celebrations, especially remembering and recognising past military glory and sacrifice.

Bryant defines this process as liberal and not communitarian or authoritarian, making a distinction between 'political religion' and 'civic religion'. Political religion is defined as those rituals and symbols that 'sacralise' the current political order to place it beyond challenge, and legitimise its authority over private life, whilst the rituals and symbols of civil religion reinforce values necessary for civil interactions and negotiations in liberal democracy. The first, Bryant (1995: 149–50) argues, is imposed or constructed by the state, whilst the second emerges from society. However, this is rather vague about how such 'authentic' attachments emerge, are circulated and reinforced, and many of his examples would be classed as the 'flagging' of banal nationalism by Billig (1995). The comparison with theological religion does hint at a less spontaneous and more imposed form of ideology.

> For Durkheim, the unbelieving son of a rabbi, no avowedly secular system of values and norms could easily secure the respect due to a system believed to contain the word of God. Nevertheless, those who would establish secular ideologies could still be expected to try to vest elements of their systems with sacredness, thereby placing them, in so far as they succeeded, beyond criticism. (Bryant 1995: 151)

Whether such ideologies are liberal or communitarian, of the left or the right (hegemonic or 'counter-hegemonic'), they are still undemocratically established and perpetuated through such sacralisations. The undemocratic nature of civil religion is justified by the dubious notion of authenticity.

The Habermasian school of civil society theorists, in contrast, argue that the values of any given society or nation can be agreed in the public sphere (Edwards 2009, Kaldor 2003). However, Habermas' (1996) own conception of the public sphere was not one in which shared values were discussed, but merely assumed and appealed to, "as though political deliberation primarily involved an authentic appropriation of already shared values or political ideals" (Rehg and Bohman 2002: 33). Again, the problematic assumption of authenticity occludes the question of how to deliberatively address the disputes of multicultural society and "dilemmas of difference" (Baynes 2002).

Multiculturalism presents a challenge to the normative basis of liberal democracy as a universalising value system, revealing its implicit values by asserting multiple conflicting and equally universalising belief systems. At the same time, this apparently irresolvable clash of (again) *authentically*-felt beliefs reinforces the conviction that difference can only be accommodated by a liberal tolerance that relegates such attachments to the private sphere. However, there is "a limit to how far a religious group can accept religious pluralism internally and externally without feeling that it compromises its identity" because of the nature of divine truth in terms of a "suprahuman agency and transempirical sphere" (Riis 2007: 253).

For some multiculturalists, the assertion of religious identities in particular is consistent with "postmodern" social movements, in that both resist the assimilationist nation-state and claim a space in the public sphere for "hitherto subdued identities" (Eisenstadt 2007: 241), but ultimately reconstitute modernity in plural form, as multiple modernities that address the same problems in different ways. This doesn't resolve the tensions, however, simply frames them in different terms. The problem is not with religious freedom as non-interference in personal beliefs, but in the ethical dimensions of religions that guide religious practice in public and social interactions (Riis 2007). Riis summarises trends identified in sociological theory as privatisation (exclusion from the public sphere), democratisation (according a greater role to the laity), and marketisation (competing in a marketplace of belief) of religion, which "implies that world views are relativised and that plausibility structures become precarious" (Riis 2007: 256–7). Furthermore, he argues that the religious marketplace is skewed in countries that still have an established religion that is accorded a privileged position, especially in the provision of its own social services (such as marriage). One response has been to award similar privileges to other recognised religions, but this too is contentious, bringing the danger of *essentialising* ascribed identities in all individuals' institutional relations.

This is the principal basis of liberal discomfort – that it might be required to tolerate practices that it considers intolerant or oppressive, such as forced marriage and female genital mutilation, even if practiced 'privately' only on their own members, and also discriminatory practices that affect the public such as Christians refusing to provide services to gay couples. Hall specifies that "Diversity is attractive only within a shared framework which values the worth of the individual" (1995: 15). However, the appeal to "the worth of the individual" would be rejected by Keane as "the bad monist habit of philosophically justifying civil society by referring back to a substantive grounding principle" (1998: 53), including natural rights, associating such ideology with "cruel hubris" (1998: 59). Other liberal scholars have accommodated postmodern and multiculturalist critiques of Kantian universalism, rejecting the justification of virtues on the basis of natural law or natural rights, but on democratic dialogue and agreement.

Multicultural forms of liberalism employ some communitarian ideas about the self, rejecting the deontological notion of state neutrality, universalist rationalism, and assimilationist ambitions of liberalism. Instead, Parekh (2005) emphasises "reasons" for being persuaded by universal, global ethics – which are not limited to truth claims but may be substantive and diverse, and argues that the application of such principles may vary according to context. He also advocates the preservation of the diversity of culture on the basis that allowing or encouraging people to "experiment with diverse visions of the good life" (2005: 30) and fostering dialogue between them is likely to produce more critically reflexive cultures. However, his suggested solutions seem to seek to "protect" cultural products and industries (2005: 31), which could be interpreted as reifying minority cultures and failing to account for the contingent and changing nature of culture – the substance of Kenny's (2004: 26–8) critique of Kymlicka's liberal multiculturalism. In any case, if accommodation can be reached through moral debate, this still leaves the question of whether this debate is political or social, and where the boundaries of the political lie.

The role of the state in regulating virtue

Both neo-liberals and communitarians argue for very narrow bounds of the political, but whilst the former prefer to leave values to private individuals, the latter argue for *social* regulation of the good. For neo-liberals, freedom from state regulation is a central defining principle in itself, that "the only legitimate purpose of the state is to safeguard individual, especially commercial, liberty, as well as strong private property rights [...and] a belief that the state ought to be minimal or at least drastically reduced in strength and size" (Thorsen and Lie 2010: 14). In as far as neo-liberalism is understood as drawing on or returning to early modern liberalism, this could be seen as consistent with J.S. Mill's (2003 [1869]) contention that only that which harms another's liberty should be legislatively, *or* socially, proscribed, and that the virtue or otherwise of an individual's "self-regarding" behaviour should be judged only by other individuals.

However, more particularly, privacy is argued to be essential for virtue to develop through intimate emotions, with friendship and other personal relationships forming the basis of "valuable moral qualities such as intimacy, affection, generosity, and trust" (Silver 1997: 43). Silver argues that these qualities depend on being shielded from public scrutiny, as their moral value can only be subjectively judged by those involved, and that the aggregation of such personal attachments produces a virtuous outcome not by design but by the same mechanism as markets, simply with "sympathy and sociability" replacing the motivation of utility (1997: 63). Silver suggests that voluntary acts of charity and the emotions that inspire them arise from their being private arrangements, and are poisoned by state coercion such as redistributive state welfare.

Powell (2007) presents a neo-Marxist critique of the ideology behind voluntarism and charity more broadly, as operating as a safety net for capitalism whilst reinforcing the justification of wealth as an indicator of moral virtue, with poverty blamed on the poor. This can be also seen in the obsession of contemporary British politics with 'hard-working families' as the 'deserving' poor, in contrast to the 'workshy' who need to be incentivised through punitive measures such as the withdrawal or reduction of benefit, rather than supported or enabled. In contrast, it is argued that the wealthy need to be offered positive incentives to meet their social responsibilities, as was asserted during the debate in the UK over tax breaks for charitable donations in March 2012. In this, communitarians are in agreement with neo-liberals: Etzioni illustrates the difference between social pressure and state coercion "by comparing the transfer of wealth via charity to a system of taxes" (2004: 154), suggesting that the former is preferable because it is voluntary. However, as Powell argues, it is also egoistic and allows the philanthropist to exert his own values and priorities rather than contributing to meet democratically-agreed needs.

Whilst Etzioni is not entirely against state legislation on moral issues – since, he argues, most of politics does involve values – he does agree that too much moral judgement over individuals' choices is authoritarian. However, he insists that social interference is less oppressive than state interference.

> Granted, developing and sustaining a good society does require reaching into what is considered the private realm, shaping behavior that does not directly relate to the state or to the state-mediated relationships with one's fellow citizens. (Etzioni 2004: 150).

He specifies altruistic relations of charity and care, but also intimate relations of marriage and children, limited only by an assurance that the community should deliver no diktat over *how many* children the individual should have (but apparently seeing it as acceptable that they should be expected to have *some*). The incursion of the community into the private is not authoritarian because it "seeks to cultivate only a limited set of core virtues rather than have an expansive or holistic normative agenda" (2004: 150).

Etzioni seeks to distinguish responsive communitarianism from social conservativism, and religious conservatives in particular, who seek state enforcement of their moral values, such as bans on abortion, homosexuality and so on, which he argues are "not good-citizen issues, but good-person issues" (2004: 149). This distinction is difficult to sustain in consideration of those issues on which he does argue in favour of social pressure, unless we regard marriage and childbearing as "good-citizens issues". It is possible that you could justify this in terms of other-regarding versus self-regarding behaviour, but that would be to accept elements of Mill's liberal-utilitarian argument, which opposed *all* forms of social pressure on self-regarding behaviour, not just the socially conservative. Arguably, however, Etzioni's attempts to salvage communitarianism from accusations of oppressive moral imposition have made it rather less distinct from the liberal position, especially in his insistence that community membership and compliance is voluntary (2004: 154). Still, this does not acknowledge the potential for problematic power-differentials in private relations.

Most obviously, feminist theory has challenged the definition of the domestic realm as not only private in terms of visibility but also in terms of being outside the bounds of the political. Second wave scholars such as Carol Hanisch (1969), credited with popularising the phrase "the personal is political" (although she attributes the title to the editors of the collection) pointed out that the exercise of power and domination is not restricted to public interactions – indeed Weintraub points out that in the classical polis, domination was reserved for the domestic sphere, explicitly understood as being "structured by relationships of natural *in*equality" (1997: 12). Therefore, designating the domestic as private shields abuse from political or legal redress, and excludes debate on gender relations in the home from serious consideration in the public sphere. However, this focus on domestic relations as political is criticized for essentialising women's domestic role (Weintraub 1997: 29), undermining women's personal agency in their personal and intimate relations, and eroding or displacing legitimate politics (Elshtain 1997). Liberal criticisms of community as undemocratic would seem to recognise the cultural forms of ideological domination claimed in feminism and other emancipatory or identity movements, but are conflicted on the jurisdiction of the state over such issues.

Conservative and progressive views on state regulation of private virtue conflict, but not along consistent lines. The left are broadly comfortable with interventions in the interests of social justice, whilst the right dismiss this as the 'nanny state'. Conversely, the right see 'tough' law and order measures that monitor and regulate social behaviour as necessary public order, whilst the left express concern about civil liberties.

The definition of virtue: Liberty, justice and equality

Judgements on the substance of the values of the good society are also divided along left-right ideological lines, and in correspondence with the neo-liberal and activist models of civil society.

Economic liberty
Neo-liberalism emphasises economic liberty as the central freedom that guarantees personal autonomy. As Thorsen and Lie (2010) point out, this is variously theorised in utilitarian terms and in more deontological terms as based in natural rights. Tara Smith (1995) combines the two, arguing that "the right to lead one's life" is a natural right derived from the essence of what life is – that what distinguishes human life is the capacity for "self-generated" action. From this she derives "rights to life, liberty, property and the pursuit of happiness" (1995: 185). The libertarian focus on whatever makes the individual happy makes no judgement on what the individual takes pleasure in, and is only concerned with how it affects the overall utility – so if one individual takes pleasure at another's expense, or even takes pleasure in another's pain, this pleasure offsets the damage to the other's utility to some extent, when moral instinct suggests that it should be judged worse (Scarre 1996). More pertinently, the focus on *maximisation* of utility ignores its *distribution* within society.

Since wealth creation is assumed to be the source of most utility for neo-liberals, however, the market is prioritised. The assumption is that the market allows each individual to maximise their own utility, and therefore produces the best aggregate outcome for the society, principally through economic growth. In practice, this means that business interests are conflated with the national interest.

> Neoliberalism is perhaps best perceived of as a radical descendant of liberalism 'proper', in which traditional liberal demands for 'equality of liberty' have been bent out of shape into a demand for total liberty for the talented and their enterprises. (Thorsen and Lie 2010: 16)

Negative liberty theoretically grants each individual equal liberty from interference, but that doesn't mean that they have equal opportunity to act. Furthermore, Thorsen and Lie suggest that greater liberty is intentionally demanded for some individuals. Arguably, this "total liberty" is not claimed for *all* those we might judge "talented", but those who are well-resourced and enjoy advantage. This is the direct opposite of John Rawls' (1971) notion of justice as fairness, which adds to the primary principle of equal liberty the equality principle – a stipulation that there should be fair equality of opportunity and that any inequality should favour the *dis*advantaged.

Powell (2007) argues that the consideration of social as well as civil and political rights reflects a willingness to view the individual in terms of their humanity rather than as commodities defined by their market position. Whilst citizens are increasingly regarded as consumers, they are also increasingly located in a diverse range of communities, not only of locality, but of interest, identity, and political agenda. For Powell (2007: 16), "strong democracy", in which citizens engage in political decision-making via civil society, builds community without sacrificing individuality, and ensures that the political arena is not dominated by powerful interests.

Interest politics and redistribution
Sectional interests can be variously conflated with the national interest; legitimised as minority or marginalised interests whose needs should be met; or delegitimised as self-interested and counter to the national interest or public interest. The first position is the traditional hegemonic relationship of elites to society, whereby powerful agents manufacture consent, not least through the media (Herman and Chomsky 1988) by constructing their own interests as those of society as a whole – in particular in terms of the conflation of business interests with the national interest, where the latter is principally defined as economic growth. The second corresponds with social democratic and redistributive positions, which recognise some interests as valid, whilst rejecting more powerful interests. The third is most typically attached to organised interests such as on the one hand corporate lobbyists and on the other trades unions, where these groups are interpreted as excessively powerful and influential in contrast with the public interest.

Cohen and Arato (1992) are sceptical about the existence of a general interest, and prefer to see contingent consensus (or at least acceptance) as based in common identity that grounds commitment to the procedures of political decision-making. Whilst decisions may be reached by compromise rather than consensus, they are stable precisely because of this recognition of a fair process based on equal participation. This, they argue, is consistent with the focus on justice and solidarity at the heart of Habermas' discourse ethics. Whilst this is a procedural account, they reject criticisms that it is merely formalist with no concept of the good.

> The institutionalization of any norm that might cause irreparable damage to the integrity of the identities of individuals and groups who are willing to discuss and abide by the procedural principles of symmetric reciprocity is proscribed. (Cohen and Arato 1992: 380)

This could be interpreted as similar to Mill's notion of harm to the liberty of others as the constraint on the exercise of liberty, but incorporating a positive interpretation of freedom and requiring commitment to procedural metanorms. However, this assumes "that there are no intractable conflicts between different types of discourse" (Rehg and Bowman 2002: 43), such as between morality, utilitarianism and social bond, or between liberty and equality, or indeed conflicting rights claims, and the extent to which his theory can address the recognition claims of identity politics is the subject of rather more debate (Baynes 2002, Rehg and Bohman 2002).

Identity politics and recognition
The rise of identity politics is frequently associated with the decline of the politics of class or other interest or ideological positions. The new politics associated with new social movements has been distinguished as a shift from economically-motivated to culturally-motivated advocacy, from a concern with equality to a concern with recognition of difference. Kenny (2004:18) argues that the emergence of identity politics in the US in the 1960s was defined by groups such as Students For a Democratic Society (SDS) rejecting their socialist forbears, and focusing instead on counter-cultural politics of difference.

However, this distinction is not as severe a break as is often suggested – identity movements such as women's and gay liberation share emancipatory goals with class politics, including a fight against prejudice and discrimination (Kenny 2004: 4). The key points of departure are that identity groups' claims on state and society are related more to social and cultural recognition than material and redistributive justice, that they often seek to preserve difference rather than gain equality, and that they challenge the liberal ideal of the disinterested, public-spirited participant in public life.

The liberal ideal of detached and disinterested orientation to the 'good' is rejected as unrealistically deontological as it doesn't acknowledge the reality of individuals' situatedness in their culture and background, and confuses neutrality with the hegemonic imposition of liberal beliefs and marginalisation of others. This is argued to be a conditional form of tolerance, whereby liberal democracies accommodate different value systems as long as they are relegated to the private sphere and that they "respect the public value of tolerance and the procedures for interaction between individuals and groups in the public sphere" (Widdows 2005: 80).

> Yet the relegation of value to the private sphere cannot ultimately be successful, as public forms of moral decision-making are essential and value judgements cannot be purely a matter of individual choice. [...] As a consequence of their privatisation of value, liberal democracies have difficulty in giving reasons for their positions and value judgements. (Widdows 2005: 79)

The liberal concern, however, is that the politics of identity may be more prone to an uncompromising militancy that is indifferent to the claims and values of others, and that demands for recognition of non-liberal cultural practices may include those that breach basic human rights (such as forced marriage or female genital cutting).

For liberals equality means being treated equally regardless of difference, whilst critics argue that this simply reflects a dominant normativity (white, male, straight, middle class assumptions and sensibilities), therefore institutions should be sensitive to difference. Identity politics calls for stereotyping and assimilation to be acknowledged as causing particular forms of harm, such as humiliation, that are not recognised by liberal state neutrality and tolerance, yet have significant implications for liberal democracy since cultural marginalisation that is damaging to groups' sense of self-worth can undermine their capacity for cooperation in civil society and politics (Kenny 2004: 34).

However, a focus on recognition of cultural authenticity can lead to groups essentialising their own difference through a sense of injury and defensiveness. Kenny argues that there is a broad consensus across the ideological divide that the growth of insular forms of identity politics is divisive, breeding a sense of entitlement based on offended injury (Kenny 2004: 75). This is amplified by policies that seek to award special rights to groups that have been historically marginalised or oppressed, since this incentivises such claims. Instead, Kenny argues, the harms of "discrimination, unfairness or humiliation" on the basis of a shared identity should be addressed in the same way as other threats to civil rights – on an individual basis, rather than through affording special group rights (2004: 173–4).

Indeed, the similarities and overlaps between interest and identity politics have suggested the possibility of a liberal theory that accommodates the insights of identity politics without compromising its key principles. Firstly, economic and cultural statuses are clearly related:

> Recognition is mediated through forms of signification, that is, through modes of intelligibility, and ideological frames of sense making that organise individuals and groups into socio-economic hierarchies of power and privilege. (Powell 2007: 132)

Therefore redistribution is a key resolution to discrimination, and recognition can be sought for non-essentialist identities. Nancy Fraser (1997) attempts to combine theories of redistribution and recognition into a new critical theory of recognition that deconstructs group identities to challenge dominant signification, and applies principles of socialist solidarity. This non-essentialist approach to identity is also crucial for Kenny (2004: 171), who emphasises the dynamic and hybrid nature of particularistic attachments, and the capacity of group members to challenge the dominant group identification from within. Cohen and Arato (1992: 383–4) also argue for a critically reflexive approach, through discourse, and a civil solidarity that includes reciprocal recognition, whilst insisting on support for universal human rights wherever those claims are asserted as a normative imperative intrinsic to discourse ethics.

Summary

There is a range of thought on the capacity of individuals for virtuous thought and action, how the potential for public virtue can be fostered or imposed, and whether the regulation of virtue by moral or legal authority is even in itself morally valid and consistent with the common good. Where different values are appealed to in the same debate, there can be no resolution unless the basis, relevance and implications of those values are also open to discussion. However, debate often instead shifts to the legitimacy of the *form* of the message rather than its *content*, in terms of the legal limits to the exercise of civil rights, adherence to proper democratic procedures and principles, and socially acceptable behaviour in accordance with dominant expectations. These will be taken in turn, starting with the relationship of law, rights and legitimate dissent.

Dissent: Law and order, civil rights and moral challenge

Much like the civil economy is facilitated and legitimated by legal concepts (Bryant 1995), and both civil society and the public sphere depend on the rule of law (Habermas 1996). Laws also derive legitimacy from their origin (to some extent) in popular sovereignty through the democratic system of representation. However, they are also fallible, open to revision and therefore to moral challenge. Since violence is almost universally rejected as part of civil society, and since this is the paradigmatic form of delegitimising protest activity, this will be addressed first, but this will be followed by more subtle and contested disputes over the extent of the protection against legal redress afforded by civil rights, and the moral case for law-breaking as legitimate civil disobedience. The section will conclude by considering the role of the police in enforcing public order in the context of dissent.

Violence

Edwards (2009: 29) argues that whilst it is "intellectually dubious" to exclude "uncivil" groups on the basis of moral or ideological disapproval, violent and coercive groups must be excluded as incompatible with civility. Kaldor (2003) defines civil society as "an answer to war", in that it is a way of achieving reform without violent revolution. Even Keane – associated with the most inclusive model, postmodern civil society – argues that although civil society is not in itself a universal ideal, as a particular form of organisation it is incompatible with violence, which would undermine the rules of "solidarity, liberty and equality of citizens" (1998: 139). However, his main concern is not violent groups within society, but the violence of the state as a threat to civil society.

There is an inherent contradiction in the state monopoly on violence as the guarantor of civility – that violence is prevented by the threat of violence (Keane 1998, Powell 2007). The horrific state violence of the Holocaust demonstrated the fragility of that arrangement, leading to international human rights agreements, which continue to be the basis of challenges to the violent and extra-judicial abuses of contemporary authoritarian states. However, Keane argues that this is only one of a "plurality of strategies" that should be employed against violence. "Cultures of civility" in civil society are essential, he argues, to avoid a "drift into authoritarian 'law and order' strategies" of 'tougher' solutions, but instead cultivate *"public spheres of controversy,* in which the violent exercise of power over others is resisted initially by civilian-citizens' efforts to monitor it non-violently" (Keane 1998: 156 [emphasis in original]).

Violence by the state may inspire a violent resistance or response from protesters, but this is broadly rejected. Whilst Powell acknowledges that there is a problem with a commitment to non-violent action, faced with state power with its monopoly on legitimate violence, he argues that violent protesters "are fundamentally at odds with the ethical basis of civil society and are without moral justification" (Powell 2007: 125). However, his examples are of dissent within more or less democratic societies such as animal rights and pro-life "extremists", who employ threats, assault or terror tactics. He argues that these tactics inevitably undermine the cause that they are employed to advance.

Cohen and Arato (1992: 454) explicitly address the issue of revolution aimed at the "overthrow of an oppressive system", but argue that they tend to be self-defeating as "revolutions in the modern sense are carried out, or at least won, by organizations of power that, in a genuine rupture with the old society and in the inevitable chaos and power vacuum that follow, are driven to increase rather than limit sovereign power". This insight would seem to be supported by the aftermath of some of the so called Arab Spring uprisings.[2]

Violence as a protest tactic is not always aimed at human targets, and is often used to refer to public disorder and property damage as part of direct action repertoires. Some of those involved in the 1990s anti-globalisation and contemporary anti-capitalist movements emphasise this distinction and do not define property damage as violence, complaining that media coverage conflates the two (Ackerman 2000). Others do define it as violence, and complain that the media focus on it at the expense of peaceful tactics and argumentation (Joyce 2002). Gitlin's (1980) account of the anti-Vietnam War movement, furthermore, found that the news media's focus only on the most 'violent' or provocative tactics (burning draft cards, then flags and eventually buildings) incentivised a more violent repertoire, and the representation of the movement as violent became a self-fulfilling prophecy. The consequence, Gitlin argues, was that the movement

---

2   The situation is, of course, rather more complex than that, with Egypt's comparatively bloodless revolt and democratic elections nevertheless followed by accusations of centralisation of power, a coup and further unrest, whilst some commentators attribute the instability in Libya following the more violent ousting of Gaddafi to the *weakness* of the state and its inability to control warring militias (http://www.newyorker. com/online/blogs/comment/2013/08/can-libya-be-saved.html).

isolated itself as increasingly militant, just as mainstream public opinion was turning against the war, aiding the media's elevation of a 'moderate alternative' that was pit against the 'militant' New Left.

This highlights another distinction, in that property damage is often not spontaneous violence sparked by anger or aggression, but purposefully employed as a symbolic form of protest – this will be considered under political legitimacy – and as civil disobedience, where law-breaking is morally justified as highlighting or preventing greater wrong-doing.

Disruption and disobedience

The more conventional, primarily peaceful repertoires of dissent include marches, rallies and strikes, all of which are not only legal but an expression of civil rights – freedom of speech and association – that are fundamental to liberal democracy. Nonetheless, various legal constraints have been placed on these activities (see below), ostensibly to ensure that such rights are exercised responsibly and democratically. In addition, the legal and democratic status of such forms of protest does not necessarily translate into the public perception of legitimacy. Strikes in particular have been framed in delegitimising frames both in politics and media (Glasgow University Media Group 1976, Philo 1990), but the most common undermining factor has long been noted as the tendency to ignore, underplay, or misrepresent peaceful protest (Halloran et al. 1970, Gitlin 1980). This is one explanation for the increasing use of direct action.

Direct action includes consumer boycotts, civil disobedience and obstruction, where "groups have gone beyond activities seeking to 'sell' their cause to the general public and have utilised various forms of physical action to implement their objectives" (Joyce 2002: 16), although they do also aim to influence public opinion through symbolic actions and spectacular (but peaceful) events. Some direct action disrupts corporate activity from within the logic of capitalism, such as consumer boycotts, which introduce a moral criterion to rational choice within the market. This increases the cost of the behaviour by affecting revenue, whilst other interventions attempt to disrupt production more directly. Obstruction is the most common method of preventing the activity that is opposed, such as blockades, sit-ins, or occupations. This has been used to prevent live animal exports (peaking in the mid-1990s), road-building (most famously the Newbury by-pass protest in 1996), and even fossil fuel energy production (including at Ratcliffe on Sour in 2007 and 2009). Occupation has a long history, with campus sit-ins a common tactic of the anti-Vietnam war protests, especially by Students for a Democratic Society (Gitlin 1980) and peace camps such as the Greenham Common Women's camp. Both obstruction and occupation often involve activities that are illegal, such as trespass and breach of the peace.

The moral justification of preventing a greater social ill has been successfully asserted as a defence against prosecution for law-breaking civil disobedience (Joyce 2002: 17). This is distinct from conscientious refusal, where an individual breaks a law because they believe it to unjustly breach their rights. Conscientious refusal is a less political act than civil disobedience, as it only seeks an exemption from law on the basis of personal, particularistic moral objections, whilst civil disobedience appeals to public opinion with reference to shared principles of justice (Cohen and Arato 1992).

Cohen and Arato dedicated the final chapter of their *Civil Society and Political Theory* (1992) to a consideration of civil disobedience, since they believe that it is through this that the radical potential of civil society as a theory of political participation can be best understood. They regard this as a useful alternative to cold reformism on the one hand, and hot revolutionary fundamentalism on the other (1992: 565). However, civil disobedience means breaking laws that have been democratically agreed through majority rule, so a strong moral case needs to be made in justification. Most obviously, whilst majority rule is an essential democratic principle, the majority may be mistaken, prejudiced, or otherwise make law that breaches the principles of justice, not least in the transgression of minority rights. However, Cohen and Arato criticise Rawls (1971) for only recognising this as grounds for non-compliance when the law breaches existing rights, not in the assertion of a new, unrecognised one, making it a narrowly defensive gesture, with no meaningful political role for civil society.

Dworkin (1978), in contrast with Rawls, argues that the moral rights of individuals are too complex and open to interpretation to be fully encapsulated in a constitution, and therefore civil disobedience is a useful way of allowing citizens to challenge the validity of law in relation to shared principles through test cases in the highest judicial courts. However, civil disobedience does not always, or even usually, involve breaking the law that is the subject of challenge – often the law transgressed is some element of public order or property law. Cohen and Arato also object that law testing is more generally aimed at testing procedural validity than moral legitimacy. Nonetheless, Dworkins' view includes a role for civil society in asserting new rights rather than simply defending existing ones. However, he does insist that principles be framed in terms of rights.

For Cohen and Arato (also Cohen 2009), Dworkins' insistence on individual rights as the basis of legitimacy limits his understanding of citizen participation and associated rights to voting and seeking electoral office, and cannot accommodate protests against policy (as opposed to in the pursuit of justice) on the basis of democratic principle (rather than individual rights). For instance, he dismissed anti-nuclear protest as engaging in a non-discursive strategy to dissuade the state from a policy of nuclear deterrent by raising the cost through obstruction. Rights-oriented liberalism fails to recognise the issues of legitimacy in questions of policy as opposed to rights. Cohen and Arato's own definition of civil disobedience theorises it as an act of political participation.

> Civil disobedience involves illegal acts, usually on the part of collective actors, that are public, principled, and symbolic in character, involve primarily nonviolent means of protest, and appeal to the capacity for reason and the sense

of justice of the populace. The aim of civil disobedience is to persuade public opinion in civil and political society (or economic society) that a particular law or policy is illegitimate and a change is warranted. (Cohen and Arato 1992: 587–8)

Like Arendt and Habermas, they embrace the normative ideals of republican democracy whilst rejecting the Rousseuian model of fully institutionalised participation and a unified 'general will'.

Arendt defines the legitimacy of civil disobedience, not in terms of "the individual's moral integrity" (1992: 594), but the political necessity of challenge where normal channels are judged ineffective. Connectedly, it is not non-violence that principally defines civil disobedience, but "the spirit of the action and the spirit of the laws to which it is addressed" (1992: 595). For Habermas (1996), civil disobedience is part of the communication between the weak and strong publics of civil and political society, and important in terms of the revisable nature of law and decision-making, which serves to reassure minorities that decisions are not fixed. However, whilst theoretical approaches associated with the activist model of civil society identify a clear role for civil disobedience as a legitimate moral challenge to power, analysis of news media suggests that legal judgements are typically privileged over the moral objections (McLeod and Hertog 1992).

Kantian liberalism defines freedom of speech and association as private rights, as part of the 'natural' right to personal autonomy as the negative liberty from interference, whereas Rousseauian republicanism recognises only positive political rights, requiring, where citizens are reluctant to participate, that they be 'forced to be free'. Between these two positions, procedural models of democracy – such as Habermas' deliberative democracy – aim to balance the private and political rights of citizens. Baynes (2002) finds Habermas' resolution of the tension between the principles of democracy (self-determination by majority rule) and of justice (rights, especially those of minorities) rather abstract, but Cohen and Arato argue that "the institution of rights represents the majority's promise to the minorities that their dignity and equality will be respected" (1992: 583) and thereby underpin the legitimacy of majority rule.

> Although individual rights to speak, assemble and associate are the precondition for institutionalizing public spaces within civil society, their animating principle is deeply political: It is the principle of democratic legitimacy itself. (Cohen and Arato 1992: 590)

They argue that the principle of democratic legitimacy relates to the political system via the public sphere in the same way that the principle of rights relates to the legal system, as a parallel and complementary process. However, the proliferation of rights claims can pit rights associated with negative liberties (personal autonomy and so on) against the right to protest. Therefore, the boundaries of legitimate dissent and legitimate public order policing are shifting and contested.

Boundaries of legitimate dissent, legitimate public order policing

Public order policing in the UK has been subject to several legislative changes since the seventies. Changes to industrial law in 1980 and 1982 that placed restrictions on picketing and weakened the closed shop followed the 1979 'Winter of Discontent', which the Conservative government and media blamed for high taxation and inflation (Joyce 2002: 81), and remains a touchstone of anti-union rhetoric. The changes claimed to increase the accountability of unions to their members, but critics argued that they sought to weaken working class association.

The 1986 Public Order Act criminalised various dissenting activities and placed more onerous requirements on others, effectively placing conditions on the civil right to public assembly (Joyce 2002: 49). Critics have queried whether the need for prior negotiation between protest organisers and police represents efforts to ensure policing by consent or unnecessary police restrictions on legitimate protest (Joyce 2002: 54). Certainly public order legislation is vulnerable to reactionary responses to moral panics, such as the 1994 Criminal Justice and Public Order Act that attempted to circumscribe 'rave culture'. More recently, the 2001 Anti-Terrorism, Crime and Security Act and 2004 Civil Contingencies Act extended the use of the military in civil emergencies, as part of the post 9/11 "security regime" aimed at monitoring and controlling dissent (Price 2011).

The increasing scope of police powers and sophistication of their tactics are often argued to signal the close relationship between police and state, and their antipathy to left-wing causes in particular. However, it has been noted that the police have shown restraint in *exercising* those powers, which Joyce (2002) attributes to the countervailing influence of the 1998 Human Rights Act, whilst Marx (1998) explains it as a reciprocal restraint, with protesters also more conscious of media representation and the potential for backlash.

Della Porta (1998) argues that, whilst the political environment has an impact, with a 'law and order' framework and 'harder' tactics associated with conservative governments and concern with civil rights and 'softer' tactics with the left, this isn't a consistent or deterministic relationship and she identifies a broader range of factors at play than the legal and political structures, including a strong cultural component. Cultural factors include the extent to which the police understand their job as crime-fighting or peacekeeping, how they perceive society, and the extent to which they rely on stereotypes to make decisions on intervention, but also social perceptions of moral legitimacy and proportionate policing.

Public opinion, not least as represented by the media, on the police's use of force is also significant, though it can also work in both directions, sometimes critical of police 'overreaction' and other times pressing for 'tougher' containment. The public understanding of proportionate policing is closely related to perceptions of legitimate protest.

> [...] public opinion seems to be less tolerant of disruptive protest behavior when other protest channels are available. Moreover, coercive policing is better

accepted, or even advocated, if directed against violent protesters. (della Porta
and Reiter 1998: 19–20)

This suggests that the news framing of protest and its policing is significant for the
cultural context of public order strategy.

Della Porta's study of Italian policing of protest in the 1990s identified different
models of non-confrontational public order strategy dependent on the type of protest:
a 'cooperative' model for trade union and other political marches, a 'negotiated'
model for more disruptive forms of protest such as obstruction, and 'ritualized
stand-off' for more radical groups, whilst 'total isolation' is limited to contexts in
which there is judged to be a high risk of disorder, such as football hooliganism.
The cooperative model involves a large scale of police presence, but with the aim of
facilitating protest rather than preventing disorder, which may mean refraining from
arresting marginal disruptive elements if it would likely lead to escalation (although
they may be identified through surveillance and arrested later), and even relying
on the majority or organisers to marginalise them. This is facilitated by a common
perception that "the degeneration of a demonstration is now seen as a failure of the
demonstration itself" (police chief officer quoted in della Porta 1998: 237). The
negotiated model is more interventionist, aiming to prevent or limit the disruption,
"reducing inconveniences for other citizens" (della Porta 1998: 233), but this may
be achieved by arranging for the media attention that is the key aim of the protest,
in order to shorten it. Whilst riot gear is often deployed in ritualised stand-off, the
helmet will be carried until there is a tangible threat, and a policy of low-profile
policing may be employed where there is a danger of appearing confrontational.

However, Reiner's (1998) analysis of British public order policing in the same
volume identifies an opposite trend of greater militarisation and use of "heavy-
handed" tactics, even against "respectable middle-class" protesters such as those
opposing live animal exports. He predicted that policing methods would "become
a major political issue" (1998: 48), which arguably occurred with the death of
newspaper vendor Ian Tomlinson at the G20 protest in London, which resulted in a
report by Her Majesty's Chief Inspector of Constabulary (HMIC) called *Adapting
to Protest* (HMIC 2009) recommending a more consent-oriented approach.[3]
Reiner's particular concern is with the increasing sophistication of riot equipment,
which can give the impression that the police are expecting and even looking for
trouble, and appear confrontational, but the police claim that a more professional,
confident and disciplined policing operation is in the interests of protesters (Joyce
2002). A police force that feels vulnerable to attack may be more brutal in its
use of force to contain the perceived threat (della Porta and Reiter 1998: 12).
Nonetheless, the widespread use of such equipment as a matter of course prior

---

3   Although when the Metropolitan police finally offered the Tomlinson family
an apology they focused on the actions of the individual officer and "failures in vetting
procedures" rather than public order policing policy (http://www.theguardian.com/uk-
news/2013/aug/05/ian-tomlinson-apology-met-police).

to the Tomlinson incident suggests less discretion of the part of the British police between different types of protest.

Such distinctions are not necessarily, in any case, always clear cut, since the organisers of demonstrations cannot fully control the intentions of all those who attend, and factions can diverge from the official plan. A tendency has been noted to characterise this as a distinction between 'professional' protesters for whom (violent or disruptive) protest is as end in itself, and 'legitimate' protesters who are availing themselves of their right to protest with clear and credible ends (Della Porta and Reiter 1998: 25). However, this is a shift toward stereotyping a minority of protesters, where previously whole movements (such as the labour movement) were regarded as a hostile 'other' (Della Porta and Reiter: 31). Where peaceful protests are "infiltrated" by radical minorities the police response needs to achieve "a difficult equilibrium between control of the radicals and respect for the rights of the moderates" (Della Porta and Reiter 1998: 21), often through the use of containment tactics (Della Porta 1998).

Containment tactics, now known as 'kettling', were used against anti-capitalist demonstrators as early as Mayday 2001, which Joyce (2002: 51) regarded as "potentially illegal", especially since the mass detention was followed with a search and photograph of each participant, without the strong grounds for suspecting criminal activity required. The use of surveillance has since increased significantly, not least through the continued development of specialist policing units. These emerged in the 1960s in large metropolitan areas such as London and Greater Manchester, and were later consolidated into formal structures and provided with increasingly sophisticated equipment (Joyce 2002). The structure and accountability of these police units was called into question in 2011 when the undercover activities of officers – most notably Mark Kennedy – seconded to the National Public Order Intelligence Unit, part of the National Domestic Extremism Unit, under the purview of the Association of Chief Police Officers (ACPO) – an independent association not accountable through standard police structures (see Chapter 5).

A decade prior to the Mark Kennedy scandal, Joyce (2002) noted that the development of transnational protest had led to calls for increased international cooperation in police intelligence-gathering, which would seem to have been heeded, given the embedded officers global activities. Surveillance of protest groups is not new – it was employed during the Cold War, including by the security services, on the basis of communist links or support – however, there is an increasing demand for intelligence. Gary T. Marx (1998: 260) argues that "Information begets the need for more information and one can never be fully sure of its validity, nor with the movement of time, its currency". Accordingly, there are moves to extend the surveillance by GCHQ to monitoring internet activity.

Summary

Whilst violence against human targets is universally excluded from definitions of legitimate civil society, other law-breaking occupies a more ambiguous position.

Theorists associated with the activist model of civil society make a strong case for civil disobedience as a moral challenge to unjust law, but public acceptance of its legitimacy is highly contingent on a number of factors, including dominant perceptions of the impact on the rights of others, proportionality of police tactics and threat to stability and security, as well as the potential for challenge through formal political channels. However, even when protesters do address the political system, the legitimacy of their contributions can be challenged.

Procedure and participation: Political legitimacy in the public sphere

Legitimacy in the political public sphere is defined in terms of the structures of decision-making and representation, and the procedural norms of rational deliberation, corporatist negotiation, rhetorical advocacy, and spectacular ideational disruption. The first legitimises collective action in ways that may or may not mirror aspects of the political system. The second relates to the ways in which they address formal politics and its publics.

Democratic structures and orientation to the political system

Assessments differ on the legitimacy and effectiveness of the structures of civil society associations and movements. Neo-liberals and other neo-Tocquevillians assume that autonomous voluntary associations are intrinsically more effective and therefore legitimate than state-run services. Edwards (2009: 55) counters that effectiveness in service delivery is dependent on the same structural factors in the third sector as in state institutions and market-led corporations, that is, accountability, responsiveness, and the least hierarchy that is consistent with efficient operation. From the perspective of the activist model of civil society, however, effectiveness is not measured in market-based criteria of efficiency, but social, political, and communicative goals.

Some politically-oriented civil society associations are hierarchical and relatively professionalised, although their relationship with the grassroots membership differs widely. Organisations such as the RSPB that combine political advocacy (although largely from a position of expertise rather than opinion representation) with charitable service provision don't tend to consult their members on emerging ornithological issues, but instead offer other member benefits such as discounts (Grant 2000). Trade union leaders, in contrast, are legally obliged to consult their membership on matters of industrial relations, with tight regulations around strike ballots delineating legitimacy in a legalistic way. To some extent this may reflect differences between the aims of 'cause' and 'sectional' groups, but it is more specifically related to status and strategy, with the former a "specialist insider" group (Grant 2000) that engages pragmatically through formal processes such as government consultation, whilst the latter are more peripheral in status, sometimes engaging in negotiation, other times in disruption and direct action. Other elements of civil society, meanwhile – social movements in particular – reject hierarchical structures that mirror the structures of political institutions, preferring participation over representation and symbolic expression over instrumental rationality (Cohen and Arato 1992, della Porta and Diani 2006: 239) and choose a status as "ideological outsiders" (Grant 2000).

Social movements have been described as operating with "dual logic of contemporary collective action" (Cohen and Arato 1992: 556), combining a system orientation that seeks political influence with a lifeworld orientation that seeks cultural recognition for the movement's identity and alternative organisational forms. Hierarchical structures of representation are regarded as more valid by those who favour an elite model of democracy, which regards politics as necessarily a specialism due to technical-pragmatic complexity in the contemporary political economy (Held 2006). This assumption is reflected in a 'stage model' of social movements that regards a more institutionalised form as signalling the maturity of a movement, culminating in the participation of leaders in formal party politics and parliamentary representation (Cohen and Arato: 557). However, Cohen and Arato (1992) argue that this undervalues the cultural function of social movements, and the need for a dual politics that addresses both logics.

An important aspect of collective action, according to this view, is to present a challenge to moribund forms of remote and unresponsive democracy. Alternative structures of participation include horizontal, leaderless networks; decision-making by assembly; and affinity groups connected to the wider movement through 'hubs and spokes' arrangements (Klein 2001, della Porta and Diani 2006, Rojecki 2011). In practice there remains the potential for the most committed or effective communicators to dominate, and decision-making can be laborious and even inconclusive (della Porta and Diana 2006: 244). These organisational forms are, however, aided by the network structure of digital media communications, especially in terms of low-level participation (such as via a Facebook page), more active mobilisation, and direct dissemination of information, arguments and images (Cottle and Lester 2011), although "issues of selective exposure, credibility, self-interest, and sheer audience reach continue to make the mainstream media a relevant factor in the new politics of dissent" (Rojecki 2011: 95). They are not simply technologically-determined forms directed by the opportunity structure of the internet, but part of a transformative strategy promoting populist, bottom-up democratisation (della Porta and Diana 2006: 246).

Therefore, cooptation by the system is thought to undermine the aims of the movement and its continued mobilisation, whilst continued resistance can undermine recognition of its legitimacy in pragmatic terms.

> To the extent that these processes involve cooptation, deradicalization, professionalization, bureaucratization, and centralization, "success" in institutional terms of inclusion signals the end of the movement and the dilution of its aims (the famous law of oligarchy). Since, in its original form, this dilemma flowed logically from the revolutionary rhetoric of the labor movement that

has subsequently been abandoned, life cycle theorists can dismiss it as utopian, unrealistic, or dangerous. When movement fundamentalists articulate such fears today, in the absence of any claim to be engaging in revolutionary politics, they can be accused of an unwillingness or an inability to learn. (Cohen and Arato 1992: 557)

Conventions of news-framing, certainly in the mid-late twentieth century, tended to regard outsider organizations, associations and movements as politically illegitimate. The positioning of contentious politics was most thoroughly set out by Daniel Hallin (1989) in his study of news coverage of the Vietnam War. The anti-war movement were framed as outside mainstream opinion and therefore located in the 'sphere of deviance', where rules of balance did not apply, so their views need not be accommodated, whilst the war was situated in the 'sphere of consensus' and need not be questioned. A central part of the strategy was to misrepresent, attack and undermine student leaders of the movement. When *elite* dissensus emerged within government on the case for war, and especially on the likelihood of 'winning' the war, opposition became part of the 'sphere of legitimate controversy', a more 'moderate' anti-war movement was identified who were portrayed as having a more conventional relationship with the establishment, further marginalising the more radical movement and amplifying the split between 'militants' and 'moderates'. This would suggest that there is a strategic advantage to more horizontal and leaderless structures as well as a democratic one (Klein 2001). Interestingly, however, most studies of the media framing of protest and the politics of dissent tend to focus on the reporting of tactics and repertoires more than the democratic structures and deliberative arguments.

Procedural democracy and protest strategies

Scholars who advance the activist model of civil society tend to take a more or less Habermasian position on legitimacy within public deliberation, that is, as determined by the procedural ideals of deliberation that is free, equal and reasoned, and aimed at consensus on the basis of the common good (Cohen and Arato 1992, Kaldor 2003, Cohen 2009, Edwards 2009). The only binding values or principles are those required as preconditions of deliberation, and a commitment to be bound by the outcome of deliberation. As noted above, the model does not specify any particular conception of the good society, but is does assume that there *is one* agreed conception of the good to which participants can refer. In the context of this discussion, the problem is how the legitimacy of civil society actors' contributions to the public sphere can be judged if they each appeal to different values, or different conception of the same values, in justification of their arguments.

The fragmentation of the public sphere has been often raised as a critique of Habermas' model (Curran 1993, Keane 1998). In *Between Facts and Norms* (1996), Habermas attempted to resolve the issue by defining public opinion as decentred, as "an emergent property of a diffuse network of discourses" (Rehg and Bohman

2002: 39). Within the public sphere there is a pluralism of participation, with different procedural roles along the axis of *centre/periphery* (Habermas 1996: 354–5). The idea is to strike a balance between the efficient decision-making of the political system with influence from the democratic but complex public sphere.

However, the distinction between centre and periphery is not binary, but a gradation of status and influence, with individuals and civil society associations who are recognised and respected for their expertise in certain areas (Habermas 1996: 303) providing "information shortcuts" (Rehg and Bohman 2002: 38) for other citizens. This sacrifices some democratic legitimacy in the interests of pragmatic effectiveness, and assumes that the status is earned rather than based in established power. This suggests that deliberative democracy doesn't quite succeed in overcoming the problems associated with liberal pluralism, that powerful sectional interests can prevail over minority, marginalised or subordinated interests.

Sectional interests, deliberation and negotiation
Joshua Cohen (2009), whose work draws on Habermas' earlier writing, assumes that self-interested individuals will be incapable of concealing their real interests behind reasons that refer to the common good and are commonly acceptable, but are misleading or mistaken. For instance, in relation to his example of hiding "a desire to become wealthier come what may" (2009: 26), this may be concealed behind a trickle-down argument that suggests that their own wealth will benefit others, as opposed to adjusting to a more socially-acceptable objective. Cohen underestimates the distorting potential of power discourse (Foucault 1980, Price 2007).

Whilst an analysis of Habermas' more recent work concludes that he avoids "the elitist contempt for interest-based politics that typically distinguishes conservative theory" (Maus 2002: 123), popular understandings of legitimacy tend to focus on the public or national interest – or "generalizable interests" in Habermasian terms (Cohen and Arato 1992: 363) – as more valid than sectional interests, regardless of the validity of their subordinated claims. Trade unions are arguably most successful in advancing their concerns if their case appeals to a wider political audience than that of their own members, otherwise they tend to be viewed as concerned only to protect their own sectional interests (perhaps by retaining unnecessary jobs and restrictive practices) regardless of the national interest. (Joyce 2002: 74–5). Furthermore, the rhetorical construction of the public interest can be used in conflicting ways, such as the interests of 'taxpayers' versus those of 'public service users', who are identical, yet framed in (self-)opposition.

Another significant problem arises in relation to liberal neutrality. Habermas underestimates the potential for disagreement on moral norms and substantive values, and therefore "that on some justice issues, citizens could find themselves in irreconcilable but reasonable disagreement" (Rehg and Bohman 2002: 45). Whilst it is not necessary that agreement be based on the same reasons, and different groups may accept the same solution for different reasons, even this more abstract level of consensus will not always be possible. Where claims are not epistemic and therefore disagreement cannot be resolved through rational discourse,

Habermas concedes that bargaining and compromise may be necessary, but Rehg and Bohman (2002) question the extent to which citizens are able to distinguish between these types of issue, and question whether compromise is possible in cases where participants do not share a definition of justice.

Instead they propose a "weaker" model that places less onerous requirements for consensus, but instead regards deliberation as simply making it more likely that at least unreasonable disagreement will be resolved, or at least that substantive arguments will be supported by better reasons. Where minorities' values do not prevail they can be assured that decisions are open to revision, allowing them to recognise the legitimacy of the decision on the basis of the legitimacy of the procedure, and to continue to cooperate on the basis that their arguments may be accepted in future. This version does not see reasonable disagreement as a problem, and accords it a legitimate place in the public sphere. Cohen and Arato also argue for "a broader, or more differentiated model of civil society than either Arendt or Habermas offers" (1992: 603), since they include a role for identity-based solidarities. However, there is some disagreement over the role of particularistic identification in social movements.

Counter-cultural identity and performative politics
The solidarity of social movements is often based in shared culture and identity: "A collective actor cannot exist without reference to experiences, symbols and myths which can form the basis of their individuality" (della Porta and Diani 2006: 106). New social movements, and direct action tactics especially, have been closely associated with counter-cultural identities and alternative lifestyles such as communes and cooperatives, but also with the middle classes. In particular, students and the "economically 'decommodified'" middle class – highly educated but precariously employed – are associated with counter-cultural activism (Joyce 2002). Nonetheless, della Porta and Diani argue that the struggle for recognition of that identity is a form of engagement with the wider society that reaches beyond defensive self-legitimacy. Inevitably, this emphasis on identity makes movements vulnerable to stigmatising discourses from opponents, who seek to frame them as outsiders, unable to conform to mainstream norms and expectations (2006: 106).

Kenny argues that these "identity oriented social mobilizations" (2004: 111) are not simply another type of identity group, but a mode of practice. He cites Touraine and Melucci as giving an account of how this practice can be exploratory rather than defensive, aiming to "expand the possibilities for subjects to live autonomous lives: legitimating new ways of living, questioning established traditions and offering resources for participants to enhance their sense of self-worth" (Kenny 2004: 115). This practice is communicative and discursive, but unlike the Habermasian formulation it takes the values and principles of the good society as its subject of contestation, as opposed to as uncontested legitimating referents. The use of public space is interpreted as resisting the commodification of the social realm, and associated narrow notion of normal civility.

This is an account of social movements as underpinned by identity, but not rooted in a particularistic recognition claim, however, some groups such as the anarchist Black Bloc express a more "'embattled' activist subjectivity" (Juris 2011: 105), which may generate solidarity within a movement but can operate to exclude outside publics who may otherwise be sympathetic. Conversely, others argue that the shared activist identity is weak and superficial, that the diverse and contingent identifications of "the consumption-driven lifestyle and identity politics of postmodern society" has led to "low commitment and weakness of self-identification", that potentially undermines political and ideological commitment and sustained cooperation (Rojecki 2011: 93).

Castells (2010: 9–10) distinguishes 'resistance identities' that are defensive and communal or communitarian, from 'project identities' that build identity "expanding toward the transformation of society", but argues that latter increasingly emerge from the former in the context of the network society.

> While in modernity (early or late) project identity was constituted from civil society (as in the case of socialism on the basis of the labor movement), in the network society, project identity, if it develops at all, grows from communal resistance. (Castells 2010: 11–12)

The disconnection between the core and periphery as a result of networked global power has undermined civil society in its more formally organised sense. Identity is therefore less often based on a reflexive account of the individual's personal narrative, but on an injured communal identity, changing the nature of the project identity. However, increasingly, diverse, networked social movements challenge globalised capital through new forms of democratic engagement (Castells 2012), suggesting that the demise of civil forms of attachment and cooperation may not have been so terminal. However, new media technologies are also argued to have presented a challenge to the rationalist stipulations of the public sphere, and fundamentally altered the communication landscape and effective strategies of political address.

Symbolic protest: Image events and the public screen
DeLuca et al. (2011) theorise symbolic protest as an effective alternative to the rational civility of the public sphere, and a tactic that is well-adapted to the contemporary image culture of the "screen age". The "public screen" is defined in direct contradistinction to the public sphere, as characterised by "dissemination, images, hypermediacy, spectacular publicity, cacophony, immersion, distraction and dissent" (2011: 144). They argue that contemporary media culture does not lend itself to the public sphere, so all that the perspective can offer is a critique, not a strategy. The public screen, in contrast, can create a space for dissent within a communication landscape otherwise dominated by the discourses that have mastered its language – especially PR and advertising.

It is a strategy that is expressly pragmatic rather than normative, although they do attempt to suggest that it is a more natural or "fundamental" form of communication than dialogue, but no reasons or explanation for this are offered. They also claim a departure in recognising the public as something that comes into being through interaction, but unlike Bourdieu's (1979) prior assertion that the public does not exist (see also Splichal 2003), it is brought into being through rhetoric rather than argumentation. The power of the public screen is in the ontological power of the image to create its own reality – the world is experienced as images, and therefore they are as real to us unmediated 'reality'. However, the political power of this postmodern resistance of meaning seems to be in contradiction with their assertion that the Seattle WTO protesters were engaged in a struggle to define events – to *contest* meaning is quite different to *resisting* it altogether. Additionally the contestation of meaning is associated as much, if not more, with language, undermining the significance of image.

However, the argument that spectacle is an effective means of drawing attention to an issue must be taken seriously. DeLuca et al. (2011: 151) contest the objections of non-violent activists: "counter to the charges by peaceful protesters, then, such image events did not drown out their message but enabled it to be played more extensively" by manipulating media imperatives. However, they argue that this attention for the arguments advanced through traditional repertoires of protest is not the primary role or power of spectacular image events – instead they are "mind-bombs that expand the universe of thinkable thoughts" (2011: 151). Whilst their depiction of viewing as immersive is convincing, the specific example of smashed corporate windows as breaking the spell of the logo rests on a simplistic notion of cultural reception as passive perception in a state of distraction.

The established repertoires of marches, rallies and strikes, they argue, produce "moribund public spaces and an apathetic public" (2011: 154), however, the wild sense of risk engendered by violent disorder may not be because the images produce an intrinsically "primal sense of being", but due to a sense of novelty and shock that may dissipate over time. Juris (2011) instead distinguishes the direct experience of such confrontational and risky forms of protest, from their mediated form as image events, and argues that there is a tension between the two. For Juris the expression of anger, amplified through "embodied performance", leads to "affective solidarity" (2011: 100). Even then, however, he argues that the greater the use of emotion to mobilise, the more time-limited the action, since activists tire and novel repertoires become routine, and of course there is no direct link between an internal *feeling* of emotional empowerment and *effective* power and influence in external relations. Although Juris considers the combination of confrontational and discursive potentially effective in terms of media attention, he also cautions that the prominence of the more subversive elements could damage broader recruitment.

Summary

The criteria for mainstream political legitimacy may in some cases conflict, or sit uncomfortably, with countercultural attachments, but civil society actors, especially in contemporary social movements will often in any case challenge those legitimating structures. Alternative structures and strategies include forms of direct, participatory and/or deliberative democracy instead of hierarchical representation, and spectacular publicity in place of rational deliberation. The contested values of the good society are a problem for all approaches, however, whether as an unstable point of reference in the legitimating role for deliberative democracy, or as an excluding pressure for the embattled subjectivities or resistance identities of performative politics.

Civility and the public sphere: Social legitimacy

The legitimacy accorded to civil society associations is not limited to legal and democratic judgements, but also social judgements. Public opinion carries the legitimacy of democratic popular sovereignty, though it is generally constructed to a significant degree by news media. The particular social expectations and judgements on civil society actors (especially protesters) include those of public decorum, good manners and shame, the authenticity or sincerity of their argumentation, and either giving offence or taking it too easily.

Public opinion

The politics of protest are centrally concerned with influencing and mobilising public opinion. Broad support demonstrates political legitimacy in terms of reaching out beyond a sectional interest or marginal value system, and also potential political effectiveness, possibly in terms of direct electoral impact, but more likely in terms of the general reputation of the government if faced by a lengthy protest. To some extent publics can be addressed in a physical space, especially in terms of a locally-specific protest such as against a certain development or road-building project, but to gain broader currency requires mediated space. Cottle and Lester (2011: 20) argue that one of the ways in which "the social movement paradigm" is outdated is its "relatively under-developed recognition of how media and communications are now deeply implicated within the structures and opportunities of both social movements and the play of contentious politics more generally". Again, digital communication technologies offer new opportunities for associations and movements to represent themselves directly.

In order to gain mainstream media attention, civil society associations need to conform to the requirements of dominant news values, framing conventions, and newsgathering routines. However, the strategies for attracting attention will not necessarily be the same as those that would be judged and represented sympathetically (but, as noted above, largely ignored). Of particular significance here is the way in which representations of public opinion are used to support media assessments of the social legitimacy of the protest, and often of the protesters personally. Such representations include unsubstantiated judgements of the public 'mood' and dominant norms of proper conduct, the comments of bystanders or 'vox pops', and opinion polls (McLeod and Hertog 1992, Lewis et al. 2005).

Public opinion polling is the most obvious way in which the media measure public opinion, however, Lewis et al. (2005) found that although references to publics on UK TV news were very common (around a third of news items), just 3% of these were substantiated by opinion polls or demonstrations. Far more common were 'vox pops' (39%), but the remainder were unsubstantiated inferences, the vast majority of which were made by the news reporter presenter.

Polling in any case constructs a very specific conception of public – it measures an aggregated mass opinion, and indeed *produces* that opinion by the act of questioning, drawing spontaneous but concrete responses on issues that the respondent may never have previously considered, and which they may not consider important, a problem compounded when newspapers exclude 'don't know' responses from the figures to produce a more decisive result. For these reasons, Bourdieu (1979) argued that "public opinion does not exist" – it is not an extant entity, but something that is constructed by polling.

Similarly, 'vox pops' typically express reactive approval or disapproval, and tend to make less reference to policy than polls, with an emphasis on politicians approval ratings and on problem-identification – issues on which 'something should be done' but without specifying *what* should be done (Lewis et al. 2005: 67–9). They are also far from representative, and subject to journalistic selection and framing, and can therefore be used (as with other sources) as a demonstration of objectivity as strategic ritual – as a protective ritual by which the journalist can put across their own opinion without overtly compromising their professional norms. In any case, since most references to the public are entirely ventriloquising – as 'the public will be asking…' or 'most people don't want…', journalists clearly don't feel that great a need to substantiate such claims, but "feel an obligation – and an ability – to either speak for or about the public" (Lewis et al. 2005: 27).

Traditional letters to the editor, however, are a more participative forum, allowing readers to contribute on their own terms, within the format and discourse of the newspaper. However, research on letters pages in US newspapers found that letters editors "privilege individual expression over the expression of activist groups" since they "prefer the emotionally-charged stories of individuals", whilst the overtly political views of activist groups were regarded as "political rhetoric", lacking "sincerity, authenticity and truth" (Wahl-Jorgensen 2001: 313), and as a "manipulative discourse" (2001: 311) that advocates an argument that can be contradicted rather than a feeling that cannot. We will return to this notion of personal authenticity below, after considering another form of social or cultural legitimacy in relation to more tacit expectations.

Dominant social norms: Manners and shame in social space

Consideration of social norms of personal conduct and appearance in public space takes us back to civility or civic virtue, and to the public/private divide. In this case, 'public' is understood as visibility – in public view – and perhaps as a common right of access to, or use of the space. Sociability is not, however, regarded as public in the political sense, being related neither to collectivity or solidarity, but merely the coexistence in close physical proximity of heterogeneous people, especially in cosmopolitan cities (Weintraub 1997). Both Weintraub (1997) and Seligman (1995) define sociability in terms of civility, but Weintraub's version draws on a notion of pre-modern community attachment that has diminished in modern, individualistic society, whilst Seligman (1995: 207) sees it as intrinsically modern and as a *departure from* communitarian civic virtue.

The distinction rests on the nature of the internal moral voice – the communitarian account is of an individual considering the moral expectations of specific people with whom they have an emotional connection or whose approval or acceptance they seek (Etzioni 2004: 153), whilst the liberal approach is more abstract and reflexive and related to settling conflicts of interest rather than cultural belonging. Adam Smith's internalised other is an impartial observer (Bryant 1995), and Rawls (1971) defined ideal moral judgement as the decisions that individuals would make from behind a 'veil of ignorance' about their own interests and position in society. In contrast, the communitarian perspective is more interested in the cultural context of expectations, which may include tradition, ritual or etiquette.

The characteristic virtue of this form of public space, which it both requires and reinforces, is civility – which is a matter of codes and conventions, no less important for being largely implicit (Weintraub 1997: 23). Proper public conduct may relate to the secular sacred rituals of civic religion that tie the nation together as an imagined community (Bryant 1995, Berezin 2002), such as respect for symbols such as flags or rituals in remembrance of war dead, and also observance of cultural customs such as queuing and turn-taking, deference to elders or authority figures, or wearing clothes that cover certain parts of the body.

Such rituals of sociability are commonly understood as good manners or politeness. Elias (1969) traced the origin of manners and etiquette back to late Medieval Europe, where increasing social complexity and interdependence produced a need for rules and self-restraint. Initially overt rules of behaviour were internalised to the degree that they became second nature and were often followed in private as well as in public, the most powerful being motivated by a sense of shame or disgust. However, Elias also noted that etiquette could be used to exclude those who had not been initiated into the rules and rituals of refined behaviour, and to distinguish between 'established' and 'outsider' communities by stigmatising the other as unrespectable (1994 [1965]). This suggests a distinction between rules that have a social function of regulating equal respect and consideration, and those that are arbitrary codes of belonging or status.

The attempt to present oneself as a person worthy of status and respect is seen as a more conscious and contingent process by Goffman (1959), a public performance that relies on a backstage for individuals to be their 'true' selves, free of the anxiety of constant self-monitoring. In other words, whilst Elias, in common with most theorists of civic virtue and civility, argues that the scrutiny of the observer, whether internal or external, changes the proclivities of the individual, Goffman argues that the performance of self is an inauthentic ritual. The metaphor of stage performance is also reflected in the "dramaturgy" of contemporary protest repertoires.

The dramaturgy of counter-cultural and symbolic protest can be read in different ways in relation to civilised public behaviour and authenticity. In one view such protesters are expressing their authentic, individualistic identities, in which case they may be criticised for an impolite lack of restraint – as childishly "projecting one's urges and rages directly onto the world" (Elshtain 1997: 178) – or more favourably interpreted as challenging the hegemonic social control of dominant norms. However, if protesters seek recognition for their cultural identities, and even more if they understand their identity as intrinsically oppositional to the acceptable mainstream, they risk being dismissed as "marginal squatters and punks committed more to their subcultural lifestyles than political change" (Juris 2011: 108).

A more political view is that the presentation of protest identity is a conscious performance, strategically appealing to popular culture, such as Greenpeace's marketing of their anti-whaling activities with signifiers of "pirate chic" (Crouch and Damjanov 2011: 189). The presentation therefore may be transgressive of social norms, but in a way that is paradoxically acceptable or appealing to mainstream publics as rebellious or edgy. Their public conduct is therefore confrontational to authorities but not to 'the public', although it is notable that this example takes place in a remote space that is not public in the sense of physical proximity and inconvenience. However, this professionalisation and popularisation of protest can attract criticism for inauthentic and manipulative rhetoric that, in tackling political PR on its own ground, fails to rise above it.

Dramaturgy therefore assumes a contrast between politeness and authenticity; between individualistically but authentically doing as one pleases, and politely (whether through consideration of others or conformity with social control) performing a publicly acceptable political persona. This presents a difficulty in attributing legitimacy to civil society and other discursive actors, since both civility and authenticity are valued in politics.

> The fact that action is dramaturgical does not mean that the public sphere is
> impoverished [...but] nonetheless manages to convey the sense that authenticity,
> if it is ever to be found in modern society, is more likely to be found in the
> shadows than the sunlight. (Wolfe 1997: 184)

That is not, however, to say that the interpretation and value of authenticity as a legitimating concept is uncontested.

Political authenticity and sincerity

The notion of the 'authentic self' is a product of individualist modernity, defined as the internal essence and potential of the individual, and therefore the moral ideal is self-realisation and self-fulfilment through free choice, which is criticised by communitarians for narcissism and viewing relationships with others as purely instrumental (Taylor 1991). In political terms, then, authenticity is the expression of a personal (instrumental or emotional) response to individual experience.

Accordingly, protesters pursuing their own instrumental interests are regarded as more legitimate (and also more predictable) in their motivations than those "who protest about issues that do not concern them directly, and whose themes are more "abstract" and easily 'manipulated'" (della Porta 1998: 242). For instance, whilst in the UK the Stop the War Campaign against the 2003 Iraq invasion was a broad protest movement, driven by a point of principle and a feeling of moral responsibility, in the US it was centred around families of soldiers, since "Grieving relatives have a particular moral purchase on the right to protest" (Powell 2007: 122).

This definition of authenticity is even reflected in deliberative democratic accounts of legitimacy.

> The political public sphere can fulfil its function of perceiving and thematizing encompassing social problems only insofar as it develops out of the communication taking place among *those who are potentially affected*" (Habermas 1996: 365 [emphasis in original])

The role of the media audience is to distinguish between established organisations that appear "before the public" (representing sectional interests and identities) and less formally organised actors who "emerge from" the public and are more "authentic" because less distorted by vested interests (Habermas 1996: 375).[4]

The understanding of authenticity as resisting the exertion of power from the system is shared by Marshall Berman (1971), although he frames it in less instrumental terms and rather in terms of feelings of alienation and repression. Alienation is not only a product of powerlessness but also the humiliation of the othered. Taylor (1991) argues that identifications such as homosexuality can be seen in liberal terms as a choice – a preference – but that this demeans the significance to a trivial matter of taste. He proposes a more communitarian sense of authenticity in which significance is imbued from an intersubjective social context, that is, from recognition. However, Kenny (2004: 157–60) criticises Taylor for failing to recognise the difference between groups' identities that are freely asserted and those that are ascribed and resisted, and for understating the

---

4   However, being affected by the issue is in itself a form of interest in the outcome, so he also stipulates that such concerns must be translated into the disinterested terms appropriate to the public sphere.

role of individual autonomy in defining a moral sense of the good. He concludes that authenticity is "morally dubious and practically unwise" (2004: 167) as a definition of legitimate claims for recognition, which should instead be based in "the principles and values pertinent to democratic citizenship – stability, self-worth, equal respect and capability".

Much as Kenny seeks to resolve divisions between liberalism and communitarian identity politics, McAfee (2000) attempts the same between deliberative liberalism and postmodern subjectivity, proposing an emphasis on intersubjectivity as an inclination of the individuals toward others through an open-minded deliberative practice. However, this more subjective and particularist version of political debate is rejected by Kantian liberals and neo-liberals. Elshtain (1997: 177), for instance, objects to any notion of 'private' identity as political.

> [...] such notions die hard in a therapeutic culture like our own, where personal authenticity becomes the test of political credibility [...] this version of identity absolutism shares with other modes of twentieth-century expressivist politics a celebration of "feelings" or "private authenticity" as an alternative to public reason and political judgement. (Elshtain 1997: 177)

Elshtain's overall argument is a neo-liberal rejection of positive rights claims, but it also suggests a neo-conservative objection that the assertion of sexual identities transgresses the "boundary of shame" (1997: 176) in invites disapproval.

There can therefore develop a stand-off between those who assert an identity that others find offensive, and those others who criticise or talk disparagingly about that identity in a way the group find offensive. The increasing awareness of the offence caused by certain terms that connote racial slurs, sexist attitudes, and other prejudicial language has produced a counter-accusation of 'political correctness' as a form of censorship or imposed liberal orthodoxy. The apocryphal nature of many examples of political correctness has in turn led to a vigorous defence that argues that the whole notion has been invented by neo-conservatives to discredit the left, higher education, and in particular the discipline of cultural studies (Wilson 1995, Feldstein 1997). However, Kenny (2004: 19) expressed concern about identity groups' definition of any criticism of their cultural behaviour and practices as an affront to their dignity. This defensive form of identity can lead to stalemate between conflicting rights and recognition claims, and fear of causing unintended offence could cause some issues to become taboo.

Political emotion
The accommodation of moral perspectives as legitimate contributions to the public sphere covers the substantive, but skirts the issue of the affective. Whilst reasons can be given in support of value judgements, even if they are not epistemically conclusive, emotions are thought to be the opposite of reason. Liberal and neo-liberal theorists in particular argue that "To project one's urges and rages directly onto the world is to eradicate altogether a prime requisite of politics – the need

for judgment based on criteria that are public in nature" (Elshtain 1997: 178). However, social movement scholars have noted that emotion is an important factor in the mobilisation of collective action as they play a significant part, not only in solidarity (Juris 2011), but in motivating "moral indignation and anger" (della Porta and Diani 2006: 12). Indeed, even liberal theorists saw a role for emotion, such as Smith's 'moral sentiment'.

Aristotle theorised both reason and emotion as essential for social and political virtue, and whilst he recognised that untamed emotion can be hot and impetuous, he categorised a lack of emotion as a form of vice (Sokolon 2006). Marlene Sokolon's analysis of Aristotle's thought on political emotion concludes that few emotions are intrinsically positive or negative, but can be "habituated" into positive dispositions. For instance, anger tempered by reason and gentleness is essential for the virtue of courage, though without such constraint it can lead instead to rashness (2006: 63). This habituation is dependent on the political context which influences citizens' emotional judgements of virtue through laws and education. Under a good political regime, "individual experience within a political environment can modify or educate those natural tendencies towards virtuous action" (Sokolon 2006: 30). Contemporary theorists influenced by Aristotle tend to be of a communitarian persuasion, regarding liberal individualism as antithetical to virtuous dispositions.

> Democracy, for example, as a rule tends to create character types that yield frequently to their desires and emotions. In consequence, in democracies in which freedom is defined as living as one wants, the typical citizen has excessive emotional responses. (Sokolon 2006: 30)

This position would interpret challenges to mainstream or dominant culture by social movements as emotion untempered by reason rather than a 'moderate' ethical position (but also suggests that neo-liberals should be accepting of political emotion). The need for political emotion to be habituated or tempered is often expressed in terms of politeness.

Politeness and offence: Contentious politics and civility

Edwards (2009: 77) identifies the "understanding of "civility" as politeness and the conflation of civil society with "consensus" not debate or disagreement" as a threat to the public sphere. He argues that the discourse of offence has a "deadening" effect on debate, especially in the United States, where research "found that public debates about politics were frowned on as "divisive" or "uncivil" so that people's most important thoughts were relegated to their private interactions" (2009: 78).

This is particularly associated with defensive forms of identity politics, whose sense of injury blocks their willingness to participate open-mindedly or discursively.

> And because the group is aggrieved, offended in a way that permits no compromise, civility – rule-governed activity that allows a pluralist society to

exist and to persist over time because not everything is up for grabs and because
I cannot always get what I want – is scornfully rejected. (Elshtain 1997: 175)

However, Elshtain assumes that all identity politics employs a discourse of
offence, whilst using a non-discursive rhetorical construction of such activists as
spoilt children unwilling to play nicely and recognise the quasi-parental authority
of peacekeeping social rules. If that means withdrawing all value-based issues
from public discussion, on the basis that we cannot discuss them without causing
or claiming offence, then the effect would surely be to maintain the status quo on
these issues, or to refer simply to tradition in support of existing values, principles
and universalising belief systems.

Liberal theorists Rawls and Ackerman both exclude some issues from public
discussion to avoid moral conflict and controversy (Baynes 2002: 24), whilst
Etzioni's new communitarianism places moral debate in the social realm, relieving
it of procedural rules of legitimate participation, but is as vague as proponents of
deliberative democracy on how this produces a "truly shared consensus" (Etzioni
2004: 156). Kenny's compromise position aims to combine substantive and
ontologically grounded values with procedural principles of openness and mutual
respect.

> […] it is paramount to establish a public sphere in which individuals can speak
> critically and playfully about their own and others' identities; be free to explore
> and amend the identities imposed upon them; and treated with a presumption of
> respect when they do relate to, and draw upon, group cultures and experiences.
> (Kenny 2004: 167)

Neither is this limited to the politics of recognition, as if the politics of redistribution
were unrelated to deeply-held values and beliefs. The avoidance of controversy
and offence can equally be applied to traditional left/right ideologies, class
identities, and disputes over resource allocation that are deeply principled in their
basis, despite the pragmatic and managerial discourses of neo-liberal capitalism.

Summary

Definitions of legitimacy are contested on grounds of legal, moral, political, social
and cultural criteria, not only between different normative models of civil society,
but within different versions and iterations of the activist model. All of these criteria
are interrelated, with moral or ethical values playing an especially central role,
including as a context legitimising challenges to law and law-breaking for a higher
purpose, and as a common reference point in political appeals from sectional or
particularistic positions. Nonetheless, these various grounds are distinct enough to
be a useful way of approaching the case studies in the following chapters.

Chapter 3
Civil Society in the News:
Case Studies

The various ways in which civil society can be defined, enacted and delegitimised are circulated in society via news media. The following chapters will explore the media representation of various individual and collective actors that could be understood as part of civil society, their values, repertoires, structures and personal qualities. Through this analysis it is hoped that a picture will emerge of the mediated definition of legitimacy in and of civil society, and the extent to which news media reflect the contested ground of the concept in social, cultural and politics terms.

The presence of civil society as a topic in news media is difficult to discern as a reference point in day-to-day news reporting, and it is not a term frequently used (or not in the context of British politics) but as a topic it rather lends itself to case studies. Civil society has, in fact, been discernable in UK news coverage over the period of this study, 2010–2012, in a broad range of prominent stories.

Case studies

Five stories have been selected for analysis, all but one of a broadly similar scale of coverage. The sample of news articles on these stories is not exhaustive, but focuses on the period in which the story appeared every day in many newspapers, up until such point as coverage became more sporadic, and excluding the long tail of articles following up aspects such as the outcome of court cases. The sample in each case aimed to cover the key incidents in the timeline of the story.

The student anti-tuition fee protest was chosen to represent coverage of political 'violence' and public order policing. It would have been interesting, with more time and space, to compare this with the 'summer riots' sparked by the police shooting of Mark Duggan, but within the constraints of this study the more overtly political, and less comprehensively delegitimised conflict was chosen. Connectedly, the Mark Kennedy scandal was chosen as an examination of the policing of public protest from the perspective of police surveillance, which is a growing concern for civil liberties.

The Occupy movement was chosen as the most prominent case of the growing respectability of 'anti-capitalist' protest against unaccountable corporate power. Most obviously this could be set in the context of the broader coverage of the global movement against austerity measures in which the London camp had its origins – the Greek riots, the Spanish Indignados (or 15M movement), and Occupy Wall St,

Table 3.1 Total coverage by case study (number of words)

Newspaper title	Pope n	Pope vert %	Students n	Students vert %	Kennedy n	Kennedy vert %	Unions n	Unions vert %	Occupy n	Occupy vert %	Total n	Total vert %
Guardian	13,374	12.7%	17,448	17.8%	26,474	36.7%	19,529	19%	32,105	25.1%	108,930	21.5%
Times	15,012	14.2%	9,436	9.6%	6,278	8.7%	7,690	7.5%	14,436	11.3%	52,852	10.4%
Daily Telegraph	5,775	5.5%	9,568	9.8%	4,037	5.6%	12,539	12.2%	13,289	10.4%	45,208	8.9%
Daily Mail	7,119	6.7%	6,916	7.1%	8,491	11.8%	10,524	10.2%	6,906	5.4%	39,956	7.9%
Independent	4,809	4.6%	7,104	7.3%	2,771	3.8%	11,394	11.1%	12,296	9.6%	38,374	7.6%
Express	6,794	6.4%	2,604	2.7%	1,831	2.5%	9,209	8.9%	6,071	4.8%	26,509	5.2%
Independent on Sunday	9,053	8.6%	3,888	4%	3,187	4.4%	0	0%	9,868	7.7%	25,996	5.1%
Herald	7,526	7.1%	4,267	4.4%	1,314	1.8%	3,755	3.6%	6,789	5.3%	23,651	4.7%
Western Mail	3,758	3.6%	4,974	5.1%	792	1.1%	7,549	7.3%	3,884	3%	20,957	4.1%
Mirror	5,759	5.4%	3,460	3.5%	917	1.3%	8,651	8.4%	1,903	1.5%	20,690	4.1%
Observer	2,590	2.5%	7,131	7.3%	2,171	3%	0	0%	8,775	6.9%	20,667	4.1%
Sunday Times	7,653	7.2%	2,743	2.8%	4,703	6.5%	0	0%	5,165	4%	20,264	4.0%
Sun	3,099	2.9%	2,880	2.9%	208	0.3%	7,760	7.5%	1,372	1.1%	15,319	3.0%
Belfast Telegraph	4,609	4.4%	3,817	3.9%	789	1.1%	2,556	2.5%	1,265	1%	13,036	2.6%
Sunday Telegraph	5,605	5.3%	4,567	4.7%	1,961	2.7%	0	0%	394	0.3%	12,527	2.5%
Mail on Sunday	0	0.0%	3,526	3.6%	5,102	7.1%	0	0%	866	0.7%	9,494	1.9%
Daily Star	779	0.7%	1,122	1.1%	0	0%	1,879	1.8%	1,325	1%	5,105	1.0%
Sunday Express	1,203	1.1%	1,822	1.9%	635	0.9%	0	0%	624	0.5%	4,284	0.8%
Sunday Mirror	377	0.4%	643	0.7%	207	0.3%	0	0%	204	0.2%	1,431	0.3%
People	493	0.5%	0	0%	177	0.2%	0	0%	0	0%	670	0.1%
Sunday Star	303	0.3%	0	0%	0	0%	0	0%	182	0.1%	485	0.1%
Total	105,690	100%	97,916	100%	72,045	100%	103,035	100%	127,719	100%	506,405	100%

but that could be a book in itself. Similarly, the movement took inspiration from the Arab Spring uprisings, but it would be impossible to do justice to that issue as just a single case study. The UK context includes the 'Democracy Square' occupation, and Brian Haw's one man protest, as well as UK UnCut, who have brought the issue of corporate tax avoidance to mainstream prominence, including the interrogation of Google, Amazon, and Starbucks CEOs by the Public Accounts Select Committee. However, the global context and local impact of Occupy in shifting discourses and representations of public opinion made it impossible to exclude.

The public sector trade union strikes were selected to represent the traditional organisations of civil society, and the legitimacy of interest politics, whilst the state visit of Pope Benedict XVI represents the role of values, the legitimacy of identity politics and also the Big Society. Other candidates for the Big Society were difficult to identify, with few concrete policies and sporadic coverage at best.

Pope Benedict XVI: Three speeches on the role of religion in public life (17th–19th September 2010)

During a state visit to the UK in September 2010 Pope Benedict XVI made three key speeches (among other visits and smaller addresses) that all touched on the central theme of the role of religion in public life. The visit generated a huge amount of news media coverage, including discussion of broader issues involving the Catholic Church, especially the child abuse scandal, as well as colour pieces about the Pope's reception by various dignitaries and crowds of well-wishers. The selection of a manageable sample therefore necessarily excluded some of this contextual material in favour of those articles that made fairly substantial (more than a passing) reference to the three speeches.

The first day of the sample covered the Scottish leg of the visit, and the addresses at Holyrood in Edinburgh and Bellahouston Park in Glasgow (on 16th September, reported the following day), the second reported the Westminster Hall speech, and the third day picked up the Sunday newspapers' analysis. The 105,690 words over 158 articles in those three days make this the second largest sample of all the case studies, despite being the shortest time-frame.

Holyrood: Opening speech at the royal reception in Edinburgh
This being a state visit, the Pope was formally received by the Queen and Prince Philip at the Palace of Holyroodhouse in Edinburgh, the Queen's official Scottish residence. There were the customary formalities of thanks and acknowledgement of the various dignitaries present and fulsome praise for the host country, though broadly framed in relation to the role of Christianity in the monarchy, history, traditions and culture of the UK. The Queen also made a speech in reply, praising the international role of the Holy See[1] in peace, development and charity, and

---

1   The Holy See is recognised as a sovereign entity, which controversially allowed this visit, unlike visits by previous popes such as John Paul II, to be given the status of a

expressing support for efforts to overcome sectarian conflict, and a conviction that "freedom to worship is at the core of our tolerant and democratic society".

Bellahouston Park: Homily to the faithful in Glasgow
The Pope then travelled to Glasgow to conduct an open-air mass, reportedly attended by around 70,000 people, in the same park where his predecessor Pope John Paul II had given a similar mass in 1982, but to a reported 300,000 people. He referred to the social and cultural changes since then, including work to overcome sectarian conflict in Scotland, and the tradition of Catholic schools in the country. The latter was linked to an "evangelisation of culture" and "the promotion of faith's wisdom and vision in the public forum" set against those who would "exclude religious belief from public discourse". The homily then moved on to the inspiration followers should draw from various Scottish saints, and specific messages for the bishops, priests, and young Catholics of Scotland, with instructions for service to god and avoidance of sinful temptations.

Westminster Hall: Speech to 'civil society'
The following day, Benedict delivered his keynote speech at Westminster Hall in London to an audience including MPs, religious leaders, and members of 'civil society'. The arguments alluded to in the previous addresses were elaborated on far more fully in this speech, arguing for the role of religion in promoting the common good, and discussing its relationship with government, reason, and secular human rights. He also developed his theme of the "marginalisation of religion" by "secular rationality" (in rather more conciliatory terms than the previous day's reference to "atheist extremism").

Student anti-tuition fees protest: NUS march and breakaway Millbank action (10th–15th November 2010)

The first of a series of student protests against the proposed increase in the cap on university tuition fees took place on 10th November 2010, and was followed by further protests on 24th and 30th November and 9th December.[2] A march and rally had been officially arranged and sanctioned by the Metropolitan Police, passing Whitehall, Downing Street, and the Houses of Parliament. A breakaway

---

state visit. It has Episcopal jurisdiction over the Catholic church throughout the world, as opposed to the Vatican state which is simply a city state.

2   Later protests were organised by the National Campaign Against Fees and Cuts, smaller and far more heavily policed, with more arrests. On 24th November, protesters were kettled from the early afternoon until late in the evening, so the following week protesters dispersed when police blocked their route, but repeatedly blocked by police lines, many returned to be kettled at Trafalgar Square. Notable incidents included the vandalism of a police van, which was then encircled by school-girls who prevented further damage (24th November), and an attack on a car carrying Prince Charles and his wife (9th December).

group broke into and occupied 30 Millbank, where the Conservative Party has its headquarters, causing damage to property and staging a rooftop protest.

The cap on tuition fees had been fixed at £3,000, rising with inflation to £3,290 at the time of the protest, but the Browne review recommended raising this to £9,000. In opposition, the Liberal Democrats had opposed the measure, and leader Nick Clegg had personally signed an NUS-authored pledge to vote against any proposed increase in fees. Once in coalition government with the Conservative party, the Liberal Democrats dropped this policy and instead negotiated measures to provide support for students from a low income background. Opposition and anger was such that Clegg was later moved to issue an apology in a statement scheduled for broadcast during the party conference (though only for making the pledge, not breaking it), which promptly appeared in an edited, auto-tuned spoof version on satirical website *the poke*.

The main march and rally was organised by the National Union of Students (NUS) and the Universities and Colleges Union (UCU), and attracted a much larger turnout than anticipated. Organisers told police that they expected 24,000, but police expected just 15,000. In the event, organisers estimated attendance at 50,000, and the police put it at half that number. Only 225 police officers were deployed to police the march, at which police judged there to be little risk of violence.

It was estimated that around 200 protesters occupied Millbank, cheered on by a further 1,000 outside. One student threw a fire extinguisher off the roof, and was later given a custodial sentence for violent disorder. There were 35 arrests on the day, and a further 19 in the following days. Fourteen people were reported to have been injured, most of whom were protesters.

On the day of the protest coverage was dominated by sympathetic, left-leaning newspapers, mostly reporting the large number of expected participants (*Guardian*, *Independent*, *Times*, *Western Mail* 10/11/10). The following day, the story was picked up by all of the newspapers, with a predictable focus on the instances of violence, and the scale of participation cited in problematic terms, in relation to inadequate police presence. Columnists only picked the story up from around 13th November, when controversy had emerged following expressions of support from academics and Labour MPs, who were then accused of condoning violence.

Mark Kennedy: Police infiltration of environmental protest (10th–19th January 2011)

The extent of police infiltration of protest movements came to light with the collapse of the court case against a group of environmental protesters accused of plotting to occupy the Ratcliffe on Soar power station near Nottingham[3]. Mark Kennedy had

---

3   Twenty of the protesters charged with conspiring to break into the power station had earlier pleaded guilty and received a light sentence from a sympathetic judge who concluded that they were acting with "the highest possible motives", but a further six denied that they had agreed to be involved in the action.

already been unmasked as an undercover police officer on Indymedia in October 2010 by members of the protest group he had infiltrated, but it was when his role in planning the occupation was about to be raised in the defence case by lawyers acting for the activists that it reached public prominence.

Kennedy had spent seven years living undercover, and had developed personal and intimate relationships with activists whilst in the guise of Mark Stone, a "freelance climber". He was also accused of operating as an agent provocateur by supplying resources, including a van, and taking a prominent role in organisation and strategy. There was controversy over the extent to which he had acted as a rogue officer or was acting under the instruction of his superiors, the extent and effectiveness of supervision, and the legitimacy and accountability of the undercover unit in charge. There was a political response on 19th January 2011, when ACPO's powers were withdrawn.

Whilst all but two newspapers in the sample paid some attention to this story, coverage was patchier than the other cases, spread out over 10 days, and lower overall in word count. It was also, perhaps predictably, the story on which the *Guardian* most emphatically dominated the coverage, accounting for 37% of the total word-count on the story and with over three times the volume of the next greatest coverage (rather more surprisingly, the *Daily Mail*). Otherwise the coverage was mostly in the *Times, Telegraph* and the Sunday papers (picking up the *Mail on Sunday's* exclusive interview in the later editions), whilst the *Sun* practically ignored the story, with only two news in brief items on the story, and the *Mirror* ran one article focusing on Kennedy 'going native'. The tabloids, especially the *Sun* rely heavily on the police as a source of news, and are likely to be reluctant to displease their contacts.

Public sector union strikes (27th June–1st July 2011)

Four unions representing public sectors workers held coordinated strike action on 30th June 2011 in opposition to changes to pensions. The government proposed, following recommendations from Lord Hutton's report, to change pensions from final salary to career average, increase contributions and raise the retirement age at which workers qualify for the full pension. Unions opposed the latter two measures, accepting the change to career average, which is still a defined benefit scheme with a guaranteed level of income, rather than the money purchase schemes that are now more common in the private sector, where the investment risk is borne by the worker.

The unions involved were the Public and Commercial Services (PCS) union, the National Union of Teachers (NUT), the Association of Teachers and Lecturers (ATL), and the Universities and Colleges Union (UCU), who collectively had around 750,000 members. Turnout for the various unions ballots ranged from 32% to 40%, and the proportion voting in favour of strike action from 61% to 92%. On both counts the lowest were the PCS, and the highest the NUT. The PCS represent a broad range of public sector workers, including civil servants, some of whom are very highly paid and accrue substantial pensions, whilst leader Mark Serwotka insisted that the average pension among his members was just £6,000.

In comparison with the student protest, where there was little attention prior to the action, followed by fall-out extending for several days after, coverage of the strike started early with news of anticipated disruption to services and Q&A sections on the background of the dispute, peaked on the day of action, and fell off sharply after a single day of coverage of the strike action.

Occupy London Stock Exchange: Occupation at St Paul's Cathedral (15th–30th October 2011)

The Occupy movement emerged in the USA in September 2011, inspired by the Spanish 15M movement (also known as the Indignados) which had been active since May that year, and came to widespread prominence with the Occupy Wall Street (OWS) camp in Zuccotti Park in New York, established on 17th September 2011. By October, the movement had spread across the globe, and the London encampment at St Paul's Cathedral began at the end of a march as part of a Global Day of Action on 15th October. The initial target had been Paternoster Square, directly outside the London Stock Exchange, but the City had been able to secure a High Court injunction preventing access, as it is private property. The chance involvement of the Church of England may have had a significant impact on the policing of the protest, and on the development of the story in the news.

On the first day, the Canon Chancellor of the cathedral, Dr Giles Fraser – a prominent church figure and regular contributor to the Thought for the Day slot on BBC Radio 4's flagship current affairs programme, Today – asked the police to leave the steps of the cathedral and expressed support for the right to protest. However, when around 150–200 tents were erected over the first few days the cathedral authorities made it clear that they wished the protesters to leave. On 21st October the Dean of St Paul's announced that the cathedral would close its doors for the first time since the Second World War, citing health and safety concerns, but following minor changes to the arrangement of tents, and having failed to fatally undermine the protest, re-opened five days later.

Giles Fraser resigned on 27th October, in disagreement with moves to initiate legal action (in cooperation with the City of London Corporation, the Local Authority for the square mile) to have the occupation evicted, followed by the Chaplain, Fraser Dyer on 28th and finally the Dean, The Rt Revd Graeme Knowles, following criticism of the cathedral's decision to proceed with legal action. Legal action was eventually taken by the City of London Corporation alone, and the eviction took place on 28th February 2012.

Occupy was by far the slowest-burning story, with the greatest amount of coverage overall, but spread over 16 days. Interestingly, the peaks and troughs in coverage didn't follow the development of events, apart from the resignation of Giles Fraser reported on 28th October, as the story was dominated by feature articles, comment and opinion. This is perhaps also the reason that coverage petered out, even though there were still developments such as new sites, events, music concerts and so on. The absence of clearly-defined aims may have helped the newsworthiness of the politics, as intrigued journalists tried to make sense of the protest. However, this curiosity and caution gradually shifted over time as new delegitimising frames were established.

Again, coverage was dominated by the *Guardian*, which accounted for a quarter of all coverage, and twice as much as the next most attentive newspaper (*Times*). The coverage was also more concentrated in fewer titles than the other stories, with 94% of the coverage in 11 of the 21 newspapers, and 71% in the top six (*Guardian, Times, Telegraph, Independent, Independent on Sunday*, and *Observer*). Of the most attentive papers, the *Guardian* were strongly supportive, the *Times* rather ambivalent, and the *Telegraph* in opposition. The most fervently critical newspaper, the *Express*, was ranked only ninth in terms of coverage, and only really picked up the story when the cathedral closure presented an opportunity to undermine the legitimacy of the protest. Conversely, the *Mirror* gave the occupation limited coverage until the counter-backlash around the 28th and 29th October.

Newspaper sample

The sample included all of the main national daily and Sunday newspapers included in the Nexis UK press category, except for the *Morning Star*, which does not have a broad circulation. In addition, the sample included the largest national newspaper in each of the devolved nations of the UK – the *Herald* in Scotland, the *Belfast Telegraph* in Northern Ireland, and the *Western Mail* in Wales, since there is a distinct political climate in each, although the particularity of the media is being eroded by competition from the 'tartanised' Scottish editions of the UK papers, who can take advantage of economies of scale, and by the general cost-cutting pressures on the regional and local press across the UK.

Thematic/framing analysis using CAQDAS

The research used a form of thematic analysis that is principally qualitative but also has a quantitative element. Within a broad framework of general themes informed by the theoretical exploration in Chapter 2 (such as virtues, incivility, interests and so on), the more specific thematic categories emerged from the text, rather than being precisely defined at the outset as in purely quantitative content analysis. However, those themes could also be quantified in terms of the number of newspaper titles, articles and words, and their significance in indicated in the context of other themes and as a proportion of overall coverage.

The articles in the sample were downloaded in electronic form from the Nexis database, which allowed for computer-assisted analysis using NVivo. The use of computer-assisted qualitative software programs (CAQDAS) as a data management tool to facilitate (but not perform) analysis is time-saving, transparent, and allows checks on consistency (Bringer et al. 2006). 'Code and retrieve' functions allow data to be categorised (as hyperlinked 'nodes') and for the categories to be worked into a framework as suggested by grounded theory (Glaser and Strauss 1968) but whist retaining a direct and accessible link with the original text and the extract in context.

Nodes were used as both "resource" for qualitative analysis of contextually grounded meaning, and "representation" of framing as dominant, contested, or marginal in comparative context. In other words, the coding functioned both to gather material for analysis and to summarise how representative each analytic unit was of the overall sample. This prevented the subconscious selection of content that supported a particular hypothesis, or an impression that the selected frame was more prominent than others would perceive it.

All material directly quoted from or paraphrased and attributed to a source was coded, under categories including civil society, politicians, and police, which were then 'coded on' to subcategories. This made it possible to contextualise the news-framing in terms of source access, and to judge the extent to which the established theories of elite or official sources as a filter on news angles (Herman and Chomsky 1988) or as primary definers (Hall et al. 1978) still hold, or whether the hierarchy of credibility (Becker 1969) has been overthrown in the new media age as argued by Cottle (2011).

In one of the stories, the Pope's state visit, much of the quoted material was drawn from the same three speeches, which were the central topic of the story. In that instance it was practical to use the node of newspaper quotes from the Pope to code transcripts of *the speeches themselves* by newspaper, showing the pattern of selection from the source material, including that which did not make it into the news. Although it would be impractical to similarly code all sources in all cases, without the expertise and resources of Lewis et al. (2008) to root them out, this is a useful contextualisation where there is a clear primary definer.

The search function was used to measure the frequency of specific terms and phrases such as 'hardworking' taxpayers, 'fat cat' bankers or union leaders, and 'softly-softly' policing, and metaphors such as 'siege' of St Paul's, anarchist 'hijack', and 'gold-plated' pensions. Matrices were used to cross-tabulate thematic nodes against newspaper titles (coded as 'cases'), date (collected as 'sets' of documents), or against other coding categories such as sources. Data was tabulated by 'coding reference' if measuring the incidence of a term, or by word-count if measuring the volume of coverage dedicated to a particular news-frame or angle. However, the use of specific terms was also examined in context, for instance to judge whether a term was being used uncritically, in sceptical or distancing quotes, or being directly challenged as misrepresentative or delegitimising.

Chapter 4
The Good Society:
Virtues, Interests, and Justice

Media discussion of the good society inevitably focuses on the perceived shortcomings of the lived experience, the incivilities and injustices that suggest social breakdown, and the deterioration of authority, trust, or the social contract. Political discourse has reflected and responded to these moral panics with talk of a 'respect agenda' (Blair) or 'broken Britain' (Cameron). There have also, however, been news stories about individuals or groups in civil society advocating a particular vision of the good society.

Debate over common values and morals in Britain – and elsewhere in Western Europe – has been dominated in recent years by arguments over the role of religion in public life. Recurrent themes include the established position of Christian traditions (such as prayer in council meetings), the right to express religious observance through dress (including the veil but also Christian jewellery at work), and above all the conflicting rights of religious observance and freedom from discrimination on the basis of gender and sexuality. Pope Benedict XVI delivered three speeches during his state visit to the UK in September 2010 that addressed all of these issues, albeit obliquely in some cases, and generated extensive debate on personal conscience, national identity, and the state regulation of virtue, as well as the recognition claims of identity politics.

In contrast, the values and principles of social justice and equality are often disparaged as piously moralising rather than upstandingly moral. The Occupy LSX encampment in the grounds of St Paul's Cathedral inadvertently revealed the tension between the Church of England's establishment position and its stated values, and the distinction between charity and social change. The protest, along with more traditional sources of dissent, in the form of the student tuition fees protest and public sector strikes, prompted debate on the nature of justice, fairness and the public interest. It explored the relationship between idealism and pragmatism, with particular attention to the virtues (wealth creation) and vices (greed, inequality) associated with negative economic liberties and the withdrawal of the state from public services.

This chapter will explore the range of mediated debates on sources of civic virtues and values, and on the role of civil society in its various forms in generating and reproducing them, starting with the question of whether our shared moral values should have a collective, institutional, or individual origin. The second half of the chapter will examine the ways in which particular values are appealed to in political debate. The first addresses the tension between individual liberty and a collective notion of virtue, the second the tension between economic liberty and a social democratic notion of justice. The first pits broadly liberal perspectives on the role of civil society against communitarian and socially conservative views, the second neo-liberal against activist understandings.

Virtue and liberty

The origin of virtue in society is a topic inevitably most clearly defined by religious groups, given that religion offers, in the abstract, the clearest answer to the question – it comes from, or is at least inspired by God. However, the conflicting moral authority from increasing religious pluralism and democratically-agreed secular values are not easily resolved with a strong role for religion in public life. This was the task Pope Benedict set for himself in a series of three speeches during his state visit in September 2010.

The Pope's first speech was at Holyrood in Edinburgh, following a formal greeting by the Queen, where he argued that Christianity is the "foundation" of "traditional" British values. Later that day, he delivered a homily at an outdoor mass in Glasgow's Bellahouston Park, which addressed the faithful on matters of faith, but also introduced the theme of the role of religion in public life and its compatibility with principles of equality and liberty, but with a particular slant on the "evangelisation" of British culture.

The speech at Westminster Hall the following day expanded in far more detail on the role of religion in public life, and in particular the extent to which religious conscience should be subject to state regulation, as well as making the claim that Christian voices are marginalised in contemporary public life. This was more extensively quoted than the two preceding speeches – over half (51%) of the speech appeared somewhere in the press, in comparison with 39% of the Holyrood speech and 30% of the Bellahouston Park address. The Westminster Hall speech also accounted for twice the volume of coverage of either other, though partly because it was twice as long as the Holyrood speech.

Table 4.1   The proportion of the Pope's speeches reported in the press

	Westminster Hall		Holyrood Palace		Bellahouston Park	
	n	vert%	n	vert%	n	vert%
Pope Benedict's speeches	1,814	100%	972	100%	1,562	100%
Quoted by any newspaper	925	51.0%	384	39.5%	475	30.4%
Times	583	32.1%	94	9.7%	305	19.5%
Herald	354	19.5%	217	22.3%	112	7.2%
Guardian	366	20.2%	228	23.5%	70	4.5%

	Westminster Hall		Holyrood Palace		Bellahouston Park	
	n	vert%	n	vert%	n	vert%
Express	249	13.7%	184	18.9%	42	2.7%
Daily Mail	202	11.1%	163	16.8%	88	5.6%
Daily Telegraph	147	8.1%	133	13.7%	62	4.0%
Sun	103	5.7%	23	2.4%	169	10.8%
Independent	102	5.6%	91	9.4%	55	3.5%
Belfast Telegraph	105	5.8%	84	8.6%	55	3.5%
Mirror	106	5.8%	77	7.9%	43	2.8%
Western Mail	35	1.9%	142	14.6%	42	2.7%
Independent on Sunday	93	5.1%	6	0.6%	3	0.2%
Observer	17	0.9%	4	0.4%	21	1.3%
Daily Star	0	0%	37	3.8%	0	0%
Sunday Times	0	0%	33	3.4%	0	0%
Sunday Mirror	0	0%	6	0.6%	0	0%
Sunday Express	0	0%	4	0.4%	0	0%
Sunday Telegraph	0	0%	4	0.4%	0	0%

Traditional values and moral authority

Taking as his opening theme the "Christian roots" (quoted by *Independent* 17/09/10) and "Christian foundations" (quoted by *Belfast Telegraph*, *Telegraph*, *Guardian*, and *Independent* 17/09/10) of Britain's traditional values, Benedict's Holyrood speech was likely to appeal to a royal and royalist audience. In particular, Pope Benedict argued that the virtues of "truth, mercy, justice and charity come to you from a faith that remains a mighty force for good in your kingdom" (*Express*,[1] *Guardian*, *Herald*, *Western Mail*, and *Daily Mail* in part 17/09/10). He praised historical British figures for their good works "inspired by a deep faith born and nurtured in these islands" (not directly quoted). There was also, however, a more negative account given, that contrasted Christian virtue with individualistic secular values, which were portrayed as hedonistic and self-involved.

The homily at Bellahouston Park made the most specific reference both to proper conduct and sinful behaviour, ostensibly as advice addressed to the congregation of worshippers. However, Benedict was probably aware that his guidance to young people urging them to avoid seeking happiness in "drugs, money, sex, pornography and alcohol" (quoted by *Daily Mail*, *Herald*, *Mirror*, *Sun*, and *Times* 17/09/10, Observer 19/09/10) would appeal to common contemporary media anxieties and moral panics, such as Cameron's 'broken Britain'. His broader point may have

---

1 Although the Scottish Express quoted only "force for good" and framed it as praise for Britain, rather than Christianity.

been expected to be less attractive to right-wing politicians and press, however, suggesting that (neo-)liberal individualism is selfish and self-destructive, and that the problem with utilitarianism is that people don't make rational choices due to their "weakness and fragility" (quoted *Guardian* and *Times* 17/09/10).

Those comments were sympathetically but infrequently commented on. Peter Stanford, writing in the *Observer* (19/09/10), argued that "he was voicing the fears of many parents at the value-lite culture their children so often readily embrace in a secular society", and a *Sunday Mirror* editorial claimed that "It is widely accepted that the ills of society are caused by a break-down in morality yet it is rare to hear anyone, even a churchman, link that to the loosening of religious beliefs" (leader, *Sunday Mirror* 19/09/10). Ian Jack in the *Guardian* (18/09/10) reported that worshippers said that they had attended the Bellahouston Park mass "because British behaviour and values were going to the dogs and Benedict's message might help re-moralise society" (though he also suggested that a more common reason was his sheer authority – or celebrity – "because he's the Pope").

Paul Vallely's account of travelling to the mass with a bus-load of the faithful (*Independent* 17/09/10) suggested that they shared the Pope's critique of individualistic society, as "a bald secularism" that does not provide meaning to life but reduces existence to pragmatic imperatives and basic desires.

> The Pope's key message is that people should be thinking of others before themselves. But we live in a society that encourages people to focus on themselves and they don't want to hear the church saying that they should be focusing on others. The Pope's message is a threat to their comfort zone.
> (Bellahouston Park pilgrim quoted in *Independent* 17/09/10)

Vallely – a theologian – also contributed an opinion column in the *Independent on Sunday* two days later, which framed this in more political terms. He argued that Benedict's "insistence that some of our freedoms can be self-destructive was thought-provoking; he could usefully expand on that idea" and praised "his insight that modern society cares too much about rights and not enough about responsibilities" (*Independent on Sunday* 19/09/10). 'Rights and responsibilities' is the discourse of communitarianism,[2] reflecting the belief that civic virtue is a product of social expectation and duty, not love or friendship (in Aristotelian terms), moral sentiment or humanitarian respect (in liberal terms).

The source of this individualism was portrayed as a shallow and superficial culture, but less often connected to the consumer culture of free market neo-liberalism. The *Guardian* warned of the "danger of creating a society in which only man and materialism hold sway" (*Guardian* 18/09/10), whilst Janice Turner in the *Times* (in an otherwise critical article) argued that secularists "might concede that the Pope has a point that secular values have struggled in the past decade when

---

2   And also the Blairite 'Third Way' and Cameroonian 'Big Society'.

morality was wholly defined by the free market." (18/09/19). Turner specifies the neo-liberal belief that the market is a neutral mechanism that facilitates the greatest liberty and utility for the greatest number and as therefore producing virtue, but whilst accepting the Pope's critique, she locates the solution in the institutions of the democratic state, rather than religion.

Rather than focusing on Christianity as a source of virtue in society, however, most of the media coverage focused on the Pope's account of the threats to these traditional Christian values. By far the most extensively quoted sections of the Holyrood speech referred to threats from "multiculturalism" and "aggressive secularism", with the latter related to "atheist extremism" of the past. Similarly, the Bellahoustoun Park homily referred to a threat from "relativism". Between them these remarks accounted for just 6% of the three speeches (by wordcount), but they made up 30% of the quoted text in the press; the sections on aggressive secularism and atheist extremism alone made up almost a quarter (24.4%). We'll take moral relativism first, as a general comment on the argument between liberalism and communitarianism, postmodernism and universalising narratives, then address the others in relation to the more specific claims about the imagined community of nation.

Moral relativism and personal conscience

The argument about the threat to Christian truth from moral relativism was most explicit in the Bellahouston Park homily to the faithful.

> The evangelisation of culture is all the more important in our times, when a 'dictatorship of relativism' threatens to obscure the unchanging truth about man's nature, his destiny and his ultimate good. ("Dictatorship of relativism" quoted in *Belfast Telegraph, Guardian, Herald, Independent,* and *Times* 17/09/10, *Independent on Sunday* 19/09/10, but none quoted the preceding remark about the "evangelisation of culture")

This was one of two references (both at Bellahouston Park) to Catholic doctrine, or perhaps Christian belief more broadly, as absolute, objective, and universal truth, and also presented the church's paternalistic moral authority as operating in everyone's best interests. This would appear to reject the notion that individuals can make 'correct' moral decisions without the discipline of faith.[3]

The Pope's critique of moral relativism was more often quoted than commented on, regarded as unhelpful "jargon" by Paul Vallely in the *Independent on Sunday* (19/09/10), and as an "awkward phrase" of obtuse meaning by Ian Jack in the *Guardian*:

---

3   At Westminster Hall he was more conciliatory toward the notion of secular ethics: "the role of religion in political debate is not so much to supply these norms, as if they could not be known by non-believers" (quoted in *Guardian* 18/09/10).

And yet, when his homily came, I wonder how many of us understood it? Benedict has been trotting out "the dictatorship of relativism" since 2005, as though that awkward phrase was a clincher. Only when he reached the temptations of the young that must be resisted – drugs, money, sex, pornography, alcohol – did his audience seem to perk up with a greater understanding. (Ian Jack, opinion column, *Guardian* 18/09/10)

Jack suggests that the remark was a comment on personal morality and social breakdown in the absence of religious civic virtue, rather than the accommodation of Christianity alongside other religions.

The same connection was explicitly made by Jerome Taylor, in a news article printed in both the Independent and the *Belfast Telegraph* (17/09/10), who interpreted it as "a term coined by Benedict to describe the way modern societies tend to pick and choose which morals and teachings they adhere to", and suggested by the *Herald* (18/09/10) through syntactic proximity of the propositions: "Rejecting 'the dictatorship of relativism', he urged young Catholics to resist the destructive temptations of drugs, money, sex, pornography and alcohol". Finally, a Catholic letter-writer in the *Guardian* (18/09/10) contrasted "the easy culture of relativism" with "the strength of faith".

All of these interpretations suggest firstly that secular culture and (civil) society is intrinsically market-dominated and individualistic, hedonistic even, and secondly that doctrine is ignored out of convenience or self-indulgence rather than rejected through principled objection based on personal conscience. The terminology of "relativism" suggests a critique of postmodern acceptance of all cultural traditions, lifestyle choices, and values, but it is equally a critique of liberal value-neutrality and tolerance, suggesting that this leaves a moral vacuum at the heart of society. As Andrew Brown, editor of the Belief section of the *Guardian*'s online comment pages, interprets Benedict's point: "he does not think [pluralist democracy] is or can be stable without an explicit and worked out moral and ethical dimension based on absolute principles – for him, obviously, Catholic Christianity" (Andrew Brown, *Guardian* 18/09/10).[4]

---

4   A very similar argument was put by David Cameron the following December, in a speech about the role of religion in public life, to mark the 400 year anniversary of the King James Bible in which he railed against "moral neutrality".

> Put simply, for too long we have been unwilling to distinguish right from wrong. "Live and let live" has too often become "do what you please". Bad choices have too often been defended as just different lifestyles. To be confident in saying something is wrong is not a sign of weakness, it's a strength. But we can't fight something with nothing. As I've said if we don't stand for something, we can't stand against anything. (http://www.ewtn.com/library/SCRIPTUR/kjv400.htm)

This distinction he describes as between a "passively tolerant society" and a "much more active, muscular liberalism" that is explicit about its values. And he argues that those values come from Christianity – at least in as far as he sees it as useful in countering youth unrest, irresponsible banking and Islamic extremism. However, he reserves the right to dissent

There are two objections, then, to the Pope's argument. The first is that other-oriented values come from within, rather than being the result of religious instruction, countering the communitarian argument with an assertion of the possibility of ethics in individualistic liberal democracy. The second is that the imposition of a moral code on the basis of tradition or submission to authority is oppressive and undemocratic.

The first argument was asserted by five commentators, largely, but not exclusively, in the left-leaning press. Four of these referred to 'goodness' or 'decency' as a natural disposition within humanity. Gay rights campaigner Peter Tatchell asserted "You do not need religion to be a good human being and to show compassion for others" (quoted in *Daily Mail* 17/09/10), and columnist Fiona McLutosh in the *Sunday Mirror* (19/09/10) similarly objected "Some of us don't need organised religion to lead good, moral lives". McLutosh's qualifier "some of us" implies that those who *do* need moral instruction are lacking in their personal qualities.

Comment in the *Guardian* and *Mirror* was more explicit about liberal secular morality as a 'natural' individual quality.

> Then there is our stubborn attachment to the notion that all you really need is decency, rather than theology. This too the Pope denies, and the sections of his [Westminster Hall] speech dealing with that were the most interesting part [... but reflected] a deeply conservative and pessimistic view of human nature. (Andrew Brown, *Guardian* 18/09/10)

> Atheists – decent ones anyway – are people who believe in the inherent goodness of humanity as a whole, as opposed to those who use religion to promote the values of a tribal, exclusive club with narrow beliefs which cause more harm in the world than good. [...] I believe in good human values such as compassion and treating others (who/whatever they are) as I would wish to be treated. I just don't need religion to tell me that. (Fiona Phillips, *Mirror* 18/09/10)

Phillips' argument is distinct from the others in that she contrasts 'natural' human virtue with the strategic use of moral rules to exert power. This draws in the liberal discourse of the 'authenticity' of the individual, regarding a pro-social other-orientation as part of the project of self-realisation, which is restricted by social

---

against religious moral authority on matters such as "equality and tolerance", presumably a reference to homosexuality – an issue on which Cameron is socially liberal. Whilst he makes some fairly sophisticated philosophical points, Cameron essentially – like Etzioni (2004) – fails to give a convincing account of how to distinguish between those issues on which traditional morals should be asserted and those on which dissent against the moral authority is legitimate – in other words between his own social conservativism and social liberalism. Cameron only suggests that the church "must keep on the agenda that speaks to the whole country". This either suggests majority values, which could lead to the majority oppressing minorities, or tolerance of all *legitimate* "lifestyle" choices, which doesn't take us any further forward.

rules. However, to locate morality entirely within the individual, and deny or resist any social or structural influence, by extension implies that those who transgress the rules and norms of society are intrinsically 'bad' or 'evil'.

Finally, one commentator defined secular morality in more social terms, locating 'the good' in "a common-sense decency that I've never found in the obscure language of religious texts" (Joan Smith, *Independent on Sunday* 19/09/10). 'Common sense', however, is an unreflective received wisdom that is not explicitly defined and considered. The Enlightenment notion of 'moral sentiment' as a more conscious reflexivity was only hinted at by Giles Fraser, the then Canon Chancellor of St Paul's Cathedral, later to find himself at the centre of the stand-off between the cathedral and the Occupy movement. He told the *Guardian* (17/09/10) "Most people arrive at the great truths of life by quietly thinking about things".

All of these assertions of secular morality did, like the Pope, refer to moral truths or universal values, distinguishing only their source. Tatchell's reference to "compassion" and Phillips' principle of recognising other human life and dignity as worthy of equal respect to oneself, such as that proposed by Rawls (1971) and Dworkin (2011), adopts a universalising liberal principle that is rejected by postmodern theorists as foundationalist (Keane 1998: 53–4) and communitarian perspectives as neglecting the ontological context of the external social and political environment.

The second objection – that community imposition of morals is oppressive – was made by four commentators, including two secular civil society sources who were quoted in five newspapers between them. Andrew Copson, Chief Executive of the British Humanist Society, (quoted in *Belfast Telegraph*, *Daily Mail* 17/09/11, and *Sunday Times* 19/09/11) argued that the church "exerts itself internationally to impose its narrow and exclusive form of morality and undermine the human rights of women, children, gay people and many others", portraying religion as coercive and not pluralistic, and therefore uncivil. Terry Sanderson, President of the National Secular Society, also talked of dogma, and contrasted it with a common national identity that is chosen (or, again, 'authentic') not imposed: "The secular identity of the British people is not something to criticise, but celebrate. We have rejected dogmatic religion devoid of compassion" (quoted in *Telegraph* and *Guardian* 17/09/11).

Less often, this was also framed in explicitly democratic terms. Polly Toynbee contrasted the relativism that Benedict opposed with the absolutism she argued that he sought: "The "moral relativism" he has railed against will seem to many like moral irrelevance when points of mystical belief and dogma take precedence." (*Guardian* 18/09/10). This also suggests that the "mystical" is an irrational basis for political argumentation. Finally, a letter-writer in the *Express* offered a mix of individual rights and collective tradition as a legitimating discourse for secular morality: "In Britain we have a proud tradition of questioning beliefs and having the courage and legal right to speak out if we do not agree with religious dogma" (letter to the editor, *Express* 17/09/10). However, the meaning of Britishness was of course highly contested, especially in relation to cultural diversity.

National identity, cultural cohesion, and multiculturalism (ethnic nation)

Benedict's comments on the Christian basis of British national identity were followed by a comment on multiculturalism that, in that context, seems to frame cultural diversity and pluralism as a threat to national cohesion.

> Today, the United Kingdom strives to be a modern and multicultural society. In this challenging enterprise, may it always maintain its respect for those traditional values and cultural expressions that more aggressive forms of secularism no longer value or even tolerate. (quoted by 12 newspapers)

Benedict accuses the British authorities of being illiberal towards religion, by liberal democracy's own criteria of tolerance and respect. However, instead of seeking recognition and accommodation of the faith alongside other others, albeit as a private and non-political identity, he seeks to validate the privileged position of Christianity over other religions, and indeed over secular humanism. It is difficult to see how his preferred Christian monoculture embodies tolerance and respect for non-Christians. There is also, of course, a discourse of injured identity here, used to legitimise claims for special recognition and particularistic rights (Kenny 2004), which we will come back to, but it is worth noting that this is an argument associated *with* multiculturalism rather than against it.

Although the reference to multiculturalism was broadly quoted (508 words in 12 newspapers), there was surprisingly little comment on it (432 words in four newspapers), although there was some implicit comment in connections made to a senior Vatican aide's comment prior to the visit, whose comment was more explicitly derisory (comparing Britain to a "Third World country" on account of its ethic diversity) and had attracted direct criticism[5] (a further 274 words).

The *Guardian* mildly observed that Benedict's remark "might be regarded as a less than warm endorsement" and "struck an odd note" (*Guardian* 17/09/11). The only criticism of the Pope's argument for Christianity to be privileged as more traditionally British came from a representative of secular civil society, Terry Sanderson of the National Secular Society, who called it "veiled attack on the rise of Islam".

> He keeps emphasising that this is a Christian country and is very tolerant, but that it must remain a Christian country – he is setting up the battle lines between his religion and Islam. (quoted in *Daily Star* 17/09/11)

The Star framed this comment within the sensationalist frame of a "race row" ("THE Pope's state visit was rocked by a race row last night when he was accused of an attack on Britain's Muslims"), although Sanderson appeared to be the only

---

5   Cardinal Kaspar's absence from the state visit following his comment was explained as owing to illness, though this was treated with scepticism by much of the press.

source in support of the assertion that the comments "were perceived as a guarded dig at the UK's growing number of Muslim communities".

On the other hand there was one comment that criticised Benedict for being too *conciliatory* toward multiculturalism.

> However, in so doing he sadly fell into the old trap of talking about our "multicultural" society. We do not want a multicultural society, rather a multiracial society which embraces all peoples and allows them to celebrate their many religions and enjoy their Hanukkah, Eid, Diwali or whatever else it might be, while all the time accepting that this is a Christian country with Christian core beliefs and values. (Nick Ferrari, *Sunday Express* 19/09/11)

This most faithfully reflects Benedict's belief that other religions should be private, but the Christian church(es) should remain established within the ruling tradition. Although open to racial diversity, this emphasis on assimilation suggests to some extent an ethnic conception of nation, which is hostile to pluralism and based in "organic unity" (Bryant 1995: 140–41), as opposed to an associational civic nation.

Ferrari's use of the inclusive 'we' constructs a consensus on nation that does not exist, but the *Guardian*'s Andrew Brown points out that neither is it a marginal view.

> According to the British Social Attitudes survey, 45% of us believe that religious diversity is harming Britain and more than half of irreligious Britons believe that "Britain is deeply divided on religious lines". So the pope's worries about multiculturalism – and for that matter Cardinal Kasper's – are by no means confined to a kooky minority. (Andrew Brown, *Guardian* 17/09/10)

This reflects concerns about the possibility of a culturally neutral liberal state and public sphere in the context of such diversity, and the implication for coherence and stability of the nation. Janice Turner (*Times* 18/09/11) was alone in putting the case that secular liberalism allows for religious tolerance of multiple faiths, and therefore represents a "more profound tie that unites us" in British society across religious divides. Nonetheless, as Bryant (1995) argues, that commitment to the civic nation requires a set of symbols and rituals to invest it with sufficient sentiment. For Britain, the collective memory of the Second World War and associated civil sacraments is probably the strongest or at least most frequently invoked in news media.

National identity and shared historical narrative (civic nation and civil religion)

Benedict's references to WWII were probably mindful of its place in British identity, and it must have been no surprise that the most contentious argument against the value-neutral liberal democratic state, was that it had led to "Nazi tyranny".

As we reflect on the sobering lessons of the atheist extremism of the twentieth century, let us never forget how the exclusion of God, religion and virtue from public life leads ultimately to a truncated vision of man and of society and this to a 'reductive vision of the person and his destiny'. ("atheist extremism" quoted by eight newspapers, in full by *Mail, Express, Telegraph, Guardian,* and *Times* 17/09/10)

The Pope is not alone in associating the total wars of the twentieth century with rational, technocratic modernity, however the two main political-philosophical responses to the horrors of the Holocaust were the UN's Universal Declaration of Human Rights on the one hand and postmodern relativism on the other – both of which the Pope rejects (though not entirely consistently). His response is a retreat to traditional values before the cold rationalism and instrumentalism of modernism, but without the eclecticism of traditions accommodated by postmodernism. Benedict's argument, again, implies that there is a need for stable and universal morals in society, which cannot come from democratic politics as the realm of (Enlightenment) "reason", therefore *one* religion should inform British values and laws, and Christianity has the strongest claim on the basis of tradition.

Coverage of the "atheist extremism" remarks either remarked on its controversial nature or was explicitly critical, with the latter falling into three types of objection. Most frequently, commentators responded with the inevitable historical objections against the claimed correspondence between religion and anti-fascism. Evidence was reviewed in terms of the faith of key figures ("Hitler was not an atheist, Winston Churchill probably was" (Donald McLeod, *Observer* 19/09/10), and the part played by various religious and secular institutions (in five newspapers[6]) – though there was some limited, largely qualified recognition that there were courageous Catholics and other Christians who paid with their lives.[7]

Secondly, several newspapers objected to the broader implication that religion is a protection against evil, presenting counter-evidence of sinful Catholics (*Herald* 18/09/10) and religious fundamentalism (*Sunday Mirror* 19/09/10). Polly Toynbee in the *Guardian* (18/09/10) scoffed, "as if belief in God were any protection against monstrous human tyrannies". Even a senior commentator from the Jewish community argued that "the enemies of humanity are the intolerant, and intolerance exists among people of faith as well as those of no faith" (Jon Benjamin, chief executive, Board of Deputies of British Jews, quoted in *Guardian* 18/09/10). Immoral or inhumane behaviour, like its positive equivalent, is predominantly understood as coming from the moral disposition of the individual.

Finally, there were three affronted reactions to the remark as an insult to the moral qualities of the irreligious. The British Humanist Association released

---

6   *Daily Mail* 17/09/10, *Guardian* 18/09/10, *Herald* 18/09/10, *Times* 18/09/10, *Observer* 19/09/10 and *Sunday Times* 19/09/10.

7   There were 510 words across four newspapers in support of the Pope's argument, in comparison with 1,474 words across 10 newspapers in criticism.

a statement objecting to the "terrible libel against those who do not believe in God" (quoted in the *Daily Telegraph* 17/09/10, *Express* 17/09/10, *Sunday Times* 19/09/10). A protester complained of being "compared revoltingly to Nazis because we don't choose to believe in the man-made strictures of a closed and dark society" (protester, quoted in *Sunday Telegraph* 19/09/10). The author Terry Pratchett suggested that Benedict has invoked the Nazis as an uncivil rhetorical device:

> Dragging up the Nazis for a soundbite doesn't help anybody. The English don't like being hectored. We don't like being bullied. We don't like being compared to the Nazis. (Terry Pratchett, quoted in *Daily Mail* 17/09/10)

There was fairly extensive discussion of whether it is rhetorically useful or politically legitimate to make comparisons with the Nazis when making claims of injustice (see Chapter 6). Arguably the language of offence tends to operate to close down debate (Edwards 2009) or reduce the debate to conflicting rights claims of the basis of injured identity (Kenny 2004).

The political or social role of religion in public life

However, whilst the central theme of Benedict's speeches was an assertion of the legitimate role of religion in public life, he placed less emphasis on arguing for Catholic views to be accommodated in political debate (see below), than on arguing for the church to be freed from state regulation of its social roles. This is centrally about the definition of public, private and social, and the understanding of the line between them; what is of public concern, in need of political or social regulation, or to be left to individual liberty (whether in terms of personal conscience or self-interest). For Benedict, social regulation of virtue should be separate from political regulation of the pragmatic realms of law and bureaucracy.

Benedict not only argued that the state regulation of virtue is coercive, but that society is incapable of understanding true virtue, so the church alone can play this role. Connectedly, he strongly inferred that the church should be granted exemption from legal constraints that are inconsistent with Catholic doctrine. These arguments made up the greater part of the Westminster speech, and encompassed three aspects: 1) the limits of legitimate *state* intervention, especially in terms of the regulation of virtue, as contrasted with religious freedom; 2) the inability of *democracy* to define the moral or ethical values of the good society to which the rational debate of democratic politics appeal; and 3) the moral as the natural realm of religion, which should work in (equal) partnership with the state whose realm is properly limited to reason. A fourth angle can be also discerned in the Bellahouston Park homily, where he argued that Catholic values are not in any case inconsistent with dominant values. It is notable that few of these passages were widely quoted or paraphrased in the press coverage.

Firstly, in relation to the legitimacy of state regulation of virtue, Benedict framed legislation as making claims on citizens that should be limited: in part to preserve the liberty of the individual, by achieving "a genuine balance between the legitimate claims of government and the rights of those subject to it" (quoted by the *Herald* and *Times*), with rights defined as negative liberties from state control rather than positive liberties guaranteed by law; but also to allow for the duties to a higher power – "the perennial question of the relationship between what is owed to Caesar and what is owed to God" (quoted by the *Herald*). This biblical reference (Matthew 22: 17–21[8]) relates to the legitimacy of the obligation to pay taxes, but what is owed to God (and not to civil authorities) is generally interpreted as moral and spiritual conscience.

Benedict furthermore explicitly questioned the ability of the state to assert the moral values of the good society.

> Each generation, as it seeks to advance the common good, must ask anew: What are the requirements that governments may reasonably impose upon citizens, and how far do they extend? By appeal to what authority can moral dilemmas be resolved? (partially quoted by *Guardian* and *Times*)

He argued that religious 'conscience' (defined in terms of doctrinal observance) gave Catholics the strength of purpose to challenge state power, citing St Thomas More as a figure "admired by believers and non-believers alike for the integrity with which he followed his conscience, even at the cost of displeasing the sovereign whose 'good servant' he was, because he chose to serve God first" (closely paraphrased by several papers, and more loosely but faithfully by the *Guardian* (18/09/10), who said he was convicted "for refusing to put expedience ahead of his religious convictions").

Secondly, Benedict anticipates the response that legitimacy is drawn from the democratically-expressed will of the people. He argues that the shifting grounds of public opinion make it an unstable and therefore illegitimate moral basis, in contrast to the universal truth of Christian faith.

> If the moral principles underpinning the democratic process are themselves determined by nothing more solid than social consensus, then the fragility of the process becomes all too evident – herein lies the real challenge for democracy. (quoted by *Telegraph*, *Guardian*, *Herald*, *Independent on Sunday*, and *Times*, at least in part)

---

8 "'Tell us, then, what you think. Is it lawful to pay taxes to Caesar, or not?' But Jesus, aware of their malice, said, 'Why put me to the test, you hypocrites? Show me the coin for the tax.' And they brought him a denarius. And Jesus said to them, 'Whose likeness and inscription is this?' They said, 'Caesar's.' Then he said to them, 'Therefore render to Caesar the things that are Caesar's, and to God the things that are God's.'"

Paul Vallely interprets this as a Tocquevillian concern with the 'tyranny of the majority'.

> The majority are not always right, though it is usually not popular to say
> so [...] Religion should be a corrective, however unwelcome, to coercive
> majoritarianism. (Paul Vallely, *Independent on Sunday* 19/09/10)

Tocqueville's argument is that democratic mechanisms favour the majority group over the interests of minorities, and it could be that Benedict's intention is to frame Catholics as an oppressed religious minority, though it is not clear how or why religion would offer a more just outcome (religious groups, too, oppress minorities) apart from as the word of God.[9]

The reference to "social consensus" suggests that Benedict is concerned, not only with the expression of the aggregated mass of individuals through the law, but also with the *direct* social pressure of the collective community, which suppresses free speech and action by shunning those who have offended dominant sensibilities – in this case minority religious groups, women's and gay rights movements, and their supporters. This was the particular concern of J. S. Mill in *On Liberty* (2003 [1869]), however, it is unlikely that Mill would have found in Benedict's favour, for two reasons. Firstly, because Mill made a distinction between those 'self-regarding' behaviours that had no impact on others beyond offended feelings (such as sexuality), and those that are 'other-regarding' and constitute a harm to the rights of others (such as discrimination on the basis of sexuality).[10] Secondly, the Vatican itself operates on the basis of social pressure, including on its own liberal wings.

In any case, regardless of the legitimacy of dominant social values, Benedict defines the state in Kantian terms of the rational, value-neutral liberal democratic state, and therefore, *thirdly*, argues that the state has relinquished claim to jurisdiction over values.

> This is why I would suggest that the world of reason and the world of faith – the
> world of secular rationality and the world of religious belief – need one another
> and should not be afraid to enter into a profound and ongoing dialogue, for the
> good of our civilisation. (not quoted)

---

9   Tocqueville did himself embrace this argument however: "Unlimited power is in itself a bad and dangerous thing. Human beings are not competent to exercise it with discretion. God alone can be omnipotent, because his wisdom and his justice are always equal to his power. There is no power on earth so worthy of honor in itself or clothed with rights so sacred that I would admit its uncontrolled and all-predominant authority" (Tocqueville 1835: 241).

10   Mill's distinction could be read as a liberal analogue to the Christian distinction between what is owed to Caesar and to God – "To individuality should belong the part of life in which it is chiefly the individual that is interested; to society the part which chiefly interests society" (2003 [1869]: 139).

He states that there is no value consensus to which political arguments can appeal (since "moral dilemmas" exist), and since liberal democracy cannot make a legitimate claim to solve those dilemmas (being value-neutral), it follows that these values must come from a moral "authority" working in parallel to the state. Without recognising liberal democratic values as particular, its adherents cannot make an argument for them, debate them, or indeed legitimise them on the basis of being democratically agreed.

The role he envisages is not, therefore, of religious organisations taking a role alongside secular civil associations in public debate, and equally being bound by the outcome of that debate even if they do not prevail (see Chapter 6), but of religion as an independent authority on equal terms with the legislative. The humanitarian good works cited were described as "cooperation between the United Kingdom and the Holy See" (not quoted) placing the Vatican state as an equal with a democratic state. Benedict then drew the same parallel within the borders of the UK.

> I am convinced that, within this country too, there are many areas in which the Church and the public authorities can work together for the good of citizens, in harmony with this Parliament's historic practice of invoking the Spirit's guidance upon those who seek to improve the conditions of all mankind. (not quoted)

> For such cooperation to be possible, religious bodies – including institutions linked to the Catholic Church – need to be free to act in accordance with their own principles and specific convictions based upon the faith and the official teaching of the Church. (quoted in part by *Telegraph* and *Times*)

This was the most direct and unambiguous reference to the dispute over Catholic adoption agencies, and Benedict went on to make his own rights claims (against those of equal gay rights).

> In this way, such basic rights as religious freedom, freedom of conscience and freedom of association are guaranteed. (not quoted)

Like Etzioni, Benedict equates the state with moral coercion through the law (in as far as it disagrees with him), without acknowledging the liberal principle that the law is democratically agreed. The focus is therefore on negative liberties in relation to the state, and Catholic institutions as autonomous service providers with an economic (and social) but not avowedly political role (in terms of making claims on the state). In this regard the Pope's communitarian account of Catholicism's role in civil society is entirely in keeping with the neo-liberal notion of the Big Society (see below).

Fourthly, in addition to using the logic and rhetoric of secular liberal democracy against its proponents, at Bellahouston Park Benedict also sought to lay claim to its (implicit) values.

> There are some who now seek to exclude religious belief from public discourse, to privatise it or even to paint it as a threat to equality and liberty. Yet religion is in fact a guarantee of authentic liberty and respect, leading us to look upon every person as a brother or sister. (quoted by *Belfast Telegraph*, *Daily Mail*, *Telegraph*, *Independent* and *Times*)

Benedict here appears to argue that Catholic tenets are not inconsistent with secular values encoded in human rights law, suggesting an appeal to underlying principles held in common, but makes a subtle distinction of "authentic" liberty and respect. This could be interpreted as the warm attachments of religious community as opposed to the cool attachments of society, but more likely it signals a different definition of liberty and respect (such as perhaps respect for the rights of the foetus over those of the mother, or showing homosexuals respect by saving them from eternal damnation).

Either way, Benedict suggests that religion offers a way to secure other-oriented virtue that is not so different from human rights law, suggesting that both are a form of civic virtue, if interpreted differently and leading to very different outcomes. However, he distinguished Catholicism's understanding of how to achieve these values as "true", whilst strongly implying that secular human rights are "arbitrary".

> Society needs clear voices which propose our right to live, not in a jungle of self-destructive and arbitrary freedoms, but in a society which works for the true welfare of its citizens and offers them guidance and protection in the face of their weakness and fragility. (quoted by *Guardian* 18/09/10)

Again, despite warm words on "pluralist democracy", he asserts a paternalistic view of moral authority operating in the best interests of morally flawed individuals, who can't even pursue their own best interests without guidance (again, an anti-utilitarian argument).

Commentators engaged with Benedict's argument over jurisdiction of the church over the morals of the good society, but judging his political legitimacy more on the *substance* of his moral judgements, rather than on the basis that religion alone can give voice to moral value, with social liberals rejecting them as illegitimate and wrong, and social conservatives supporting their validity, even if not their religious basis. However, some arguments did relate to philosophical beliefs about civil society, especially in relation to authority versus democracy, and public versus private.

Instead of relating to the common good, three commentators argued that the Pope's arguments for jurisdiction over morals was actually about power, and should therefore be subject to public accountability. A representative of secular(ist) civil society interpreted Benedict's moral concern about threats to traditional values as a self-interested concern about a threat to religious power.

> The Pope is hardly off the plane before he launches his first attack on secularism as a threat to the power that he feels should be his alone to wield." (Terry Sanderson, National Secular Society, quoted in *Mirror* 17/09/10)

One commentator referred to the Catholic church's use of 'lobbying' – a private (in terms of both visibility and collectivity) form of political pressure that is therefore democratically illegitimate.

> The Vatican […] has lobbied for exemptions from UK employment law and the rules governing adoption agencies so that it can go on discriminating against gay people. (Joan Smith, *Independent on Sunday* 19/09/10)

Smith interpreted Benedict's argument as an unwillingness to live by the laws of the land, whilst Polly Toynbee in the *Guardian* suggested that he wants his morals to be *encoded in* British law: describing his message as principally "a dense theological exposition of why religion must be the moral basis for everything" (*Guardian* 18/09/10). A letter-writer objected to the use of concordats used by the Vatican "to promote diplomatic and religious hegemony with other states" as undemocratic, and argued that "Our MPs must ensure that concordats or any agreements following from Joseph Ratzinger's visit are open, honest and subject to public scrutiny" (letter-writer, *Guardian* 17/09/10).

These comments do not explicitly defend the legitimacy of the law as democratic, but that is implied by the accusations that the Vatican's exercise of power is undemocratic. Of course the unequal exercise of private (self-interested) power is rife in capitalist society, but Toynbee and Smith have both also made arguments for greater regulation and accountability of corporate power (see below).

The precise line between matters of public (whether defined in terms of the political or the social) and private concern was elaborated on at length by three commentators. Smith defined the good society in terms of equal rights, and a public or social role for religion conflicting with that principle.

> Has religion been relegated to the private sphere in the UK? I hope so. I believe passionately in equality – the principle that everyone should have the same rights, regardless of ethnicity, gender or sexual orientation. (Joan Smith, *Independent on Sunday* 19/09/11)

In a way, this does frame equality and human rights as tenets of a belief system that is a (progressive) secular equivalent of religion. However, regardless of the neutrality of justification Smith is clear about neutrality of treatment, which she argues should be blind to differences. Unusually, however, the framing states a belief ("I believe passionately in equality"), and does not make a claim to moral truth. Later, she more explicitly acknowledged her liberal position as value-based rather than neutral: "I'm celebrating my values – and I just wish my taxes hadn't been used to promote his".

Perhaps not unconnectedly, Smith also gave the most explicit argument in favour of her values.

> When will this sclerotic, celibate priesthood acknowledge that sex is wrong when it's coercive, not when it's between people who aren't married or who happen to belong to the same gender? When will it realise that its claim to the moral high ground has been undermined by scandal and by a puritan disdain that's demonstrably incapable of distinguishing between harmless pleasure and abuse? (Joan Smith, opinion, *Independent on Sunday* 19/09/11)

Smith does make a truth claim about moral rights and wrongs, that should be "realised" and "acknowledged", but which the church is "incapable" of recognising, however, she offers an argument in support of this judgement, appealing to a distinction between personal freedoms that do not affect the liberties of others (relationship choices, sexual preferences and "harmless pleasure") and those that do ("coercive", "abuse"). This makes a strong Kantian or Millian case for tolerance of the private or intimate behaviour of gay couples, but it doesn't necessarily make the case for positive freedoms – that Catholic adoption agencies should be legally obliged to allow gay couples to adopt children.

A *Sunday Express* columnist made a similar distinction between *private* freedom of conscience or belief and the application of those views to *public* political issues – the former is self-regarding and not of anyone else's concern, whilst the latter is other-regarding and open to public criticism.

> As a life-long atheist, I've always been of the "live and let live" opinion that, as long as people don't impose their religious views on me, then I'm happy to defend their right to believe whatever they want, whether it's God or Allah or fairies at the bottom of the garden [... However,] If wanting to expose the Pope for fighting against basic human rights and the advances of medical science while protecting paedophiles from justice makes me "intolerant" and "militant", then I am happy to say I am guilty as charged. (Julia Hartley-Brewer, opinion, *Sunday Express* 19/09/11)

Human rights are appealed to as a "basic" universal given, and opposition to them wrongdoing that must be "exposed". She implies harms to others in terms of discrimination (and avoidable death in relation to opposition to "advances in medical science" – presumably referring to research involving stem cells from human foetuses), though this argument is not explicitly made, nor the Pope's objections seriously engaged with. The child abuse reference more strongly implies harms, and of a sort that is not morally contentious. Accordingly, this was the most frequently cited criticism of the Pope, even in this sample of articles specifically about the speeches.

Hartley-Brewer rhetorically challenges Benedict's implication that her belief in universal rights and the protection of children from abuse is intolerant (by using the conditional qualifier "If", and the sceptical quotes around "intolerant" and "militant"), and, like him, refuses to accept the accusation of intolerance as a reason to abandon her beliefs. Assuming her point is that the Pope seeks to claim a right to discriminate, this reflects the central liberal argument (supported even by those like Keane [1998:64] who are of a more postmodernist persuasion) that tolerance cannot be applied to itself; one cannot logically tolerate the intolerant.

In contrast, social conservatives supported the Pope's complaint that his critics' demands for tolerance were themselves intolerant.

> I am, however, dismayed by the aggression and militancy of some of my fellow atheists, who show a shocking intolerance of him and of his faith in the interests, it seems, of calling for more tolerance from the Catholic Church for homosexuals, abortionists and the promiscuous. If this is how they define live and let live, then we really are in a mess. (Simon Heffer, *Daily Telegraph* 18/09/11)

Heffer suggests that this is a hypocritical attitude that undermines liberal principles. However, his notion of "live and let live" is not an even more morally indifferent postmodern relativism. His argument instead rests on a socially conservative definition of the bounds of the political – whilst he argues that religion "is entirely a matter of private conscience and taste and of no consequence to anyone else" and "should have no part in politics", he also suggests that sexuality (which he frames in terms of sexual deviance) is not political, and therefore not accorded positive rights, but is open to social criticism. He also, then, privileges negative liberties in relation to the rights guaranteed by the state, a neo-liberal argument that is unconcerned about the advantage of traditional and well-resourced groups in society (whilst often being concerned about the imposition of socially liberal or progressive views).[11]

Whilst the Pope was arguing for a communitarian role in public life through which to instil virtue through the moral authority of the word of God, much of the freedom and influence he sought could be supported through certain understandings of the liberal civil society. Apart from the relativistic pluralism of the postmodern model, the neo-liberal notion of civil society emphasises negative liberty above all, and whilst Benedict is clearly hostile to negative liberty as it pertains to homosexuals (among others), he does seek autonomy from the state

---

11   Social conservativism is often aligned with neo-liberalism as a generally right-wing political orientation, but it is not synonymous, and it is unclear whether Heffer would prioritise the negative liberty of freedom of speech if his socially conservative view was marginalised.

for the church. The role accorded by neo-liberalism is more limited, in that it does not recognise the universalising claims of the church, but it does allow freedom to operate within its own logic, only in competition with other associations and their versions of the good. In addition, there are often overlaps between the goals of the economic liberalism of the neo-liberal perspective and the social conservativism of religious communalism. Such commonalities can be identified in David Cameron's 'Big Society'.

The self-sufficient community and the 'Big Society'

The Conservative party, and in particular David Cameron and Baroness Warsi, have praised the role of religion, and especially Christianity, in public life as a source of (communitarian) civic virtue and morality in society. Cameron's particular focus, however, is on the virtue of self-sufficiency, and the role of churches in public (or social) life through voluntary and charitable work, and especially taking responsibility for public services that would otherwise be provided by the state, such as schools and adoption services. The neo-Tocquevillian argument that such forms of association breed civic virtues of caring, cooperation, and respect is the philosophical justification for a neo-liberal contraction of the state. The 'Big Society' rhetoric frames the state as oppressively controlling and suggests that its withdrawal from certain areas (especially responsibility for personal wellbeing) is intended to facilitate the development of strong community, as opposed to being a fig-leaf for a free-market ideology.

The Pope himself made little direct reference to the church's role in these terms – apart from the oblique references to Catholic adoption agencies, he made one reference to Catholic schools. Largely, however, his argument against legislative regulation of the church's role in providing social services was related to his battle with the state over jurisdiction over morality, rather than neo-liberal concern with a 'culture of dependency', and he disregarded secular civil society as a source of civic virtue. Nonetheless, David Cameron drew parallels between the Pope's remarks and the 'Big Society' that emphasised the social benefits of organised religion as part of pluralistic, autonomous civil society.

The *Times* (17/09/10) reported a pre-released speech by Cameron, in which he "will urge sceptical Britons to recognise that Catholic organisations working in education and welfare help to make Britain more caring".

He will also draw parallels between Catholic social teaching and his own philosophy of the big society, where everyone pulls together and works together for the good of families and communities. "I believe we can all share in your message of working for the common good [...] and that we all have a social obligation to each other, to our families and our communities," he said. (*Sunday Times* 19/09/10)

This was reflected in one newspaper's comment that political discussion may be more open to the role of religion in public life, "especially given that David Cameron's Big Society project lauds many of the values that the Pope espouses." (leader, *Belfast Telegraph* 17/09/10).[12]

However, neither the communitarian nor the neo-liberal arguments about the Big Society were frequently discussed. There was just one reference to a need for individuals to be protected from the state – not particularly as intrusive or coercive, but certainly not as a caring welfare state.

> Once religion is back in its box marked 'private' – something society tolerates as a matter for consenting adults behind closed doors – the way is clear for an individualist utopia in which people are left naked before market and state.
> (Austen Ivereigh, Catholic Voices, *Independent* 17/09/10)

However, since this doesn't allow that a secular association in civil society could perform the same role, and therefore suggests – like the Pope – that it is not the practice of association that generates civic virtue and social cohesion, but the moral authority of the church.

There were some voices that suggested that the Big Society was an economic rather than a social policy: "with its emphasis on allowing the proliferation of voluntary groups and creating economic capacity, it [the Catholic church] is also likely to prove useful to David Cameron in expounding his Big Society" (leader, *Herald* 18/09/11). This suggests that the policy is strategic and pragmatic (though it also seems to suggest that it will generate growth rather than facilitate a smaller state – the ideological element), but the tone of the article was broadly supportive to this aim.

The only *criticism* of the democratic implications of the Big Society in general, and the autonomous role of religious groups in its definition of civil society in particular, was expounded at length by Janice Turner in the *Times* (18/09/11).

> It [secularism] needs to equip itself for a cool, clean fight as the coalition government seeks to use its Big Society agenda to undermine hard-won secular principles, inviting religious groups to fill the space vacated by a shrunken state.
> (Janice Turner, *Times* 18/09/11)

Turner specifies the motivation not only as economic (as the *Herald* does) but as part of a neo-liberal economic policy to reduce the welfare state.

She also expressed concern with the exercise of power by religious organisations such as the Catholic Church – a counter-argument to the discourse of the powerful or intrusive state.

---

12   It may be significant that it is a Northern Irish newspaper making this comment given the difficulties with the role of religion in a nation riven with sectarian conflict.

And on Newsnight, Baroness Warsi, defending her "We do God" speech to bishops in Oxford, refused to answer whether religious charities taking on governmental business would be allowed to override discrimination law, perhaps by refusing to have gay clients or employees. Her irritation was extraordinary given a rational unease about unaccountability and secretive religious bodies. Should we trust their volunteers more because they are motivated by faith? (Janice Turner, *Times* 18/09/11)

Turner associates state provision with democratically-agreed principles and accountability as opposed to with oppressive bureaucratic control – and frames community as potentially more oppressive. She was joined by a handful of other critics in objecting that the segregation of communities, even through market pluralism and choice, is detrimental to social cohesion and mutual understanding at a national level.

The funding of community-run 'free schools' is the only specific policy to emerge from the Big Society, and Janice Turner pointed out that the successful applications were disproportionately from organised religion. She linked faith schools with religious fundamentalism, suggesting that such extreme views were an outcome of segregation, or at least that segregation served the interests of fundamentalists, if the free school policy produced "government-funded madrassas" (Janice Turner, *Times* 18/09/11). The Observer reported protesters opposing "segregated schools" (19/09/10), and the president of the Leicester Secular Society was quoted in the *Guardian* (17/09/10) mildly suggesting that the issue "must be dealt with through the democratic process". It is perhaps surprising, however, that this connection was not made more frequently. It may be in part explained by the general assumption that the contribution of resources to a community is always simply a neutral act of altruistic charity.

Charity and theology

Whilst the 'Big Society' rhetoric reflects concerns with the instrumentalism of a state-mediated existence (breeding entitlement), it has little to say about the individualism of free-market consumerism (breeding selfishness and greed). Rather than protecting individuals against the values of the market (which are understood in neo-liberal terms as a neutral mechanism for maximising utility), the third sector is understood as a quasi-market, providing services more efficiently than the centralised state bureaucracy. However, from a neo-Marxist perspective, charity operates as a safety net for capitalism, preventing the worst social harms that could lead to revolution.

Across 11 newspapers, 1,441 words were dedicated to the association of religion and charity, but over half reported the Pope's own remarks. Among the five newspapers that commented on the issue, the vast majority was in the *Independent* and *Independent on Sunday*, and in articles by Paul Vallely in particular. Charity was framed as uncontroversially "good", with references to the "huge good the Catholic church does in the world", its "capacity for good works" (leader, *Independent on Sunday* 19/09/10), and work for "our common good" (letter to the editor, *Telegraph* 17/09/10). This assumes an uncontroversial notion of the good society, and therefore an assumption that *direct* intervention through the dedication of economic resources and voluntary labour is not political, in contrast to the dedication of arguments aimed at state or legislative intervention, which are defined as controversial or self-interested. More specifically Catholic charity was praised as altruistic, other-oriented behaviour "for people in need" (Paul Vallely, *Independent* 17/09/10), "for the disadvantaged" (leader, *Times* 18/09/10) – in particular there were three references to fighting poverty – for which they derived no personal benefit, no praise or social status: "unsung" (Paul Vallely, *Independent on Sunday* 19/09/10), "quietly and without anyone noticing" and "It's not work that anyone praises her for" (Joanna Moorhead, *Independent on Sunday* 19/09/10). Presumably, however, they believe that their reward will come in the next life, which Powell (2007) interprets as an instrumental act in pursuit of personal salvation.

The power of theology to inspire or instruct people to act in other-oriented ways was mentioned in three articles. Two framed the influence as moral leadership, inspiring followers to voluntary acts of altruism: Priests "inspire millions of British men and women daily to try to lead better lives for our common good" through setting a good example of sacrifice and duty (letter to the editor, *Telegraph* 17/09/10); "she does it because her Catholicism inspires a sense of wanting to give something back" (Joanna Moorhead, *Independent on Sunday* 19/09/10). The Times, however, saw charity as a product of the church's moral authority over its followers, as work that "believers practise out of a simple faith that they are commanded to do" (leader, *Times* 18/09/10), and for this reason it argued that criticism of the church undermined this authority and therefore "diminishes" the charitable work done in its name. This defines the Catholic Church as virtuous on account of its good works, and for this reason argues that it should be allowed to continue to perform good works without regulation or oversight. This is a circular argument that hinges on a simplistic notion of the good.

The Herald, in an editorial, developed this point more critically by describing "the theological and the humanitarian" as "paradoxical" aspects of Benedict's personality: "In the first, Benedict represents absolutes made real; in the second, compassion", suggesting that the theological aspect is "austere and authoritarian", and that compassionate humanitarianism does not originate in theology (but perhaps instead in the associative aspects of organised religion).

The assertion that the church is uncontroversially good in relation to charitable work reflects the distinction between contributing resources, which is considered intrinsically socially useful and apolitical, and arguments for changing the system in pursuit of social justice, which is rather more contested.

Justice and liberty

The neo-liberal perspective on liberty and the good society is most obvious in the stories about protest movements that challenge its assumptions and values, including the Occupy movement, student tuition fee protest and public sector strike. These protests were characterised as opposing liberty and even democracy, and as seeking policies that ran counter to the utility of the greatest number, but there were also a significant number of challenges to this framing. The Occupy coverage in particular accommodated a significant amount of discussion about social justice and inequality, although the strike and student protest were predominantly framed in terms of 'fairness', asserting the rights or claims of 'taxpayers' in particular.

Economic liberty

The Occupy movement's focus on capitalism and the economy was picked up in a reasonable amount of coverage (9,312 words – 7% of the total word count on the protest), a quarter of which referred to the economic crisis and 14% to unemployment as its outcome. Although the context would not seem to be one that lends itself easily to a neoliberal analysis, only slightly less coverage related to free markets producing wealth creation and growth. This was fairly evenly split between those advancing the argument for unfettered capitalism and those raising problems with the argument. The former appeared in five newspapers – most frequently and at greatest length in the *Telegraph* and *Times*. The latter arose in seven newspapers, especially the *Observer* and *Independent*.

Assertions of the wealth creation role largely responded to the assumed anti-capitalist stance of the occupiers, which was generally assumed to be a radical, rejectionist position that sought to overthrow the system.[13] Even commentators that were broadly sympathetic to the movement distinguished it from "crazy" or "loony" anti-capitalism (Polly Toynbee, *Guardian* 18/10/11, Margareta Pagano, *Independent on Sunday* 23/10/11). Rejection of the capitalist system as a whole was universally regarded as unthinkable and naïve, on the basis that capitalism produces wealth, benefiting us all. Protesters were therefore portrayed as hypocritical for enjoying those benefits such as "the freedom and material comforts that are indissolubly bound up with capitalism" (Melanie Phillips, *Daily Mail* 24/10/11), or at least being "wilfully blind to the extent to which they benefit from the very system they condemn" (Hugo Rifkind, *Times* 28/10/11).

---

13   Occupy were described as anti-capitalist or protesting against capitalism 120 times, though often in absence of better descriptor – although two *Guardian* columnists tried to draw more fine distinctions, such as "anti-corporate" (Seamus Milne, *Guardian* 20/10/11), and "anti-global-finance activists" (Sam Jones, *Guardian* 28/10/11), the term was still used 15 times by the newspaper. One business diary item mentions in passing "a debate on the [Occupied Times of London] paper's theme of 'Are we anti-capitalist?'" (*Independent* 26/10/11), but the various schools of thought within the movement were rarely explored.

Table 4.2 Capitalism and the economy in coverage of Occupy LSX

	Capitalism or economy	Economic crisis		Wealth creation and growth		Economic impact of cuts or inequality		Finance or financial system		Unemployment	
	n	n	horiz %	n	horiz %	n	horiz %	n	horiz %	n	horiz %
Guardian	2495	334	13.4%	61	2.4%	138	5.5%	786	31.5%	219	8.8%
Independent on Sunday	1351	658	48.7%	21	1.6%	0	0.0%	65	4.8%	346	25.6%
Independent	1143	602	52.7%	205	17.9%	0	0.0%	244	21.3%	55	4.8%
Times	1080	309	28.6%	247	22.9%	0	0.0%	49	4.5%	139	12.9%
Observer	849	211	24.9%	180	21.2%	0	0.0%	0	0%	394	46.4%
Daily Mail	514	51	9.9%	82	16.0%	0	0.0%	73	14.2%	0	0%
Daily Telegraph	495	92	18.6%	140	28.3%	0	0.0%	41	8.3%	91	18.4%
Herald	419	65	15.5%	131	31.3%	32	7.6%	0	0%	0	0%
Express	262	31	11.8%	0	0.0%	0	0.0%	0	0%	0	0%
Sunday Times	195	99	50.8%	18	9.2%	73	37.4%	0	0%	18	9.2%
Western Mail	162	70	43.2%	0	0.0%	0	0%	24	14.8%	23	14.2%
Mail on Sunday	104	0	0%	0	0.0%	0	0%	0	0%	0	0%
Mirror	68	0	0%	10	14.7%	0	0%	16	23.5%	0	0%
Sunday Telegraph	53	0	0%	0	0%	0	0%	22	41.5%	31	58.5%
Belfast Telegraph	48	0	0%	0	0%	0	0%	0	0%	0	0%
Star	47	0	0.0%	0	0.0%	0	0.0%	0	0.0%	10	21.3%
Sun	14	0	0.0%	0	0.0%	0	0.0%	0	0.0%	0	0.0%
Sunday Mirror	13	0	0.0%	0	0.0%	0	0.0%	0	0.0%	0	0.0%
Total	9312	2522	27.1%	1095	11.8%	243	2.6%	1320	14.2%	1326	14.2%

The protesters' use of Starbucks (in implicit contrast to the stereotype of anti-capitalist aggression toward the brand) was framed as hypocrisy four times in the *Daily Mail*, *Express*, and *Sun*, and by MP Louise Mensch on *Have I Got News For You* although the *Guardian* and *Times* both rejected this argument. The son of a "millionaire property developer" was accused of hypocrisy in the *Express* and *Star* (27/10/11). These arguments suggested that the protesters were biting the hand that feeds them.

Critics countered that the benefits of economic growth are actually rather uneven, and disproportionately benefit the wealthy (110 words in four newspapers).

> My own view is not that capitalism is an inherently bad thing. It has created jobs and prosperity, but it is clear prosperity has not been fairly distributed in our society. (Dr Giles Fraser, quoted in *Daily Mail* 28/10/11)

This goes beyond a utilitarian concern with the economic growth, and introduces concern with justice and fairness in the distribution of benefit. Additionally, one critic argued that there were uneven *costs* of growth, achieved at the expense of living conditions for the majority of workers, who had been asked "to work harder and longer" on stagnant wages (James Harkin, *Independent* 18/10/11). Harkin challenges the suggestion that capitalism produces growth through entrepreneurial spirit as opposed to wage control and asset-stripping.

An editorial in the *Times* acknowledged that Occupy were concerned with the poor and powerless, but made the most explicitly neo-liberal argument that economic liberty of the privileged is in the interests of the disadvantaged.

> Critics of capitalism misjudge the causes of the financial crisis, the route to development and the recuperative power and potential of markets. [...] The protesters think that they are standing up for the little guy; in fact their mishmash of proposals makes for a muddled charter of stagnation in which he would suffer most. The fact is that economic liberty enables the little guy to stand up for himself. (editorial, *Times* 18/10/11)

This reflects an assumption that negative liberties produce a level playing field as opposed to benefitting existing power, framing freedom as empowerment.

What's more, capitalism was not only defined in terms of economic liberty, but civil liberties and democracy, with anti-capitalism as therefore a rejection of liberal democracy.

> Isn't it ludicrous they are protesting about the very system which gives them the freedom to wave their placards and chant their slogans. If capitalism isn't the answer they should try the alternatives. Try holding a sit-down protest in North Korea, Iran, China or Syria (please, anywhere but London) and see how it feels to have your head cracked open by a police baton. Prove how much you abhor capitalism by refusing to collect your dole money. They won't because

hypocrisy is part of the agitprop kit along with the juvenile slogans. (Chris Roycroft-Davis, *Express* 25/10/11)

Capitalism and democracy are conflated, not only to assert that non-capitalist societies are all authoritarian, but also – far more dubiously – that all capitalist societies are democratic. By extension, this suggests that unfettered, *laissez-faire* capitalism is the *most* democratic system, assuming that democracy is defined in terms of negative liberties rather than positive empowerment. Interestingly, some criticisms came from business columnists, though they tended to object that there was evidence of market failure in the sector, whilst accepting that the good is principally defined as economic growth.

> If these executives had been creating real value for shareholders and staff, their pay might be justified, but they are not. (Margareta Pagneto, Business Editor, *Independent on Sunday* 23/10/11)

> Wandering among the tents last week, it was not hard to share the puzzled disbelief of the capital's happy band of tent-dwellers. Their demand was a simple one: a banking sector that serves the economy. It doesn't seem too much to ask. (Heather Stewart, Business Comment, *Observer* 30/10/11)

This relates to the 'reward for failure' discourse that has gained political ground because it refers to a market distortion in incentives, such as flawed remuneration procedures, rather than a problem with the market per se. Accordingly, it is regarded as having market-based solutions rather than legislative intervention, such as the 'shareholder spring'.[14] Stewart equates the public interest with that which serves the economy, rather than serves society more generally and non-economic goals of the good society, although she did also cite a remark by the head of the Financial Services Authority, Adair Turner, that much of what the City gets up to is "socially useless" (*Observer* 30/10/11), suggesting that there are other measures of 'the good' and even of utility. More obviously, in relation to the banking crisis, there are social *harms* associated with economic failure.

For neo-liberals, however, the market is private, including harms as well as rewards. For instance, Andrew McKie made an explicit defence of the negative liberties of the bankers, in part as wealth creators, but more broadly as individuals operating in private mechanisms of gain and loss.

---

14   Around May 2012 there were reports of a "new mood of militancy" at annual shareholder meetings, when investors in banks (Citigroup, Barclays, UBS) and then insurance companies (Aviva) refused to back remuneration packages (*Financial Times* 04/05/12). It was immediately met with derision by left-wing commentators (such as Marina Hyde, *Guardian* 11/05/12), declared a "myth" by the BBC's Robert Peston in June (12/06/12), and laid to rest by KPMG describing it as an "illusion" in November (*Telegraph* 19/11/12).

> The top 10% of earners stump up more than half of the tax revenue which pays
> for the schools, hospitals and libraries the rest of us use. The best policy would
> clearly be to leave them in peace to try to make the money with which they can
> then subsidise our services, and to regard it as none of our business if they take
> home potloads of cash. But by the same token, it's none of our business if they
> go to the wall, and we should let them. (Andrew McKie, *Herald* 24/10/11)

He argues that they should be allowed the liberty to succeed in the (utilitarian)
interests of the common good without concern for the extent of their own financial
reward, or equally allow them to fail (which would presumably also veto regulation
to prevent the failure occurring in the first place). This defines the collapse of a
bank as, in Millian terms, a self-regarding harm that is pertinent to no-one but the
bankers themselves (a view not shared by Mill himself)[15]. It is unclear whether
he is disregarding the harm to customers of the bank, or whether he believes that
since that is a result of a private, voluntary and reciprocal contract, it is a harm that
needs to be privately resolved and is of no concern to anyone else.

Indeed, McKie regards the greatest harm as the broader financial crisis, which
he argues was caused by the state bailout of the banks, and claims that this is what
Occupy LSX are protesting against, but complains that:

> They then say this is a failure of capitalism. This is where they make their colossal
> howler. Handing taxpayers' money to failed businesses is not capitalism. It is
> the exact opposite of capitalism. It is, in fact, old-fashioned socialism [...] The
> enemy is not capitalism, but people who have failed at capitalism, and then
> embrace a form of special-interest socialism, expecting a subsidy from the state
> to protect them from their own failure. (Andrew McKie, *Herald* 24/10/11)

He argues that the state intervention caused harm by interfering in the functional
incentives of the market, including the potential of failure as a risk calculation, and
also by violating the liberties of taxpayers by spending their money on ownership
without shareholder rights and therefore "no effective power". Whilst this was
the only direct assertion of this libertarian neo-liberal argument, the banking
bailout did attract more attention than the arguments that the crisis was a result of
systemic problems with free-market capitalism, or even mismanagement ("people
who have failed at capitalism").

State intervention: Banking bailout

Resentment at the banking bailout was the most substantial complaint in terms of
the interests served by corporate power (1,485 words in 13 newspapers). Much of

---

15   Mill argued that "trade is a social act", in which a trader is "amenable to those
whose interests are concerned, and, if need be, to society as their protector" (cited in Ten
2008: 11).

this echoed McKie's assertion that the bailouts were an egregious use of taxpayers' money with no public benefit. Almost half (48%) argued that powerful corporate elites were being awarded preferential treatment by the government over ordinary taxpayers. Only the *Sunday Telegraph* and *Western Mail* mentioned the bailouts without mentioning this complaint, instead simply noting anger and opposition.

Of this framing, over a quarter came from occupiers, including from banner slogans such as "Bankers got a bailout, we got sold out" (quoted in *Daily Mail* 17/10/11), and otherwise as paraphrased opinions attributed to the movement: "Protesters say they are upset about corporate excess and that the billions in bailouts doled out during the recession meant banks resumed earning huge profits while 99 per cent of people suffered" (*Independent on Sunday* 30 /10/11). Corporate profit is here not assumed to represent success, fulfilling economic responsibilities, or securing jobs, but private gain which is of no public benefit.

This framing does seem to have originated with the Occupy movement, who released a statement connecting the public money received by the banks ("bailouts") with the withdrawal of public money ("austerity"), and disrupting the association of profits with jobs by associating it instead with unemployment.

> After huge bailouts and in the face of unemployment, privatisation and austerity, we still see profits for the rich on the increase. (statement from Occupy LSX quoted in *Independent* and *Western Mail* 15/10/11)

This suggests that the majority of citizens were suffering an unfair burden of cuts to public spending in comparison with wealthy banks and bankers, and frames the interests of each as separate and even competing. Other commentators furthermore argued that this preferential treatment was unfair because the bankers were to blame for the economic crisis that was the government's justification for austerity.

> The protesters strike a resounding chord when they complain that financial elites are getting rewarded with special treatment while the punishment for their mistakes is meted out on the rest of society. (Andrew Rawnsley, *Observer* 30/10/11)

Four commentators explicitly made this point, two of which cited the Occupy LSX statement: "We refuse to pay for the banks' crisis" (*Independent on Sunday* 23/10/11 and *Times* 24/10/11), and a third was from a journalist-activist who contrasted the internal democracy of the Occupy movement "against the tyranny of the financial markets which, having crashed the economy, now demand fealty in the form of austerity, privatisations and bailouts" (Katharine Ainger, *Guardian* 29/10/11). This simple message was rather effectively transmitted through the mainstream media, as it cleverly reproduced popular (and somewhat populist) news-frames of fairness, wrongdoing and blame, victims and baddies (see also Birks 2011).

A further objection to the profits and bonuses was that they demonstrated that it was 'business as usual' at the bailed-out banks, despite the effects of their irresponsible risk-taking (283 words in six newspapers, especially in sympathetic titles such as the *Independent on Sunday*, and a third in quotes from Occupy sources).

> Three years after the banks that brought the west's economies to their knees were bailed out with vast public funds, nothing has fundamentally changed. Profits and bonuses are booming for financial oligarchs and corporate giants, while most people are paying the price of their reckless speculation with falling living standards, cuts in public services and mounting unemployment. (Seamus Milne, *Guardian* 20/10/11)

This accepts the argument that a healthy economy is at least one measure of the public interest, but that this is not necessarily produced by an unregulated market, and the banks should be obliged, having accepted public money, to also accept some public responsibility for their corporate behaviour.

However, protesters' focus on the bailout over and above regulation allowed critics to retort again with the utilitarian public interest argument:

> "I'm not entirely sure what they're protesting about," says Jonathan, a 28-year-old City lawyer who has visited during his lunch break out of curiosity. "Would they rather the entire financial system had collapsed?" (Iain Hollingshead, *Telegraph* 20/10/11)

The consequentialist argument is here used to advance a pragmatic argument of 'no choice', and arguably illustrates how the belief that society is dependent on the financial markets does seem to breed a sense of entitlement that refuses to recognise other legitimate interests. The protesters rejected the argument as rhetorical, as one objected: "They rule us by fear, saying if you don't bail the banks out everything will collapse" (occupier quoted in *Mirror* 29/10/11). Although the pragmatist argument (ostensibly) involves truth claims or predictions of cause and effect that could be supported with evidence, rather than expression of or appeal to values, none is offered, and all the opposition can offer doubt is rather than disproof.

Greed and the good society

Similarly, the discussion of causes of the economic crisis focused more on the personal culpability of bankers rather than the structural failures of free markets. There was some attention to the recklessness of the banking system (11 references in seven newspapers, largely left-leaning titles) that was not overly personalised; six references (246 words) were to reckless practices ("reckless speculation", "risky casino banking" and so on), three (84 words) to reckless institutions, and just two (79 words) to reckless bankers. The popularity of the term "casino banking" following the crisis has framed the complex world of investment banking as essentially institutionalised gambling, challenging the assumption that risk-taking among the poor is a vice, but among the wealthy it is a virtue. However, the term was only used once here (Heather Stewart, Business, *Observer*, 30/10/11). There were a further 384 words on "mismanagement" of banks in four newspapers (*Observer*, *Daily Mail*, *Telegraph*, and *Herald*), including identical references to Occupy as aiming to "highlight inequalities caused by mismanagement of the economy", apparently lifted from a press release (*Daily Mail* and *Telegraph* 20/10/11, *Daily Mail* 25/10/11).

A significantly more prominent theme, however, and one that was more personalized,[16] was greed. Greed was very frequently mentioned but rarely discussed at any length – the 1,631 words were spread across 58 separate references (an average of 28 words per reference), and frequently in summaries of what the protest was about, though less than 7% was directly from Occupy sources.

> PROTESTERS descended on the City of London yesterday as part of worldwide demonstrations against "corporate greed" in the financial sector. (*Sunday Telegraph* 16/10/11)

> The problem, it maintains, is corporate greed, the bankers and government austerity programmes. (*Times* 18/10/11)

The left-leaning papers cited this concern more frequently, but the less sympathetic titles made disproportionate mention of it in relation to the extent of their overall coverage. This framing lends itself to communitarian criticisms of the uncivic behaviour of individuals undermining trust in the system, and a neo-liberal defence of self-interested behaviour as functional in the smooth-running of the system, but not a criticism of the system itself.

The most explicit framing of the banking crisis as a consequence of personal moral failure came from a *Telegraph* columnist.

> Too many banks were greedy, stupid and wicked – yes, wicked, when we look at the impact of their strategies on our pension plans, on the ability of families to get mortgages, on the capacity of small businesses to grow – and yet, intolerably, nothing of consequence has happened to the industry's leadership, which gives the impression that it's already back to business as usual. (Graeme Archer, *Telegraph* 22/10/11)

The focus on social harms signals a liberal approach – that liberty should be constrained when it negatively affects others – but the concern with the "impression" given by the lack of punishment suggests a more communitarian approach, whereby trust is instilled through visible retributive justice. Just

---

16   Diani and della Porta's definition of social movements excludes personalised politics.

as, he argues, trust and civility was restored through punitive sentencing of perpetrators after the 'summer riots', the banking industry needs to be seen to suffer consequences for its mishandling of the financial sector and damage to the economy, concluding, "This matters, because without trust, civilisation is not possible" (*Telegraph* 22/10/11).

It is possible that Archer believes that punishment of the bankers will change their future behaviour (through the logic of 'sending a message' or 'making an example'), but the principal objective is to defuse the anger motivating the protest, regardless of whether it resolves the issue *causing* the anger – interpreting the anger as resentment, not as a principled objection. The activist role of civil society, in terms of holding power to account and debating public policy, is dismissed in favour of an interpretation of protest as merely a symptom of social malaise.

Although in the coverage of Occupy LSX only one commentator raised the argument that former Royal Bank of Scotland CEO Sir Fred Goodwin should be stripped of his honour (Andrew Rawnsley, *Observer* 30/09/11), this later became prominent enough that the knighthood was annulled the following year. Such individual punishment does nothing to reform the system and arguably distracts from the argument for regulatory reform. This framing is reinforced by a cultural bias of news media toward seeking out individual wrongdoing, since the professional norm of objectivity as part of the social responsibility model of journalism, combined with the notion of their democratic role as a 'watchdog', favours attention on the transgression of rather than challenges to the rules. This argument was made by social theorist Slavoj Žižek, writing in the *Guardian* – "Do not blame people and their attitudes. The problem is not corruption or greed, the problem is the system that pushes you to be corrupt" (27/10/11).

In contrast, critics of the movement argued that greed is inevitable, functional or irrelevant to beneficial outcomes. A banker quoted in the Independent framed greed as an inevitable part of (any) social system: "Capitalism makes the world go around, to be honest. Look what happened with communism. There's always going to be greed in the world" (*Independent* 18/10/11). What's more, with the market understood as the aggregation of individual utility, the wider population are also implicated in the credit bubble.

> Fine to speak up against greedy bankers, but without any other political arguments [...] it rather seems like you're damning the millions who lived off their loans in the first place. And why would they want to do that? (James Harkin, *Independent* 18/10/11)

Harkin, an author of popular economics books, accuses Occupy of making a moralistic judgement on the free private choices made by individuals exercising their liberty. He argues that the good society is defined in terms of utility, not abstract values or a moral notion of the good: "It's lovely to imagine a world without greed, but no one ever built a movement without appealing to the real interests of ordinary people" (James Harkin, *Independent* 18/10/11).

State intervention and the public interest

However, the power implications of the negative liberties enjoyed by the financial sector were raised 11 times in relation to the private lobbying power of corporate interests – not very frequently, but perhaps more than might be expected (see Chapter 6). Three newspapers criticised deregulation and argued for reform – the *Guardian* (352 words), *Independent on Sunday* (215 words), and more surprisingly, the *Times* (264 words) though they argued that this was counter to the occupiers' "diagnosis" of the problem as one of greed. Heather Stewart (*Observer* 30/10/11) criticised David Cameron for "warning that proposed European regulations on derivatives would harm the competitiveness of London", Seamus Milne in the *Guardian* (20/10/11) blamed "an era of rampant deregulation that has created huge disparities of income and wealth, concentrated in the hands of the top 1% and secured by politicians bought by corporate interests", and Margareta Pagano, the *Independent on Sunday* Business Editor (23/10/11), criticised the "trickle-down" theory and argued that deregulation opened the way for practices that undermined competition.

A *Guardian* editorial contextualised this as part of a neo-liberal conception of the good "in a world brought low by them and in need of very different guiding principles":

> They [Conservative politicians and bankers] persuaded themselves that global deregulation, shareholder value, innovative financial products, recycled credit, inflated property prices, tax avoidance, management autonomy, the bonus culture and conspicuous consumption were the foundations of a good – because prosperous – society. (leader, *Guardian* 17/10/11)

This raises more substantial questions about virtue, including "what role finance should play in the economy and society" (Heather Stewart, Business, *Observer* 30/10/11), and the case for "a capitalism that is firmly and clearly regulated to meet the objectives of green sustainability and social justice" (leader, *Independent on Sunday* 30/09/11).

At the other end of the ideological spectrum, some neo-liberal critics of the Occupy movement suggested that the economic crisis was caused not by the banking and financial sectors, but a bloated public sector placing excessive demands on the private sector, especially the *Telegraph's* Business Editor, who expounded this argument at length.

> The recapitalisation of banks is nothing compared to the massive liabilities posed by our much loved but insolvent welfare system that has been a black hole growing not for the past few years but for the past few decades. (Damien Reece, *Telegraph* 22/10/11)

Instead of arguing that state intervention is oppressive and damaging to individual liberties (as above), Reece portrays the public sector as something "much loved" but impractical; suggesting that social democratic principles are merely sentimental and the neo-liberal belief in the small state is simply hard-headed pragmatism.

The defence of government austerity as pragmatic was far more common, however, in the coverage of the public sector strikes and student anti-tuition fees protests. Pragmatism was an especially prominent theme in coverage of the strikes (6,451 words, or 6% of the total wordcount). A quarter of this asserted an economic imperative for pension reforms, and 16% a demographic imperative. Although the framing of economic necessity was particularly prominent in the *Sun, Express* and *Telegraph*, it was common in all except the *Guardian* and *Mirror*.

> By the end of his term in office, he needs to show that the imbalance between the wealth-creating private sector and a public sector bloated by unaffordable state spending has been corrected. Unless this is achieved, the levels of tax and debt needed to sustain an unfeasibly large public sector workforce, which enjoys terms and conditions that are no longer available to anyone else, will continue to sap the strength of the economy. (leader, *Telegraph* 01/07/11)

The lexical choices such as "unaffordable" and "unfeasibly large" reflect the government's argument that the unions were not being realistic about the viability of the pension scheme or sustained public spending more generally. The *Sun* and *Express* argued that the unions were out of touch with reality, the *Express* with articles headlined "Why union leaders won't leave their fantasy island" (letters, 30/06/11) and "Striking public sector workers live in an unreal world" (01/07/11).

Against the overall grain of the pragmatist argumentation was Aditya Chakrabortty's 'Brain Food' column (a weekly column in the *Guardian*'s G2 supplement exploring a news story through academic research), which presented an economic imperative for union wage claims in terms of regulating the boom and bust economic cycle.

> This is one of the first full-blown studies of the link between inequality and financial crises, and it is explicit that there is one. What's more, Kumhof and Ranciere argue that the "restoration of the lower income group's bargaining power is more effective". Take heed, Ed Miliband: unions throwing their weight around makes for more sustainable growth. (*Guardian* 28/06/11)

This is discursively interesting, tackling neo-liberals on the pragmatist ground that they claim for themselves, rather than opposing them from an idealistic stance, but it is also unusual in referring to evidence to support an argument, rather than simply asserting truth claims.

The student protest against tuition fees and education cuts was also reported in the conservative press as a naïve denial of economic necessity, portraying the protesters as arguing for a policy that would undermine the common good in terms of utility, with utility defined as economic stability and growth. Five newspapers argued that there was an economic imperative for cuts and fees, but coverage of the argument was dominated by the *Daily Mail*.

> But the Coalition has a lesson to learn as well. With a wave of public sector strikes in prospect, ministers need to remember that whatever opposition they encounter in getting our spiralling debt under control, it's the right thing to do. (leader, *Daily Mail* 11/11/10)

> If the pain imposed by cuts will be real enough, much heavier will be the price if the public, as well as this Government, does not hold its nerve amid some broken glass. (Max Hastings, *Daily Mail* 12/11/10)

These commentators suggested that the interests of the few should be sacrificed for the benefit of the many, regardless of the political representations from civil society. But the more overt message was that the students' case was irrational. A *Times* leader headline (11/11/10) accused the students of presenting an ill-thought-out opposition to fees that "lacks economic logic", and Max Hastings scoffed that "they are protesting for a cause which suggests they left their brains at home" (*Daily Mail* 12/11/10). Cutting public spending and shifting service provision into the private or third sector is therefore presented not as the 'right thing' to do, but as the 'only thing' to do, through a discourse of pragmatism.

There were two mentions of economic growth as the common good, one of which was a tongue-in-cheek reference on Page 3 of the *Sun*:

> NEWS IN BRIEFS: ELLE was dismayed the students' demo turned into an all-out riot. She said: "They failed to realise that violent expressions of protest against major socio-political problems routinely reduce the potential for economic growth and poverty reduction in climates of financial instability." (*Sun* 11/11/10)

In the other, the *Times* (news analysis, 14/11/10) warned that if the cuts *failed* to lead to recovery "government imposed-pain" would generate broader voter disaffection, questioning the government's calculation of utility, but not its measure of the good.

Interestingly, however, the discussion of wealth creation included only one, rather sceptical, mention of private sector growth compensating for public sector cuts in investment (*Western Mail* 11/11/10). The notion of wealth creation as a public good did, however, appear to be accepted by some supporters of the protests – or at least they offered reasons that would appeal to neo-liberal proponents of tuition fees and HE cuts. A student leader quoted in the *Western Mail* (13/11/10) argued that higher education graduates themselves create wealth and "the Government is sending a clear signal that it does not value the contribution made by graduates to our economy".

However, the more common defence of the public funding of higher education was related to the value of education for its own sake, advancing a different judgement of utility. Critics argued that funding by tuition fees changes students' relationship from learner seeking knowledge and skills to customer seeking qualification and reward. The terms "privatisation" and "marketisation" were used 12 times, exclusively as a criticism, initially by the NUS president, Aaron Porter, and then adopted by students who occupied the roof of Millbank, and the Goldsmiths academics who issued a statement in support. The terms were not broadly picked up by journalists or commentators, but the general argument was discussed in 2,504 words over 13 newspaper titles.

The *Guardian* highlighted this argument in the Browne review as evidence that the government misunderstood the purpose of higher education as a source of social good.

> This report displays no real interest in universities as places of education; they are conceived of simply as engines of economic prosperity and as agencies for equipping future employees to earn higher salaries. (Stefan Collini, academic, quoted in *Guardian* 12/11/10)

There are two types of critique of the neo-liberal agenda then – a pragmatic one that tries to engage with the ideology on its own terms of market logics and imperatives, and an ideological or value-based one that challenges the underlying assumptions of neo-liberalism from a social democratic perspective. The first critique uses an economistic discourse to argue that market mechanisms do not work in relation to the provision of higher education, whilst the second argues that market logics are inappropriate to the predominantly social role of education.

Critics argue that the market does not work in this context because education is a public good and because it doesn't fulfil the microeconomic conditions necessary for functional regulation through competition. A *Herald* letter-writer pointed out that the wealthy businessmen who object to public funding of education "surely depend on graduates for much of their business success" (10/11/10). This applies the economic argument that education is a public good that benefits the whole of society, in other words – like national military defence, or environmental policies – no-one can exclude themselves from benefiting and therefore owing payment.

The notion that choice and competition would improve higher education for students was also questioned.

> One of the lowest-ranked universities is preparing to charge the proposed maximum £9,000 in tuition fees for some courses, casting doubt on government hopes of a consumer led market in higher education with a mix of cheap and expensive degrees. (*Sunday Times* 14/11/10)

Again, an economic argument lies behind this – that universities are oversubscribed because demand for university places outstrips supply, making price inelastic.

Furthermore, given the value of degree prestige, there may even be pressures towards a positive price elasticity, as associated with luxury goods.

> There are good reasons for institutions to charge the maximum, the study [by the Higher Education Policy Institute] said. "Charging lower fees risks being identified as a low-quality or low-prestige institution." (*Western Mail* 11/11/10)

This suggests that attaching a monetary value to education changes the relationship of the student to their study, along the lines of Michael Sandel's (2012) argument in *What Money Can't Buy: The Moral Limits of Markets*.

Marketisation assumes that students' instrumentalism will result in them getting value for money. However, several critics pointed out that this was unlikely to be the result of the combination of fees and cuts. As economist Will Hutton pointed out "These are not fees to raise the investment in our universities and make the student experience even better" (*Observer* 14/11/10). Student union leaders interviewed in the *Western Mail* (13/11/10) all made similar points that judged the market-led reforms on the basis of market logic – in terms of customer satisfaction ("The quality of the student experience") and value for money:

> Students face the real prospect of paying higher fees for less quality, contact time and resources in their degrees. (student union leader, quoted in *Western Mail* 13/11/10)

That these higher expectations and therefore dissatisfactions are produced by the very market logic and neo-liberal discourse promoted by the government, was an irony not lost on one of the student leaders.

> Cutting government spending on higher education, then increasing the cost for the student and driving into a further market system of education, is going to leave students expecting more for the amount they are spending, but inevitably getting less. (student union leader, quoted in *Western Mail* 13/11/10)

Given the very limited choice that students enjoy in practice when choosing between universities, including on price, there are no market pressures or incentives – students as consumers have all the costs without any of the buying power.

However, this criticism accepts the general premise that higher education is primarily of instrumental value to the individual student, through their ability to command a higher salary in subsequent employment. Another argument given reasonably broad coverage (1,209 words in nine newspapers) was that education is a social virtue in itself.

> Here lies another reason why Wednesday's events were so significant – for within the government's plans for higher education lie not just the hiking-up of fees, but an entire reinvention of the very ethos of our universities, whereby

the idea of education as a public good takes yet another kicking, and everything comes down to "choice", and whatever is meant to be good for business. (John Harris, G2, *Guardian* 12/11/10)

Harris argues that not only the interests but also the values of the market are erroneously presented as equivalent to the national interest or common good. This argument mostly appeared in the left-leaning press, primarily the *Independent on Sunday* (441 words), *Guardian* (211 words), and *Independent* (147 words), although the Times did publish several short quotes and letters making the point.

There were two further references to the "ethos" of universities, a protester writing in the *Guardian* expressed concern that "The Government's decision to ringfence science and technology while cutting the entire teaching budget for the arts and humanities, points to an alarming ethos" (Zoe Pilger, *Independent* 11/11/10), and a union representative called the UK policy "totally at odds with the Scottish education ethos" (quoted in *Times* 11/11/10). In contrast to the Occupy coverage, the student protest was framed as defending positive values (educational aspiration, concern for the needs of others) as opposed to attacking negative values (greed). However, like the public sector strikes, the student protest can also be seen through the prism of interest politics. Of course the principles of social democracy underpin specific arguments over resources and redistribution, but they can also be interpreted as divisive and conflicting.

Interest politics and redistribution

Of the three protests, it was coverage the public sector strike that proportionately gave the most attention to equality and fairness, but the emphasis was on fairness to the taxpayer and private sector worker. The coverage of Occupy LSX, by comparison, gave more attention to equality.

Table 4.3   Equality and justice in coverage of the student protests, public sector strike, and Occupy LSX

	Public sector union strikes		Student protest		Occupy LSX	
	n	% coverage	n	% coverage	n	% coverage
Belfast Telegraph	171	6.7%	142	3.7%	160	12.6%
Daily Mail	1556	14.8%	190	2.7%	119	1.7%
Daily Telegraph	1310	10.4%	536	5.6%	250	1.9%
Express	1512	16.4%	0	0%	0	0%
Guardian	3114	15.9%	605	3.5%	1490	4.6%
Herald	1259	33.5%	308	7.2%	228	3.4%

	Public sector union strikes		Student protest		Occupy LSX	
	n	% coverage	n	% coverage	n	% coverage
Independent	1222	10.7%	64	0.9%	1430	11.6%
Independent on Sunday	0	0%	414	10.6%	1478	15%
Mail on Sunday	0	0%	358	10.2%	140	16.2%
Mirror	1088	12.6%	499	14.4%	59	3.1%
Observer	0	0%	141	2.0%	830	9.5%
Star	126	6.7%	0	0%	0	0%
Sun	1018	13.1%	0	0%	64	4.7%
Sunday Telegraph	0	0%	61	1.3%	0	0%
Sunday Times	0	0%	103	3.8%	254	4.9%
Times	840	10.9%	484	5.1%	289	2%
Western Mail	744	9.9%	283	5.7%	217	5.6%
Total	13960	13.5%	4188	4.3%	7008	5.5%

There were surprisingly few references to class in the coverage of the public sector strike – just 10 references in 5 newspaper titles, totalling 384 words. On the one hand, Michael White in the *Guardian* made a wry comment comparing "the time-honoured rhetoric of class struggle" to "classroom struggle" and the *Mirror* and *Western Mail* reported a union leader calling the pension policy an "assault on our class" (01/07/11), and on the other hand, the *Express* (29/06/11) made comparisons with the "class war" of the miners' strike, arguing that it benefited no-one but Arthur Scargill. Indeed, almost a tenth of all coverage of equality and fairness referred to union leader pay (1,279 words).

The debate on equality and fairness, however, was dominated by an argument over the definition of fairness in public sector pay. The conflicting interests between which a fair bargain must be struck were not framed as those of workers and employers, but those of the public and private sectors, defining fairness as equal conditions between the two sectors (3,512 words in 11 newspapers), with the private sector representing the realistic market rate, in what the TUC called a "race to the bottom" (quoted five times). Relatedly, 1,493 words (11% of equality and fairness) referred to fairness to the taxpayer of public sector reward. 'Taxpayers' were either explicitly (57%) or implicitly (26%) defined as private sector workers, with only the *Guardian* pointing out that public sector workers were also taxpayers.

> All but a handful of private final-salary schemes closed long ago, while most in the wealth-producing sector have no occupational pension to look forward to. Yet if the unions were allowed to win, these are the people who would be milked until they drop to keep their neighbours in comfortable retirement. (leader, *Daily Mail* 30/06/11)

The dramatic and emotive language of taxpaying private sector workers being "milked until they drop" was not unusual in the framing of unfairness, including inflammatory accusations of "apartheid" between the public and private sectors from "business leaders" (*Telegraph* 30/06/11) – suggesting that it is public sector workers, rather than business leaders themselves, that have eroded the value of private sector pensions.

Business is, again, privileged as the "wealth-producing sector". This suggests that the comparison is not one of context, in terms of what the market conditions have determined as affordable or sustainable, but an argument about deservingness – pitching the "self-serving mentality" of public sector workers against 'hard-working' taxpayers (Leo McKinstry, news analysis, *Express* 01/07/11). Although the unions' claims that the proposals were unfair were given some airing (2,162 words in 10 titles, 15% of equality and fairness), just 536 words related to unions seeking or securing fair wages.

Most of the coverage of the argument for equal conditions for public and private sectors (almost two-thirds) asserted that public sector pensions are more generous than those in the private sector, but a further 22% argued, more controversially, that public sector pay and conditions were more generous, not only in the *Express*, *Mail* and *Telegraph*, but also the *Herald* and *Independent* (in a vox pop).

> With our ageing population and terrifying deficit, taxpayers just don't have enough money to go on keeping public servants – on average better paid than private employees – in disproportionately long and affluent retirement. (leader, *Daily Mail* 30/06/11)

The argument that generous pensions in the public sector compensated for less favourable pay appeared in just three newspapers – in two letters to the editor (*Western Mail* 30/06/11; *Herald* 01/07/11) and one vox pop quote (*Independent* 29/06/11). Similarly, it was just the *Guardian*, *Herald*, and *Western Mail* who reported that the unions were calling for fair pensions in the private as well as public sector.

The coverage of the student protests followed a very similar set of frames. Some attention was given to social injustice, emphasising inequalities in opportunity and the potential impact on social mobility. Some of this was framed in the explicit terms of class politics (252 words in seven newspapers – hardly extensive, but more than might be expected, almost equaling that in the strikes coverage). There were some mild comments from student union leaders about "elitist proposals" (student union leader, quoted in *Western Mail* 10/11/10), but the students who made the most clear and emphatic statement of class concerns were the Millbank occupiers who released a statement from the roof.

> We stand against the cuts, in solidarity with all the poor, elderly, disabled and working people affected. (text message from Millbank occupiers, quoted in *Guardian, Star*, and *Times* 11/11/10)

However, this explicit statement of class politics was largely ignored by critics, who only mentioned class in descriptions of protesters' privileged background, to suggest that their politics were inauthentic (see Chapter 7). Of course the low proportion of students from a disadvantaged background is in itself a class issue, but the policy that was meant to address that – the expansion of access – was only raised in negative terms, as an unaffordable expense (Richard Littlejohn, *Daily Mail* 12/11/10, Richard Ingrams, *Independent* 13/11/10).

John Harris in the *Guardian* suggested that the rising tide of protest signalled an end to political complacency that allows dominant political neo-liberalism to go unchallenged.

> Wednesday gave the lie to the idea that our young people are thoroughly post-ideological creatures, with no fight in them; if even the most fusty newspapers are worried about the chasm that separates the government from the so-called squeezed middle, you can bet that the politics of class may yet make an unexpected comeback. (John Harris, *Guardian* 12/11/10)

Interestingly, this suggests that there might be an alliance of interests between middle-earners and poorer members of society against those of the very rich, which later became the position of the Occupy movement. At the same time, the contrast with the "post-ideological" suggests that this new class politics is a rejection of identity politics.

There was, however, fairly significant attention given to inequality and social justice (4,854 words – 5% of the total wordcount) equality of opportunity (533 words in five newspapers), the fear of debt deterring poor university applicants and the implications for social mobility (630 words in eight newspapers), and growing inequality in society (429 words in eight newspapers). This coverage mostly appeared in the left-leaning and devolved titles, but also in various articles in the *Times*, and one opinion column in the *Mail on Sunday* (14/11/10).

> The demonstration was not only about fees for posh kids. It was about a future in which we know only the price of education, not its value. And the protest was made by those who know that education remains the key motor of their own social mobility. (Suzanne Moore, *Mail on Sunday* 14/11/10)

Moore doesn't see the interests of the rich and poor prospective students as inconsistent, but part of the same principle.

Social mobility was approached through the frame of generational unfairness in seven newspapers (456 words), in terms of those who benefited from progressive policies and increased social mobility in the sixties refusing the same opportunities to today's young people.

> What infuriates students is the way that my generation, which benefited from free higher education, is now pulling up the ladder of opportunity behind it. (Iain McWhirter, *Herald* 11/11/10)

This is suggestive of a discourse of hypocrisy: they were willing to take the free education paid for through general taxation by their parents' generation, but are unwilling to do the same for the younger generation.

In contrast, the conservative press portrayed students as demanding that others pay for their education.

> The economics of tuition fees are simple. As access to university rises, the bill
> to pay for universities rises. Someone has to pay this bill. Should it be those who
> benefit directly from a university education? Or should it be paid by everyone,
> including those who choose not to go to university or do not get the opportunity
> to do so? (leader, *Times* 11/11/10)

This is at best ambivalent about the principle (pursued by New Labour) of expanding access to higher education to give the opportunity to poorer young people, but rather defines fairness as not having to support the privileged few who *do* go. This demonstrates how the understanding of higher education as of benefit only to the graduate themselves results in utility calculations made in purely exchange terms; in other words that benefit is dependent on payment, and no other moral claim is valid.

> Their cause is always the same: demanding other people pay for their upkeep. In
> the case of the poll tax it was the 'rich' who should have to pay for their council
> services. (Richard Littlejohn, *Daily Mail* 12/11/10)

The focus on personal agency and negative liberties privileges freedom from the duty to support others' positive right to education, and regards social mobility as a personal achievement unrelated to material opportunity.

Once again the right-wing press represented the alliance of interests in society as those of 'taxpayers', in this case defined as 'responsible', 'hard-working' *working classes* (who are presumed to accept their position in life), who were contrasted with irresponsible and petulant students with a sense of entitlement.

> I wonder how cabbies and bus drivers passing the Millbank Tower must have
> felt, knowing their hard-earned taxes were paying for a bunch of overgrown
> schoolchildren to take a day off to protest about having to meet part of the cost
> of their further education by thumping coppers and smashing windows. (Richard
> Littlejohn, *Daily Mail* 12/11/10)

Littlejohn also suggests that going on a protest march is a nice jolly rather than a boring slog that demonstrates political commitment. Civic engagement is defined as fulfilling the social obligation to be economically useful (the neo-liberal model), not as political engagement (the activist model).

This is part of a discourse of the deserving poor, defined as those who are hard-working and cooperative. In fact, a letter to the editor in the Express suggested that experience of poverty was character-building, breeding values of thrift and restraint.

> If they don't wish to pay the debts they accumulate during their time at university they shouldn't go. Only after learning about budgeting and going without, just like the rest of us, can they be considered 'the future'. (letter to the editor, *Express* 12/11/10)

Suzanne Moore (*Mail on Sunday* 14/11/10) was alone in arguing that the fear of debt is greater among the working class (whilst risk-taking is more socially acceptable among the middle classes, as 'investment' and 'entrepreneurship'), so they are constrained by social expectations as much as their lack of financial resources.

The neo-liberal discourse was also augmented by a communitarian discourse of rights and responsibilities.

> A higher education is a privilege and not a right [...] being forced to work for a living might give them a valuable insight into how the taxpayers who fund higher education feel about having to do so. (Simon Heffer, *Telegraph* 13/11/10)

There is an assumption that left-wing or social democratic views are inconsistent with the experience of having to pay for public services and welfare. Some contributors also reflected the Conservative discourse of a "something for nothing culture" (culminating in Cameron's speech on welfare on 25th June 2012), lamenting "our workshy population" who "want everything handed to them on a plate" rather than getting a part time job to help them pay their way through university (letter, Express 11/11/10), which either rather overestimates Saturday job pay or underestimates the burden of a £27,000 tuition fee debt.

The dominant discourse in both stories combined a communitarian discourse of deservingness as dependent on responsibility with a neo-liberal discourse that defines responsibility as economic usefulness rather than political citizenship. Max Hastings in the *Daily Mail* went as far as a radical reframing of "exploitation" and "social justice" to define the oppressors as welfare recipients.

> The attempt to force the long-term unemployed to take work is represented by some as a brutal assault on people's civil rights. Yet many of us see it instead as the beginning of the righting of an historic wrong: the exploitation of millions of British workers' tax contributions to allow people to suit themselves about what work they accept. [...] But the rest of us need to keep saying again and again: there are two ways to look at 'social justice'. David Cameron is attempting to restore a fundamental relationship between effort and reward, which has been allowed to atrophy for far too long. (Max Hastings, *Daily Mail* 12/11/10)

The utilitarian, neo-liberal arguments focus on an assumed 'free-rider problem', which needs to be addressed through incentivising rational, self-interested, utility-maximising free agents.

The Occupy movement tried to counter this division of interests; specifically to present a more equitable distribution of wealth as a common, generalisable interest among the majority – the 99% – against a rich and powerful minority, attempting to align the middle classes with the more impoverished groups below them rather than the group above them that they aspire to join. However, critics in the *Express*, *Telegraph*, and *Independent* (perhaps wilfully) misinterpreted the slogan as claiming the support of 99% of the population, which they portrayed as demagoguery (see Chapter 7), despite their own willingness to generalise taxpayers' interests and opinions as against public spending.

In comparison with the coverage of the public sector strike and the student tuition fees protest, however, there was a similar amount of attention given to equality and fairness (around 5%), but it was significantly more sympathetic to arguments about social justice. The vast majority (82%) of the 2,764 words on inequality and the growing divide between rich and poor appeared in just three, left-leaning newspapers (the *Independent*, *Independent on Sunday*, and *Guardian*), but the *Sunday Times* published an article headlined "Inequality: the issue that can no longer be ignored" (30/10/11) and the *Guardian* (18/10/11) noted that even the *Financial Times* was critical of "growing inequality, rising poverty and sacrifice by those least able to bear it – all of which are failing to deliver economic growth".

References to social or economic injustice (746 words in 10 newspaper titles) were more evenly spread across a range of newspapers, largely in short quotes from the Occupy movement, or briefly summarising their concerns. The argument that ordinary people were suffering an unfair burden of the economic downturn or the government austerity measures in comparison with bankers (1,098 words in 11 titles) was also given broad attention. Even the conservative press, whilst supporting the 'fairness' of public spending cuts, conceded that it is understandable that the austerity measures would be resisted by the poor if the bankers did not pay their share of pain.

> The Government's programme for welfare reform – to reintroduce fairness to the benefits system – is at risk. Not because the ideas are unpopular; they are not. But if bankers don't pay a price for their folly, why should the poor? (Graeme Archer, *Telegraph* 22/10/11)

This emphasis relates, of course, to the dominance of the banking bailout angle as the main critique of the neo-liberal focus on economic liberty, and the personalisation of blame on greedy or incompetent bankers rather than the systemic criticisms and calls for regulation and redistribution.

Another common angle questioned the position of the church on the social justice concerns raised by the movement. For some commentators, the church's claim to be concerned about poverty and critical of consumerist values is undermined by their concern about tourist income.

> If Christianity has any role in today's secular, money-grabbing society, it is to
> champion those who have nothing and to challenge don't-care capitalism, rather
> than rake in cash for a church building, even if it is Christopher Wren's glorious
> masterpiece. (Paul Routledge, *Mirror* 28/10/11)

For others, the biblical position on the poor invalidated the occupation of the grounds of the Cathedral since they were preaching to (or inconveniencing) the converted, although one columnist's account of the church's position as "dedicated to promulgating the notion that the poor shall inherit the kingdom of heaven" (Andrew McKie, *Herald* 24/10/11) fails to recognise the distinction between promising a reward in another life and fighting for justice in this one.

Nonetheless, the most common angle on the Church of England was the relationship of the cathedral to commerce (3,862 words in eight newspapers), which was discussed at length in columns in the *Daily Mail* (21/10/11), *Independent* (27/10/11), *Mirror* and *Times* (28/10/11) and *Observer* (30/10/11). Most made comment on the commercial interests of the Church of England, and its position as part of the establishment not of the periphery of the public sphere.

> It used to be said that the C of E is the Conservative Party at prayer. And, sadly,
> the church is living up to that political stereotype: business before social justice.
> (Paul Routledge, *Mirror* 28/10/11)

Certainly, Dr Giles Fraser's sympathy for the cause and generally left-wing views were regarded as causing a split in the church (297 words, over eight references, in five newspapers).

The Cathedral's own claim for a record on challenging the excesses of free-market capitalism was judged unconvincing by one columnist.

> He [Richard Chartres, the Bishop of London] further asks them to go on the
> grounds that: "I am involved in ongoing discussion with City leaders about
> improving shareholder influence on excessive remuneration." I am sure that
> the bishop is well-meaning, but that is not going to cut it. (Andrew Rawnsley,
> *Observer* 30/10/11)

The former Archbishop of Canterbury, meanwhile, argued that the problem was *not* a conflict of interests between the super-rich and the rest, but a fragmentation of society: "We have effectively forgotten who we are because we have rejected the very faith and heritage that set us on our way as a great country" (George Carey, *Telegraph* 28/10/11). Carey also conflates distrust in political and moral authority with political "cynicism and apathy".

For Martin Samuel in the *Daily Mail*, the commercial concerns punctured the piety of Giles Fraser and brought him in contact with the "mundane" pragmatics of capitalism: "Canon Fraser, while swathed in a cloak of piety, is in fact a frontman for an organisation up to its neck in free market economics" (*Daily Mail* 21/10/11).

Other conservatives regarded the authorities' stance as hypocritical, even though they disagreed with the idealism of both the protesters and the church's moralising.

> Balls to your gift shop, Rev. You've got a small army outside your doors who agree with exactly the sort of pious idealistic impracticalities that your lot are supposed to be espousing. (Hugo Rifkind, *Times* 28/10/11)

Once again, progressive values were described, not as invalid, but as impractical and detached from economic realities.

Interestingly, the church was criticised in the Occupy coverage on the basis of its establishment status, power and resources that conflict with the values of charity and social justice that might have led it to engage with the protest issues, whilst Pope Benedict made claims in his state visit speeches, conversely, that Christianity was marginalised and excluded from public debate. The Pope's case, however, was made on a cultural basis, framing Catholicism as an embattled identity.

Minority rights and recognition claims

The most comprehensive claim for Christianity as culturally marginalised was in the Westminster Hall speech.

> In this light, I cannot but voice my concern at the increasing marginalisation of religion, particularly of Christianity, that is taking place in some quarters, even in nations which place a great emphasis on tolerance. There are those who would advocate that the voice of religion be silenced, or at least relegated to the purely private sphere. (quoted by 11, including all four tabloids, all four quality dailies and the three devolved nationals)

> There are those who argue that the public celebration of festivals such as Christmas should be discouraged, in the questionable belief that it might somehow offend those of other religions or none. (quoted by nine, including all four tabloids)

> And there are those who argue – paradoxically with the intention of eliminating discrimination – that Christians in public roles should be required at times to act against their conscience. (quoted by seven)

> These are worrying signs of a failure to appreciate [...] the rights of believers to freedom of conscience and freedom of religion. (quoted by eight, including five conservative titles)

This draws on populist arguments commonly used as an attack on multiculturalism, such as myths of a 'political correctness' so overly sensitised to potential offence that cultural festivals are purged of their religious significance (as opposed that being achieved by commercialisation). This is crucial, however, to substantiate the discourse of injured identity that underpins the claims to special rights – in this case to be able to follow their conscience and deny adoption to gay couples.

Unsurprisingly, then, the 'political correctness' theme was enthusiastically picked up by the conservative papers.

> And he launched a robust and welcome attack on the creeping culture that has seen Christmas ludicrously renamed "winterval" by pathetic councils, firms and schools pandering to anti-Christian lobbying. (*Sun* 18/09/10)

> POPE Benedict XVI yesterday made an impassioned plea for Britain to return to its Christian values and condemned the "politically correct brigade" who dismiss Christmas. Pope Benedict told an audience of dignitaries, including four former prime ministers, that religious beliefs should be protected, not discriminated against. (*Express* 18/09/10)

The *Express*' quote marks around "politically correct brigade" misleadingly suggests that the Pope uttered these words – sister paper the *Star* (18/09/10) went further in claiming that Benedict had directly mentioned "Winterval" and also Easter.

The *Telegraph* (18/09/10) also described Benedict as having "attacked the politically correct ideas that Christmas should not be celebrated for fear of offending minorities and that the faithful should be forced to keep their beliefs to themselves". To an extent, this was framed as a failure to extend cultural sensitivities to the dominant religion, or of making excessive concessions to other religions (*Daily Mail*, *Daily Star*, *Telegraph,* and *Sun* 18/09/11). Nick Ferrari in the *Sunday Express* (19/09/10) objected that "While respect is, rightly, afforded to other faiths such as Islam and Sikhism, you can be openly mocked on TV or in print for being a Christian" (citing *Jerry Springer: The Opera* as an example), and argued that there was a general "Disrespect bordering on the blasphemous" for religious people. A letter to the *Times* (18/09/10) argued that an article opposing the visit "would have been claimed as 'racist hatred'" if it had been about Islam.

More commonly, however, the discourse of 'political correctness' attacked socially liberal views. The Telegraph's leader column criticised 'political correctness' as censorship of "unfashionable" beliefs (leader, *Telegraph* 18/09/11), suggesting that these values are simply temporary cultural whims (as opposed to longstanding 'tradition'), rather than significant social change on the basis of moral sentiment and debate. The editorial went on to argue that tolerance had been redefined as tolerance for "narrow spectrum of liberal-approved beliefs" whilst "Anyone who falls outside that spectrum runs the risk of being demonised". This suggests that the progressive critique of (socially) conservative hegemony has now become reified as the new hegemony, and seeks to claim an injured identity for those with socially conservative views. The *Daily Mail*'s

Amanda Platell echoed this argument: "We have been bullied into silence so that the Liberal elite who really rule Britain can impose their atheist, politically-correct values upon us" (18/09/11).

A handful of the conservative papers also followed the Pope in using the language of human rights to assert religious rights. One commentator argued that equality law "threatens the rights of religious people to practice their faith openly, such as the right for Catholic adoption agencies to refuse their services to homosexual couples" (Jerome Taylor, *Independent* and *Belfast Telegraph* 18/09/10), similarly conflating freedom to worship with freedom to observe religious rules over secular law.[17] The *Telegraph*'s front page news noted the Pope's "reference to those adoption agencies and faith schools that felt under attack from the previous Labour government" (18/09/10).

> One may disagree with Catholics and conservative Protestants on the subject of gay adoption, but it was disturbing to witness the hounding of Catholic adoption agencies that wished to place children only with married couples. Their right to do so was abolished by New Labour. (leader, *Telegraph* 18/09/10)

This echoes the Pope's framing of the law as state coercion, not as the result of a democratic process, though it also makes a party political point, perhaps to suggest that the decision was 'ideological' – based on inauthentic or dogmatic *political* values as opposed to authentic and strongly-felt *cultural* values.

One Catholic writer complained of a "narrative that pits human rights against religion, freedom against faith, justice against the Church":

> It is, of course, a false narrative. But it is particularly appealing to Peter Tatchell and other human rights campaigners, who roll out a list of charges against the Church – as homophobic, sexist, authoritarian, and illiberal – in order to prepare the stage for the next step, an ambition long nurtured by dictators of all stripes: the exclusion of faith-based organisations from the public sphere and public money." (Austen Ivereigh, Catholic Voices, *Independent* 17/09/10)

Ivereigh denies the case put by human rights campaigners, but gives no reasons why the accusations are "false", simply a counter-accusation of authoritarianism.

Andrew Brown pointed out that the debate was dominated by assertion and counter-assertion of values as "true", which does not move the argument forward. On the one hand, he argued, human rights are value-based and socially constructed.

---

17   The wording from Article 18 of the Universal Declaration of Human Rights doesn't specify what counts as observance: "Everyone has the right to freedom of thought, conscience and religion; this right includes freedom to change his religion or belief, and freedom, either alone or in community with others and in public or private, to manifest his religion or belief in teaching, practice, worship and observance." (United Nations website: http://www.un.org/en/documents/udhr/ <accessed 21/10/12>)

Where secularists see religion as a divisive force, and their own beliefs as the self-evident and true base on which a healthy society can be built, Benedict sees that secularism itself can be challenged. Human rights are not self-evident. What rights we have depend on what kind of people that we think we are, and that is exactly the kind of question which social change and multiculturalism sharpen. It's not a question to which there is any agreed answer in Britain today. (Andrew Brown, *Guardian* 17/09/11)

But on the other hand, he added, "the [Pope's] claim that there are objective moral principles is itself controversial". Brown seems to draw a pessimistic conclusion on the potential to reach agreement on the values of the good society in a pluralistic society where each party simply asserts their own particularistic values.

The clash of such principles or their reduction into common sense, was what British society thought it had outgrown. Perhaps that, too, was an illusion of empire. (Andrew Brown, *Guardian* 17/09/11)

"Illusion of empire" hints at hubristic ideologies, in which he is perhaps including postmodern relativism and rationalist deliberative democracy.

There were two criticisms of Benedict's arguments. Polly Toynbee (*Guardian* 18/09/11) challenged the argument that the church's voice is marginalised in democratic debate.

it was an odd thought, since Britain is the only Western democracy that is part-theocracy, with its 26 unelected bishops sitting as law-makers in the House of Lords. Odd, too, was his belief that atheists and multi-culturalists threaten the national celebration of Christmas, even as decorations already start to adorn shops: how useful to the imaginary victimhood of Christians was that well-intentioned but misguided local council that chose to celebrate "winterval" a few years ago." (Polly Toynbee, *Guardian* 18/09/11)

The second took up Keane's point that you cannot logically tolerate the intolerant. A letter-writer referred to the Pope's doublethink on tolerance and discrimination as "hypocrisy":

The Pope condemns our laws as somehow marginalising Christians but what he really wants is for religious people to be allowed to discriminate against others in employment, services, education and many other areas, while not being thus discriminated against themselves. It is hypocrisy. (*Herald* 17/09/10)

However, the assertion of tolerance as a defining value of civil society may have been uncomfortably close to asserting it as a true or universal value, with the dominant associations of hubris.

Summary

Whether commentators believed that virtue originates from the personal conscience or needs to be instilled by communitarian social expectation, they still tended to merely assert their own values rather than give what we might, even generously, interpret as publicly acceptable reasons – those that could change others' minds. Even Benedict, in a densely argued speech, argued for the abstract dominion of religion over social virtue, only obliquely referring to particular values. The most obvious of those – anti-fascism, particularly in the form of anti-Nazism – was surely selected as a rare point of almost universal consensus in Britain, in part because of the status of WWII as a symbol of civic religion, binding the nation in a pride for a (mythologised) past. The more contentious, especially as regards his opposition to the values encoded in equality and human rights law, he obliquely referred to as inauthentic or lacking a legitimate basis (having been decided in the realm of reason), but his own alternatives were not explicitly stated, much less argued for.

The only available supporting argument for values appeared to be to appeal to religious rights. Those who sympathised with the Pope's opposition to the Human Rights Act asserted his right to discriminate, either under Kantian liberalism's own terms – arguing that their accusations of intolerance are intolerant (ignoring Keane's stipulation that excludes intolerance, along with violence, from civil society), or postmodern relativism of live and let live (though this was explicitly rejected by Benedict as a "dictatorship"), or, finally, on the basis of injured identity as a defensive claim for recognition and respect to compensate for "marginalisation" and discrimination. The last was surely cynically and strategically embraced by the conservative critics who reject the same claims by gay couples who want to marry or adopt. However, none of these stances would legitimise the "evangelisation of culture", which relates only to a communitarian or communal notion of civic virtue, incompatible with democracy. Benedict's argument that democracy has nothing to say about values was not widely recognised.

The defence of democratically-agreed values could appeal to procedural norms (which will be explored in Chapter 6), but rarely were. More often values were explained as personal and therefore private, in the sense of not being political. However, this either leaves just the hole at the centre of liberal democracy that Benedict identifies as the realm of religion, or locates legitimacy in a notion of personal authenticity, in the sense that the most legitimate is the one who most sincerely *feels* committed to their values or (connectedly with injured identity rights) feels more acutely a sense of injury or offence (which will be discussed in Chapter 7).

The exclusion of value from politics also simply excludes the ability to criticise the values that are assumed dominant. In terms of the citizen's relationship to the state and market, this too is defined, in part, in terms of negative liberty. But there is also a more communitarian expectation that the legitimate individual is one who contributes to the economy and succeeds in those terms. These legitimating values are promoted as merely pragmatically serving the neo-liberal meta-value of wealth creation, via the more publicly acceptable 'economic growth' that is argued to benefit all. These utilitarian calculations (or wild estimations) do not allow a space for values of social justice and equality. Nonetheless, recent waves of dissent have successfully made a space for social justice and equality to be discussed in mainstream news media, but whether this is particular to the current climate of austerity remains to be seen.

Chapter 5

Uncivil Action:
Legal and Moral Legitimacy

The traditional news-framing of protest is in terms of its legal legitimacy, that is to say, to delegitimise the action by focusing on isolated incidents of violence rather than the wider peaceful activities and their political message (McLeod and Hertog 1992). However, in as far as they do attract some coverage, orderly and good-natured marches and rallies are framed in approving terms (Juris 2011). There is a tension, therefore, between those activists who emphasise publicity, awareness-raising, and ideational disruption (DeLuca 1999) through consciously exploiting news values (drama, conflict) and the qualities of the public screen (immersive and engaging spectacle), and those activists or occasional protesters who emphasise mainstream legitimacy and acceptance. This operates on multiple levels, and the next chapters will address the *democratic* definitions of political participation and *social* conventions of 'civil' behaviour in public space, whilst here we focus on compliance with *legal* codes and the boundaries of legitimate civil disobedience – law-breaking for a higher moral purpose.

The student anti-tuition fee protest involved a strong discourse of 'violence' in relation to property damage, minor injury and the threat or risk of serious injury at the breakaway occupation of the Conservative Party headquarters at Millbank. However, the main march also benefitted from a larger turnout than anticipated, appealing to the news value of "unexpectedness" (Galtung and Ruge 1965), as well as presenting a watchdog angle attributing blame for inadequate police numbers. The extensive coverage that resulted included both traditional frames and also broad access to oppositional voices, as well as a range of commentary.

In contrast, the Occupy camp at St Pauls was marked by a complete lack of violence and disorder, and by friendly and relaxed relations with police. Instead, the legal challenge to the occupation was a complex technical question of land ownership and associated legal rights, and their moral claim to peaceful civil disobedience was challenged by conflicting moral rights to religious observance and personal autonomy. Finally, the case of the police infiltration into environmental activist groups not only questions the limits of legitimate policing in the context of civil disobedience, but also highlights an interesting area of escalating dispute – the legitimate uses of police surveillance.

Violence and criminal law: Student 'rioting'

The student anti-tuition fees protest was delegitimised in legal terms through the traditional focus on the spectacle of violence. However, there was also widespread marginalisation of the violent minority, including by the student leadership who organised the march. This was in tension, not only with the centrality of violence in the coverage, but also with a contrary interpretation of that violence as a politically significant reaction to government policy. The moral justification of destructive direct action as civil disobedience was challenged through a discourse of 'condoning' violence.

Focus on spectacular 'violence' over peaceful marching

As might be expected, there were almost four times as many words dedicated to the Millbank occupation as the peaceful march (17,125 to 4,556), and a fraction to speeches (254 words in four newspapers). The march was given a proportionately high coverage in the three quasi-national papers (the Scottish *Herald*, Welsh *Western Mail*, and Northern Irish *Belfast Telegraph*), who sent reporters with busloads of student protesters to get a local angle, and in left-leaning 'quality' newspapers, the *Guardian* and *Observer.* In contrast, the Millbank action was disproportionately reported in conservative titles across the market positions, the *Telegraph*, *Times*, *Mail on Sunday*, *Sunday Express*, and *Star*. The left-leaning tabloids were split, with the *Mirror* paying more attention to Millbank and sister paper the *Sunday Mirror* focusing on the march.

Particular attention was paid to the overlapping themes of violence (12,585 words, 13%) and property damage (4,475 words, 5%). A third of coverage of property damage defined it explicitly *as* violence, a definition contested by activists who engage in direct action (Ackerman 2000). The account of property damage was dominated by the dramatic image event of a plate glass window being kicked in. A black-clad protester in full swing, almost silhouetted against burning placards, was one of the defining images of the protest, to the extent that it was directly satirised in a cartoon by Martin Rowson (*Guardian* 13/11/10), which can be seen on the cover of this book. Nearly half of references to property damage (74 of 155, 46% by wordcount) mentioned windows being broken or smashed, with the next most popularly evoked images being bonfires and obscene graffiti (12 times each). There were six references in five newspapers (all right-leaning) to the monetary value or cost of the damage done as a measure of *legal* illegitimacy, whereas activists cited the cost to targeted institutions as central to the *political* aim of the direct action.

The conflation of property damage and violence was especially common in photo captions:

> Violent scenes: Students smash windows as they clash with police after entering Millbank Tower, home of the Conservative Party's headquarters, during yesterday's protests in London. (caption, *Herald* 11/11/10)

The Conservative Party headquarters looked as if it had been hit by an explosion, showing the extent of the student attackers' violence. (caption, *Times* 12/11/10)

However, this was also attributed to one of the students on the march:

Fellow student Simon Hardy, 23, said: "There was unfortunately a small minority of people who did do some vandalism but the huge majority of us were non-violent." (*Sun* 12/11/10)

The Oxford English Dictionary defines violence as "behaviour involving physical force intended to hurt, damage, or kill someone or something", which would seem to include property damage, and in legal terms as, "the unlawful exercise of physical force or intimidation by the exhibition of such force". Commentators in the *Western Mail* ("intimidation of ordinary workers", 11/11/10), *Telegraph* ("terrifying the 95 per cent of people working there who have nothing to do with the Tory party", Charles Moore 13/11/10), and *Mail on Sunday* ("the other people working in the building" were "frightened", and a "heavily pregnant receptionist" was "very badly shaken" 14/11/10) gave accounts that suggested intimidation.

Interestingly, however, there was marginally more coverage that distinguished property damage from violence, or at least listed them separately (349 words in seven newspapers), than that explicitly conflated it (223 words in eight newspapers).

Commentators and sources in seven titles more explicitly distinguished property damage from violent attacks on people or injuries caused.

Hurling a fire extinguisher into a crowd is clearly wrong, but the broken glass and bonfires of Wednesday were more visually spectacular than actually harmful. (Priyamvada Gopal, academic, *Guardian* 13/11/10)

Barlow argues that any violence on Wednesday was kept within reasonable limits: property was damaged, but people were not injured. (*Observer* 14/11/10)

But Mr Costello did criticise Aaron Porter, the president of the National Union of Students, on Twitter for condemning the violence. Mr Costello wrote: "Shut up Aaron Porter you dickhead. Smashing a window is not violence." (*Sunday Telegraph* 14/11/10)

These sources suggest that damage causing financial loss is "reasonable" because not "harmful", in particular with harm defined as injury to people.

Certainly, the specific accounts of 'violent' behaviour focused on the threat of injury from the fire extinguisher that was thrown from the roof (69 references, totalling 2,385 words across all but two newspapers), other missiles including eggs, flowers and placards (49 references, 1,221 words). The greatest number of references was to attacks on police (82 references, 2,267 words), although 28 of these (810 words) referred to the fire extinguisher landing near or grazing past two officers.

Some newspapers framed this as intentionally aimed at injuring (or killing) the officers, despite the crowd below being made up of many more fellow protesters than police.

> Some of the violence seen on the streets of London yesterday was murderous
> in intent with officers narrowly missing serious injury or death. (leader, *Belfast
> Telegraph* 11/11/10)

In the *Mirror* and *Herald* (11/11/10) it was dropped "on to riot police", the *Sun* had it "hurled at police", and the *Telegraph* (11/11/10) and *Daily Mail* (12/11/10) described it being thrown "at police officers". Six other references in various newspapers more accurately and neutrally noted that that the missile "narrowly miss[ed] police", and an article in the *Independent* and *Belfast Telegraph* (11/11/10), whilst specifying police as the target, noted the broader risk to the protesters: thrown "at police in the crowded courtyard below". Only the *Guardian* (11/11/10, 13/11/10), *Times* (11/11/10), and *Herald* (13/11/10) reported the hostility of the crowd of protesters outside Millbank to those throwing missiles.

> [...] when one of the people on the roof made the stupid decision to hurl down
> a fire extinguisher, they were met with an outraged chant of "Don't throw shit!
> Don't throw shit!" (John Harris, *Guardian* 12/11/10)

Other titles were more sensationalist. The *Star* (12/11/10) said the fire extinguisher "nearly killed an officer", whilst the *Telegraph's* (12/11/10) claim of it "injuring two officers", suggests rather more than a glancing graze.

Both right and left-leaning newspapers focused on the fire extinguisher, but it was variously highlighted as the most serious incidence of violence, or framed as illustrative or representative of the whole occupation.

> The incident was one of the defining moments of the four-hour stand-off after a
> breakaway group of students attacked the Millbank complex. (*Herald* 13/11/10)

The Herald's framing reflects the tension in much of the coverage between defining the direct action as the work of a small minority (a "breakaway group"), and yet as emblematic ("defining moments"). It suggests that the news media couldn't resist the occupation's status as a newsworthy event due to the drama, spectacle and conflict – which could suggest that the whole protest was violent – but were reluctant to suggest that the occupiers reflected a real or widespread sense of opposition to austerity and dissent in society – which could endorse the newsworthiness of the protesters in political terms.

On the one hand, then, there was a failure to distinguish clearly between the two protest repertoires, in three distinct but overlapping ways. Firstly, specific mention of the march was concentrated on the day following the protest, but steadily fell away, and on later days was principally mentioned as the context of the 'riot' or 'violence'.[1] However, there did not appear to be a corresponding drop-off in coverage of the substantive issues, suggesting that if not a catalyst for discussion of the issues, attention to them had at least not been subsumed by the image event of Millbank, and may have lengthened the period of attention.

Secondly, there was a small but significant frame that suggested that whole demonstration had become violent. The demonstration was described as having "turned violent" ten times, erupted in(to) violence three times, and "turned nasty" or "ugly" four times. Overall there were 30 suggestions, across 13 newspapers, that the whole protest had been transformed by the Millbank action. For instance, "within moments a peaceful protest had turned into a snarling, violent attack" (*Telegraph* 11/11/10), "A few minutes were all it took for a peaceful demonstration to turn to mayhem" (*Times* 11/11/10), and "violent protesters turned a demonstration against higher tuition fees into an ugly battle" (*Belfast Telegraph* 11/11/10). Even the *Guardian* ran a headline: "Police caught out by peaceful protest that turned violent" (11/11/10), with photos captioned "The calm before the storm" and "The day turns nasty". This portrayal does not acknowledge that there were tens of thousands of protesters that were unaware of the violence, and proceeded peacefully to the rally that concluded the march as planned.

Thirdly, some newspapers conflated the march and the Millbank action altogether. The right-wing tabloids in particular described the occupation as the aim of the whole march: "the tuition fees march on the Tory HQ" (*Sun* 13/11/10), and *the march itself* as violent: Millbank "became the flashpoint for Wednesday's violent march" (*Star* 12/11/10). This was not limited to the tabloids, but also appeared in the mid-market *Sunday Express* and quality *Sunday Telegraph*.

> The huge demonstration, attended by 50,000 protesters, caused damage estimated at £1million to Conservative party headquarters a short distance from the Houses of Parliament in Westminster when the mob forced its way in, smashing the glass doors and ransacking offices. (*Sunday Express* 14/11/10)

Whilst the causal agent of the "damage" is indeterminately defined as "the huge demonstration", the sub-clause identifies the demonstration with all of the marchers, creating a very strong implication that they were all involved in the incident. The *Sunday Telegraph* made a similar implication.

> The Lib-Con coalition reached its six-month anniversary, a milestone marked by a violent street demonstration against its £81billion of spending cuts. More

---

1   On the three days following the protest specific reference to the Millbank occupation fell off somewhat, with 36.8% of coverage on the following day (11/11/10), dropping to 23% the next day, and 14.4% on the Saturday, only increasing with the Sunday newspapers covering the story afresh. However, the drop-off of coverage of the march was significantly more marked – from 48.3% on the Thursday to 17.3% and finally 6.6% on the Saturday.

than 50,000 students marched through London on Wednesday, in protest against
plans to triple tuition fees to £9,000 a year. (*Sunday Telegraph* 14/11/10)

It is not clear what "violent street demonstration" refers to, but again, the
impression that all 50,000 marchers were involved is made through proximity.
There is no syntactic causality, but convention dictates that the second sentence
is an elaboration on the first. Interestingly, a letter-writer published in the *Times*
makes just this criticism against the newspaper:

> There is no place for violence – or for populist journalism that condemns all
> people in the same bracket. Most of the 50,000 protesters were exercising their
> democratic right, trying, peacefully, to get our Government to take a hard look
> at its policies. (church leader, letter to the editor, *Times* 13/11/10)

All of these tactics (consciously or otherwise) associated the peaceful, orderly and
well-attended march with the more radical direct action, to amplify (to varying
degrees) the impression of a vast and dangerous mob running out of control.

On the other hand, despite the disproportionate focus on the 'violence' of
the Millbank occupation, the occupiers were defined as an unrepresentative
minority. In part this reflected the insistence of the National Union of Students
(NUS) organisers of march that the two actions should not be conflated, but their
attempts to distance themselves from what they perceived as damaging also had
the effect of supporting a discourse that presented the more radical students as
marginal and distinct from mainstream society. Accordingly, this framing was
disputed by those who were involved in or who supported the direct action, who
sought to claim widespread support for their protest and its expression of anger,
and rejected the framing of the protest being "hijacked" by "anarchist" elements,
insisting that they represented a widespread anger about the overall direction of
government policy.

Representativeness of 'violent' direct action: Anarchist hijack

To some extent, the president of the NUS, Aaron Porter, operated as a primary
definer on the Millbank action, which could be interpreted as a positive reflection
on the increasing access of civil society associations, or as Porter having been
co-opted as the moderate voice against the more radical element (as explored in
the next chapter). Porter framed the march as having been "hijacked" by outside
agitators who were not 'genuine' students with an interest in the cause (reflecting
as assumption that 'authentic' political action is self-interested – see Chapter 7).

There were 47 references across 14 newspapers to the protest having been
"hijacked" by "rogue" elements. Only eight of these (227 words) were attributed
to Porter, but all were on the day following the protest, supporting the contention
that he was defining the framing of the Millbank action.

THE NUS condemns the rogue protesters' violent actions. It is despicable that a minority's actions hijacked a serious issue which 50,000 students came to protest. They seemed to be a large group headed by anarchists, who probably don't even care about fees. I suspect most weren't students at all. But until the violence erupted, it was a fantastic demonstration. (Aaron Porter, NUS President, writing in the *Sun* 11/11/10)

However, the framing of anarchist hijack has become so frequent as to constitute a new 'common sense' stereotype, so the *Herald* remarked "of course, there were the anarchists who always turn up at these events" (11/11/10), and the *Sun* "We all expect students to demonstrate and we know these protests are infiltrated by anarchists" (11/11/10).

The hijack frame was enthusiastically adopted by tabloid newspapers of both left and right.

The Battle of Millbank Tower erupted just after 1pm as a previously peaceful student demo against the increase in tuition fees was hijacked by anarchists. (*Mirror* 11/11/10)

More than 40 police officers were injured and 50 people arrested when the protest was hijacked by a hardcore of activists intent on causing mayhem. (*Express* 12/11/10)

Whilst the *Mirror* adopts the discourse in the same way as Porter, to establish the legitimacy of the mainstream protest by marginalising the protesters engaging in direct action, the Express shifts the emphasis to delegitimising the protesters, with mention of the march buried half-way down the article and mentioned only as the context within which the "violence" occurred. It is used to demonise the (radical) left as motivated by mindless oppositionalism (see Chapter 7).

Despite widespread acceptance of Porter's protestations, then, some commentary on the legitimacy of the students' protest repertoires clearly positioned the breakaway occupying group as the defining face of the protests, and as – regrettably but, for some reason, inevitably – undermining the anti-tuition fee cause. Two letter-writers (*Belfast Telegraph* 11/11/10 and *Express* 12/11/10) and two opinion writers (*Daily Mail* 13/11/10 and *Mail on Sunday* 14/11/10), whilst accepting that the 'rioters' were a minority, nevertheless argued that the minority had undermined the cause.

SIR – The student demonstration was clearly hijacked by the usual anarchists. Unfortunately, the students demonstrating lawfully will be tarred with the same brush as the professional demonstrators who would demonstrate against anything. (letter to the editor, *Telegraph* 12/11/10)

The regretful tone suggests that this may be unfair, but simply can't be helped, since the majority will have to be ignored to punish the few. A Cambridge academic in the *Guardian* ridiculed the paternalistic logic of such arguments:

> As the same few pictures of broken windows and bonfires were flashed across television screens, out scuttled the politicians to deplore "bloody" mob violence and those who "ruined it for everyone else". (Priyamvada Gopal, *Guardian* 13/11/10)

In any case, the suggestion that students were not involved in the Millbank action was quickly abandoned.

The *Guardian* was the first to quote a protester who had been inside Millbank reporting that the occupiers were "mainly young students, (with) just a couple of older guys who looked like old-school anarchists" (11/11/10). John Harris argued in the *Guardian* that his much was clear from the television clips.

> On the BBC, there was a particularly priceless moment. When Porter once again talked about "hijacking", the coverage cut to the mass of people outside Tory HQ, the presenter made the point that this was not what "a small minority" would look like – and Porter seemed momentarily lost for words. You had only to look at the crowd to know that the vast majority of them were not anarchists, but reasonably regular twentysomethings. (John Harris, *Guardian* 12/11/10)

As reports of the identity of those arrested came in, it became increasingly clear to the other newspapers that the characterisation of those causing damage as anarchists was not borne out by the evidence, with police statistics indicating that all were either students or under 18 (reported in six newspapers).

> He said a number of "anarchists" had been present but added: "I have to say there were some, especially younger, students who were doing it [the violence]". (student arrested at Millbank, quoted in *Express* 12/11/10)

> Lots in papers of student protest being hijacked. It may have been at start, but many I spoke to throwing things at front were angry students tinyurl.com/neil-mann-tweet (tweet quoted in *Times* 12/11/10)

A group claiming to represent the Millbank occupiers, including NUS NEC member Mark Bergford, defended the legitimacy of the occupation as representative of a significant number of students.

> We reject any attempt to characterise the Millbank protest as small, "extremist" or unrepresentative of our movement. We celebrate the fact that thousands of students were willing to send a message to the Tories that we will fight to win. (letter to the editor, *Guardian* 12/11/10)

Whilst Porter and many others from the NUS attempted to counter the traditional media delegitimisation of the mainstream protest by distinguishing themselves from an unrepresentative minority, these protesters sought to challenge this counter-framing of anarchist hijack that paints the minority as fringe lunatics. Instead, they suggest, those engaging in direct action represent a significant seam of authentic anger in the student body, which erupted spontaneously.

Another, less prominent framing emerged suggesting that naïve students were manipulated by hardcore ideologues, using a discourse of 'incitement'. This was expounded at greatest length in a *Times* article headlined "Students were egged on by hardcore anarchists":

> Many of those who breached scant police lines to gain access to the lobby and roof of 30 Millbank insisted that they had no interest in extremist politics and believed that the clashes with police had erupted spontaneously. But Facebook pages and anarchists' blogs were discussing how to disrupt the march up to a week before it began. (*Times* 12/11/10)

The *Mirror* also asserted that "Hoodie-wearing anarchists egged on the students" (11/11/10). In response, radical organisations denied the allegations of incitement and supported the students' claims to have acted on their own authentic anger:

> Class War had no role in encouraging or facilitating what happened at Millbank. These were the actions of students who were acting on their own spontaneity. (emailed statement to *Sunday Express* 14/11/10)

Interestingly, of the seven references to the occupation and associated 'violence' as spontaneous, three were from anarchist associations denying any role in organising or inciting the action. Spontaneity, in terms of being caught up in the heat of the moment, was understood to be a legitimating factor.

> The student, an anarchist, has been protesting for 10 years. He rejects the idea that the attack was pre-planned. "I saw 10 or 15 anarchists, but the vast majority were students." The violence was, he said, the result of spontaneous anger. (*Observer* 14/11/10)

> Luke Hawksbee, a Cambridge student and fellow ASN administrator, defended the occupation of Millbank Tower as "a spontaneous outburst". (*Sunday Telegraph* 14/11/10)

This distinction suggests that instinctive emotional responses are understood to be authentic and therefore politically legitimate, whereas premeditation on the basis of substantive principle or intellectual belief would delegitimise the protest. This will be explored in detail in Chapter 7.

Millbank protesters' objections were picked up by commentators in the left-leaning press, especially the *Guardian*. John Harris reported the impression of a colleague who had been outside Millbank to report on the protest: "Talk of cynical provocateurs, he said, was 'nonsense': the crowd was made up of 'ordinary students who were viscerally angry'" (*Guardian* 12/11/10). Paul Routledge in the *Mirror* similarly highlighted the delegitimising agenda behind the discourse of 'hijack', attributing it to the establishment.

> Predictably, the powers that be – the police, the career-seeking leaders of the National Union of Students, government ministers and their poodles in the BBC – dismissed the whole episode as the work of a hard core of politically motivated anarchists, a tiny minority, less than 1% of the protesters. (Paul Routledge, *Mirror* 12/11/10)

However, both accept the framing of "politically motivated" protest on the basis of ideological or substantive beliefs about the nature of the 'good society' as illegitimate or "cynical", and argue that the occupation was legitimate – or at the very least politically significant – because it reflected the authentic anger of those directly affected by the policy (although it would actually only affect those not due to start university until 2012).

However, the legitimacy of law-breaking as civil disobedience is based on the principle of moral motivation, aimed at challenging a greater injustice. Accordingly, McLeod and Hertog (1992) identified the news focus on legal proscriptions over moral justifications as a key aspect of the delegitimising framing of protest.

Legal arguments over moral: Crime and civil disobedience

Critics frequently asserted a distinction between legal protest and unlawful violence. Of 60 references to activities at Millbank as criminal, over half referred to specific criminal offences, including potential charges to be brought against those arrested, most commonly specifying criminal damage (18), violent disorder (14), attempted murder (11), assault (5), and trespass (5).

Half were in quotes from sources, with the legal framing led by the traditional primary definers: the police (19), and politicians (8), especially David Cameron (6).

> People who assault police officers or who smash windows or who break property are breaking the law and, yes, those people I hope ... will be prosecuted. They should be. People long in our history have gone to marches and held banners and made protests and made speeches and that's part of our democracy. That is right. What is not part of our democracy is that sort of violence and lawbreaking. It's not right. It's not acceptable and I hope that the full force of the law will be used. (David Cameron quoted in *Belfast Telegraph* 11/11/10; "full force of the law" also quoted in five other right-leaning newspapers, 12/11/10)

The Police and Criminal Justice Minister made a similar distinction but suggested that restrictions on the illegitimate activities would also restrict the legitimate action, and that to some extent that was acceptable.

> Mr Herbert said: "The police have to strike a balance between dealing promptly and robustly with violence and unlawful activity on the one hand, and allowing the right to protest on the other. Clearly, in this case, the balance was wrong".
> (*Herald* 12/11/10)

Herbert may be making an oblique reference to the previous criticisms of the police for their heavy-handed policing of the G20 protest that had led to a policy that aimed to facilitate protest, suggesting that the "balance" should be shifted back toward enforcing public order (see legitimate policing, below).

Neither Cameron nor Herbert recognise the shifting and constructed nature of legal definitions of protest, such as the criminalisation of trespass and aggravated trespass (Joyce 2002), nor that a significant aspect of democracy is that laws are ultimately challengeable (Cohen and Arato 1992). In particular, it could be argued that legal protest has been so narrowly defined as to be rendered completely ineffective, since most real disruption and inconvenience has been outlawed. The suggestion that there is a clearly defined line between legitimate legal protest and illegitimate transgressions of the law leaves no room for the grey area of civil disobedience.

There was, however, also some attention given to the moral imperative for the direct action, including explicit defence of the Millbank occupation as legitimate civil disobedience. A group of Millbank protesters gave an account of their principled motivation in terms of the damage they argued was being caused to public services.

> The mood was good-spirited, with chants, singing and flares. Yet at least 32 people have now been arrested, and the police and media appear to be launching a witch-hunt condemning peaceful protesters as "criminals" and violent. A great deal is being made of a few windows smashed during the protest, but the real vandals are those waging a war on our education system. (letter to the editor, *Guardian* 12/11/10)

> That some students took part in civil disobedience in no way detracts from the scale of today's demonstration. Their actions pale in significance beside the criminal damage the Tories and Liberal Democrats are about to inflict on our universities. (Liam McNulty, SDLP Youth member quoted in *Belfast Telegraph* 11/11/10)

Both of these quotes (to differing degrees) frame the damage to Millbank as aimed at preventing greater damage to public services, which is the definition of civil disobedience as a legal defence. However, whilst it is not necessary that the law broken is the one objected to, more typically the intervention would be more direct or literal[2] rather than purely performative and symbolic. The symbolism also appears to communicate hostility to the Conservative party rather than opposition to their policies, which suggests a discourse of blame which is not consistent with della Porta and Diani's (2006) definition of social movements.

The protesters' account of the destruction of the social democratic welfare state as a greater social threat was addressed to some extent in ten of the 19 newspapers that covered the story, especially the *Guardian* (176 words), but also the *Western Mail* (193 words) and *Telegraph* (124 words). Most of these represented the cuts to public funding as a greater act of aggression and destruction.

> The real violence in this situation relates not to a smashed window but to the destructive impact of the cuts and privatisation that will follow if tuition fees are increased and if massive reductions in higher education funding are implemented. (statement by Goldsmiths academics, quoted in *Daily Mail*, *Express*, *Guardian*, *Star*, *Telegraph*, *Times*, *Mirror*, *Sunday Express*, and *Sunday Telegraph*)[3]

In addition to this framing of austerity as "the real violence", others referred to it as "much more far reaching and systematic violence" (Priyamvada Gopal, academic writing in the *Guardian* 13/11/10), "the real vandalism" (Labour MP quoted in *Sun* 12/11/10), "trashing" (Clare Solomon, president of the University of London Union quoted in *Daily Mail* and *Mirror* 13/11/10), and "destruction" (rooftop protesters quoted in *Mirror* 13/11/10).

Of the seven brief mentions of civil disobedience (275 words) all but two quoted protesters or civil society organisations, mostly on planned future action. The other two – both in the *Guardian* – did take it seriously as a political action.

> Civil disobedience – a principled breaking of the law – can be a powerful tool. (Priyamvada Gopal, academic, *Guardian* 13/11/10)

> Were they an unruly rent-a-mob, hell-bent on violence – or well-meaning students caught up in the dizzying excitement of civil disobedience? Probably a mixture. (Tom Harper, *Guardian* 14/11/10)

There is a suggestion in both, however, that although it is a legitimate tool, its "power" and "excitement" demands careful handling, and is not necessarily one for amateurs.

---

2   As, for instance, with the planned Ratcliffe on Soar power station occupation (in which Mark Kennedy was involved) committing trespass and criminal damage to directly – if temporarily – prevent environmental damage.

3   Confusingly referred to in some cases as a statement by Goldsmiths lecturers, other times as a letter signed by 100 academics, and eventually as a petition signed by 3,000 supporters, including celebrity activists.

Although there was not a great deal of reference to civil disobedience as a legitimating frame for destructive direct action, there was more general discussion of the argument that violence was pragmatically necessary for the protesters to get their message across due to failures of representative democracy or formal politics, and making comparisons with the poll tax riots as a measure of its political significance. This will be addressed in the next chapter.

Inevitability of violent reaction to cuts

Some commentators in the more sympathetic newspaper titles argued that not only was the violence a political reaction to government spending cuts, but it was also an *inevitable* reaction. The *Independent* reached this conclusion from the comparative international context, suggesting that the surprise was that it had taken so long to occur.

> Until yesterday, the British reaction to the proposed cuts has been remarkably mild compared with mass protests in France, Greece and other countries. (*Independent* 11/11/10)

A *Sunday Mirror* columnist took a more deterministic view, arguing that the government *caused* the riots by making unreasonable decisions.

> Yet, it was everyone else but the Teflon Government who was blamed for Wednesday's riots [...] Let's remember, if it wasn't for these savage cuts there would be no protests. Now ask yourself again who was really to blame for the Millbank riots. (Fiona McIntosh, *Sunday Mirror* 14/11/10)

The reference to "the Teflon Government" recalls the nickname given to Tony Blair (Teflon Tony) when he was seemingly impervious to criticism and blame. This is a rather more populist argument that seeks to implicate the culpable (for sparking a riot) rather than challenge the policy (because it is unjust). Nonetheless, it suggests a legitimate or understandable motivation for unrest.[4]

The conservative newspapers criticised this framing of the inevitability of violence as equivalent to *approval* of violence.

---

4   A colleague from sister paper the *Mirror* adopted a slightly incongruously consumer-capitalist angle to class conflict:
> How, unless they're from wealthy stock, like most of the Cabinet, are they supposed to get on the property ladder once they're finished? No wonder they rioted. (Fiona Phillips, *Mirror* 13/11/10).

This very middle class obsession of property-ownership may be designed to appeal more broadly, but it takes an instrumental rather than principled position, and rather misses the protesters' point about the public funding of education as a public good.

> In the Commons yesterday Ed Balls issued Labour's official line that the violence
> was 'completely unacceptable'. But at a separate event, shadow chancellor
> Alan Johnson suggested Government policy was partly to blame – saying their
> 'unfair' policy contributed to the clashes. (*Daily Mail* 12/11/10)

Although blaming the government for the violence suggests disapproval, or at
the very least an understanding of it as a negative outcome, the *Mail* contrasts
this blame with condemnation of 'the violence', and therefore as sympathy or
approval. In the same issue, Max Hastings made this argument more explicitly.

> More dismaying for the future though is the fact that a substantial body of
> Left-wing opinion is constantly telling such thugs that protests are 'only to be
> expected, once The Cuts start to bite' [...] In the same vein, much Left-wing
> comment, notably from the *Guardian* newspaper and the BBC, has reflected an
> assumption that the Government's policies are so radical, so menacing to the
> inalienable rights of many British people, that strong opposition is inevitable
> and – implicitly if not explicitly – deserving of sympathy. (Max Hastings, *Daily
> Mail* 12/11/10)

Hastings seeks to depoliticise the Millbank action by interpreting any response to
the protest, including any remarks on the protesters' moral *motivation*, in terms of
legal and moral judgements on their *behaviour*. This reduces the debate to a binary
of condemning versus condoning 'violence'.

Discourse of condoning/condemning

There were 56 references to the speech act of 'condemning', just under half of
which (27) were in direct quotations, most commonly from the NUS, and Aaron
Porter in particular, distancing the main march from the Millbank occupiers. The
NUS was in turn condemned for its condemnation of the Millbank occupiers by
their supporters, who had also been condemned for that support.

> But the Goldsmiths lecturers dismissed the criticism, saying: "We wish
> to condemn and distance ourselves from the divisive and, in our view,
> counterproductive statements issued by the UCU and NUS concerning the
> occupation of the Conservative Party HQ. (*Telegraph* 12/11/10)

However, in all there were just five condemnations of the NUS's and politicians'
condemnation of the violence and, more surprisingly, only three condemning
the Goldsmiths statement of support (the same number as condemning the
government's policies), against 42 condemnations of the 'violence'.

Eleven of these referred to 'condoning' violence or property damage, eight of
which were in a negative modality, such as "[...] can't be condoned" or "I don't
condone [...]". This was often (five times) followed by "but", as in "I do not condone

what the students have done, but they have a point" (letter to the editor, *Telegraph* 12/11/10). This reflects the extent to which a range of commentators, including politicians, columnists and letter-writers anticipate the criticism and modulate their support or agreement with this condition or denial. One commentator noted this anticipation of being accused of condoning violence as breeding a timidity in opposition to the cuts and fees, as "the Labour leadership is too scared of being labelled pro-violence to do anything but bleat platitudes" (Paul Routledge, *Mirror* 12/11/10). This suggests that the discourse of condemning and condoning has the effect of closing down debate through labelling opponents.

Some of the criticisms of supporters of the protest explicitly accused them of encouraging or inciting violence. The *Daily Mail* used correlation of time to rhetorically suggest that the Labour MPs who expressed support for the protest were referring to property damage and clashes with police at Millbank.

> LABOUR MPs shamelessly encouraged students rioting over tuition fees to 'get stuck in' via Twitter at the very moment they started smashing up Tory headquarters, it emerged last night. Backbencher John McDonnell used the social networking site to tweet 'just shows what can be done when people get angry. We must build on this' as missiles were hurled at police. Then as protesters started destroying the entrance to the Westminster building, MP Alex Cunningham tweeted: 'Well done our students – thousands outside the office getting stuck into the LibDem/Tory government.' (*Daily Mail* 12/11/10)

One Conservative MP accused these Labour MPs of "appearing to justify violence" (Greg Hands quoted in *Star* 13/11/10), whilst Simon Heffer in the *Telegraph* (13/11/10) claimed that the Goldsmith academics were "people who not merely condone but celebrate criminal behaviour and physical violence".

Some commentators gave reasons for condemning the Goldsmiths statement, applying certain principles of civility.

> I can imagine what they would say, were a group from the TaxPayers' Alliance to turn up at their homes and vandalise them in protest at the way these lecturers are failing to discipline their students. (Norman Tebbit, quoted in *Daily Mail* 13/11/10)

Despite the tone of parental scolding associated with the 'how would you like it?' argument, this does relate to a Kantian recognition of the moral worth of the other (Kenny 2004: 115) and J.S. Mill's notion that no-one should support any rule that they would not be prepared to have applied to themselves. However, the relative harms are not equivalent – damage to a private home is not the same as damage to an organisation's office, and Tebbit makes the questionable assumption that lecturers are supposed to "discipline" their students.

The following day, a *Sunday Express* columnist made a very similar rhetorical argument:

I wonder if Mr trendy Lecturer would take such a casual view of violence if I popped round to his house and smashed his windows in because I don't like his point of view? I bet he'd be the first to complain if the police told him that the broken glass wasn't "real"... (Julia Hartley-Brewer, *Sunday Express* 14/11/10)

When the Goldsmiths academics say that the "real violence" is the suffering caused by the cuts the obvious interpretation is that violence is defined as harm to human life and dignity, not to property, or that such harm is more *significant* violence, but Hartley-Brewer (in a presumably wilful misinterpretation) takes it for a metaphysical statement that denies the very existence of the broken glass. More importantly, however, she suggests that the protest was about a difference of opinion that could be more reasonably expressed within conventional political means, ignoring the imbalance of power between the political core and periphery and the limited opportunities for communication from the latter to the former (see political legitimacy, Chapter 6).

The focus on 'criminal' violence or property damage as the delegitimising factor in the Millbank occupation would suggest that a *peaceful* occupation would be recognised as legally legitimate protest. However, opponents to the Occupy movement, facing a peaceful and orderly occupation of the ground outside St Paul's Cathedral, shifted the goalposts to challenge the legality of disruption through civil challenge by conflicting interests and 'rights'.

Disruption and civil law: Peaceful occupation

The legal framing of Occupy as illegitimate focused on the grounds for eviction of the encampment, which rested largely on the legal ownership of the land. This was the most extensively covered legal angle, making up 22% of text on the eviction proceedings. A high-court injunction was secured by the City prior to the protest to prevent access to and occupation of the privately owned Paternoster Square in front of the London Stock Exchange, which was regarded – in as far as it was covered (by the *Guardian* and *Express* only) – as straightforwardly legitimate and in any case as a fait-accompli. The land in front of St Paul's Cathedral, however, was a complicated mix of ownership, possibly including a section of public highway that may or may not have lapsed into private use (reported by four newspapers). The cathedral could make a legal case for eviction on the basis of trespass (complicated by the potential legal interpretation of Giles Fraser's request for the police to leave the steps as an invitation to protesters to remain), whilst the Corporation could make a case on the basis of obstruction of the public highway. The basis of the legal claim in the civil law assertion of private land ownership rights meant that the dispute was explicitly about private interests as opposed to the public interest. This appears to be the cause of concern for Fraser, since that would suggest that the church was pursuing its own interests, and violence would therefore be "in the name of the church" (four times).

Alternatively, the police could evict without court proceedings under section 14 of the Public Order Act (although the legal technicalities were again only mentioned in four newspapers), but only on the basis of serious disruption. This created an imperative for official sources to amplify the discourse of disruption, although interestingly, it was only a senior police source who framed disruption as *criminal*:

> They have got the legitimate right to protest, not the right to commit crime. That is the complexity we are trying to deal with. (Metropolitan Police Commissioner Bernard Hogan-Howe, quoted in *Daily Mail* and *Guardian* 28/10/11)

The public interest case against the legal legitimacy of the protest therefore rests on the significance of disruption to legitimate social and cultural interests or rights, and commerce.

Disruption from the scale of the occupation

Initially the frame of disruption and inconvenience was related to the size of the camp. From the outset, mentions of the scale of participation were framed in terms that implied that the growth in numbers was problematic rather than reflecting widespread support. There were 78 references to the size of the camp, largely quoting current estimates of the number of tents, occupiers, and daily visitors. These accounts seemed to imply that the numbers were deemed large ("more than...", "hundreds" or "thousands"), and "growing" (31 references). Over half of these explicitly described the numbers as disruptive, whilst only two (in the *Guardian* and *Independent on Sunday*) cited the numbers as evidence of the extent of support, whilst another cited the *small* scale of the protest as evidence of its illegitimacy. Only the *Guardian* (26/10/11) pointed out the inconsistencies in criticisms – too many protesters to be accommodated without causing disruption, too few to demonstrate real commitment to the cause.

Disruption from the Cathedral closure: Blame and backlash

The disruption framing escalated sharply with the closure of the cathedral, but despite the best efforts of the authorities, blame was not entirely or consistently attributed to the protesters. At first the Cathedral's framing was largely accepted. Even before the event, the *Times* reported the authorities' warning as "Protest camp threatens to shut St Paul's" (*Times* 20/10/11), attributing agency for the closure to the occupiers rather than the Cathedral. Following the closure the protesters were blamed 22 times for "forcing" the decision, three of which were attributed to the Dean of St Paul's (*Guardian* and *Belfast Telegraph* 22/10/11, and *Independent* 27/10/11), but otherwise reported as fact by the conservative press.

There was only one claim that the closure was "because tourists and worshippers are unwilling to pass through the tents, banners and people at its entrance" (*Times* 21/10/11). Instead the cathedral cited health and safety concerns, which rarely attracts approval from the conservative press that were the natural sympathisers with the authorities' predicament. Initially, then, news reports simply reported the claims without comment, either explicitly attributing the claims to cathedral authorities (36 times) or their health and safety officers (nine times), or referring simply to health and safety "fears" or "concerns" (five and six times respectively), but not definitive 'problems'. By 24th October, two days after the closure, these uncritical references were increasingly replaced with more sceptical ones, which dominated by 28th October.

Predictably, many of these criticisms came from sympathetic newspapers such as the *Guardian*, but as they noted, there was "near-universal criticism of the decision to shut the cathedral for the first time since the blitz, not all of it displaced to the responsibility of the demonstrators." (Stephen Bates, news analysis, *Guardian* 28/10/11). Even the *Telegraph* (26/10/11) reported that "St Paul's staff were criticised for citing "spurious" health and safety issues", and the *Times* (26/10/11) that "Questions were raised yesterday whether it had been necessary to close". From within the church, a bishop called the closure "a hysterical over-reaction" (quoted in *Telegraph* 29/10/11; *Independent on Sunday* 30/10/11; leader, *Observer* 30/10/11) and Former Archbishop of Canterbury, George Carey called it "mismanagement" (writing in *Telegraph* 28/10/11; quoted in leader, *Observer* 30/10/11).

It was in the interests of the cathedral authorities to discredit the legitimacy of the occupation on 'objective' technical grounds, in order to avoid making a self-interested complaint or critical moral judgement, which their conservative supporters recognised, but were reluctant to respond credulously to the bureaucratic excuse. Criticism grew in these newspapers once it became clear that the tactic had not been successful.

> St Paul's thought that by giving rather spurious health and safety excuses and going down the draconian route of closing down, it would all get sorted within 24 hours. Instead, the protesters have dug their heels in. It's been a misjudged attempt to take the initiative by closing. (Mark Field, Conservative MP, quoted in *Times* 26/10/11)

> Did the crisis thrown up by the occasional gaffer-taped guy rope really mean they had to close St Paul's to tourists and congregants for the first time since the Blitz? Of course not. It was a bullying strategy, designed to make the protesters all bog off. (Hugo Rifkind, *Times* 28/10/11)

Of course, these criticisms are principally directed at the cathedral having made a tactical failure, but it was deemed not only as "misjudged" but also "draconian" and "bullying", and therefore as a failure to retain the moral high ground.

Charles Moore, however, argued that the cathedral authorities should abandon their moral justifications and have the courage to act decisively in their own interests.

> But they were not brave to take refuge in health, safety and fire regulations. And it seems precious to dither about the necessary decisions, leaving these nasty things to the City Corporation. The Church needs the legal action announced yesterday, but lets others take the blame for it. (Charles Moore, *Telegraph* 29/10/11)

However, there was a rather mixed response to the cathedral's pursuit of its own interests, which were broadly agreed to be the income generated by tourism and associated commercial operations such as the café and shop.

There were just eight suggestions that this income had been damaged by the occupation, primarily in the *Times* and *Daily Mail*, along the lines that "Tourism usually brings in 80 per cent of that figure but has slumped since the city of tents sprung up last weekend." (*Times* 22/10/11). In fact there was an equal number of references to the occupiers' counter-argument that they were themselves becoming a tourist attraction, though six of these were in the more sympathetic newspapers.

The main criticisms of the cathedral's financial concerns, however, was that it wasn't seemly for a religious institution to be commercially motivated. It was noted that the humble-sounding 'café' charged £25.95 for a set lunch and the shop merchandise included "a set of deeply religious cufflinks for £180" (*Daily Mail* 21/10/11), and that what they called a "donation" was actually a compulsory £14.50 entrance fee (letter to the editor, *Express* 25/10/11). One commentator used this to undermine Giles Fraser, the Canon Chancellor of St Paul's whose support for the right to protest led him to resign:

> Canon Fraser, while swathed in a cloak of piety, is in fact a frontman for an organisation up to its neck in free market economics. (Martin Samuel, *Daily Mail* 21/10/11)

Samuel is less concerned with reasserting the 'true' cultural and philanthropic role of the church than undermining it as a hypocritical posture.

However, more commonly, and especially in the left-leaning press, it was argued that prioritising the cathedral as a tourist attraction mistook its primary purpose.

> A cathedral isn't really there for the tourists, even if it can charge visitors £14.50, as St Paul's does. It is a place for prayer and worship. (leader, *Guardian* 26/10/11)

In a later leader column (28/11/10), the *Guardian* went on to argue that the inconvenience was to powerful commercial interests, and that pandering to them threatened to undermine the church's moral authority.

> Jesus denounced his Pharisaic enemies as whited sepulchres, or shining tombs; and that is what the steam-cleaned marble frontage of St Pauls will become if the protesters are evicted to make room for empty pomp: a whited sepulchre, where morality and truth count for nothing against the convenience of the heritage industry. (leader, *Guardian* 28/10/11)

Even the Bishop of Buckingham (quoted in *Telegraph* 29/10/11 and *Sunday Mirror* 30/10/11) called the cathedral a "self-important tourist Disneyland". The specifically commercial institutions in the area were deemed more legitimate interests, however.

Disruption to commercial interests

There were initially some assumptions that the occupation was a form of direct action aimed at disrupting city trading, such as the *Mirror's* characterisation of the occupation as "part of a global movement designed to stop traders getting to work" (21/10/11). The *absence* of disruption was therefore interpreted in some quarters as a *failure* of the protest repertoire, including Damian Reece in the *Telegraph* (22/10/11), Giles Hattersley in the *Sunday Times* (23/10/11) complaining that protesters were lazy because he "hadn't seen anyone confront a banker", and Andrew McKie in the *Herald* (24/10/11) similarly scolding that the occupiers "seem never to have got up early enough to inconvenience anyone who works in the City." It is likely, of course, that any disruption of trading would have been taken as evidence of its moral illegitimacy – much like the public sector strikes, where anticipated widespread disruption proved that the unions had too much power which must be curbed, and the reported lack of disruption was indicative of union weakness and therefore illegitimacy (see Chapter 6).

There were 27 references to the claims of loss in trade and takings for local businesses, mostly those located (where specified) in Paternoster Square, which was cordoned off by the Corporation of the City of London to prevent the movement gaining access, rather than directly by the protest itself. The *Guardian* (29/10/11) mentioned the cordon in passing, and the *Express* explained it as "because of the protest camp" (26/10/11). More often it was general claims that "There are a lot of shops feeling the pinch as a result" (Mark Field, Conservative MP quoted in *Daily Mail* 25/10/11), and "nearby businesses also hit." (*Sun* 25/10/11). Nonetheless, this was significantly fewer references to business interests than might be expected. Again, there was also a minority argument that the camp was having the opposite effect: "Public hygiene may be a concern, but it does not appear to worry tourists overmuch, who are flocking to see the camp – and boosting local businesses, even as they find the cathedral doors locked" (leader, *Independent* 27/10/11).

Other efforts to portray the camp as inconveniencing 'ordinary' people were undermined by their flat refusal to complain. Seven newspapers reported on the first post-closure wedding at the cathedral closure, but largely in terms of the colour added by the story, since the bride seemed to rather enjoy the attention and "drama" (*Times* 22/10/11) and moment of being "famous" (*Sunday Express* 23/10/11). She was described as "sneaking" (*Times* 22/10/11) and "being bundled" (*Independent on Sunday* 23/10/11) and having to "slip in" (*Sunday Express*) through a side door, but even the *Sunday Express* quoted her as saying "there hasn't been any disruption at all". The *Mail on Sunday* suggested that it was the intention of the protesters to prevent the wedding taking place – "couple defy protesters to marry at St Paul's" (23/10/11) – though they did quote a protester saying that they did not want to spoil the couple's day. Only the *Sunday Times* accused the occupiers of being disruptive:

> By 1.30pm members were ranting over the loudspeakers. One was a member of the "Sex Workers Open University", who yelled "There are no bad whores, just bad laws!" Just what you want to hear as you're walking down the aisle. (*Sunday Times* 23/10/11)

Again, however, the newspaper quoted the bride as saying "it's actually been really nice having all the extra wellwishers" and calling them "friendly and peaceful".

Disruption, rights, and civil law

Despite the mixed and inconclusive accounts of the disruptive effects of the encampment, there were some efforts to portray the occupation as breaching other people's rights, in order to justify legal action to evict. Of 12 references to conflicting rights (challenging the right to protest), two specified the obstruction of a public highway, six asserted a threat to the right to worship, and the rest referred more generally to "other rights and responsibilities" (Giles Fraser, quoted in *Guardian* 23/10/11), "the needs of our communities" (City Councillor, quoted in *Times* 24/10/11), "the effects on those around you" (local business owner quoted in *Times* 25/10/11 and *Express* 26/10/11), and, more obliquely, "priorities" (City Councillor, quoted in *Daily Mail* 24/10/11).

In contrast, the disruption that would have been caused by the planned occupation of the Ratcliffe on Soar power plant by environmental protesters in the Mark Kennedy case was barely mentioned, and in only one instance criticised.

> But supporters said tackling such groups was exactly what the police should be doing as they often disrupt vital services and businesses. (*Western Mail* 11/01/11)

It is unclear who exactly these "supporters" of the police infiltration are, and this attribution could be a ventriloquisation of the public.

The legal and moral legitimacy of direct action was established by the judge who handed down "lenient sentences" (*Guardian* 10 and 11/01/11, *Express* 11/01/11) to the 20 protesters who had admitted intending to occupy the power station. His remarks that they were "decent people" who were acting "with the highest possible motives" were quoted in the *Guardian* (twice and six times respectively), and – more surprisingly – in the *Express* (11/01/11). This may not be sufficient attention to suggest that the judge acted as a primary definer legitimising the intended direct action, but in as far as the morality of the protest was discussed it was in positive terms.

The protesters' solicitor, Mike Schwarz, directly argued that the moral motivation justified the action as civil disobedience.

> The police need to answer some serious questions about their conduct relating to protesters. This is a serious attack on peaceful, accountable protest on issues of public and pressing importance like climate change. One expects there to be undercover police on serious operations to investigate serious crime. This was quite the opposite. This was civil disobedience, which has a long history in this country and should be protected. (quoted in *Guardian* and *Times* 11/01/11)

Schwarz appeals to a public interest defence and to traditional national values, and therefore to both civil and communitarian reasoning.

Jenny Jones, Green Party MP and member of the Metropolitan Police Authority, was the most explicit about the disruption, but also appeared to justify the publicity-related aims as equally valid as the direct prevention of environmental damage: "they simply wanted to halt production at a power plant for a day to get some media coverage and help save the planet" (quoted in *Western Mail* 11/01/11). This recognises the symbolic aspects of civil disobedience, as a legitimate justification for trespass and minor property damage, as does Schwarz when he defines it as a "peaceful" protest, but this does not necessarily extend to more generally destructive property damage.

Moreover, the dominant framing of the story favoured a focus on the right to protest, rather than any competing rights to personal autonomy or freedom from disruption to power supply. However, the right to protest was frequently contextualised and conditionalised in relation to both Occupy LSX and the student protest.

Boundaries of legitimate dissent – the discourse of rights

The right to protest was mentioned more frequently in relation to the student protest than the police infiltration of environmental protesters. There were just four references in the latter case, three of which were in the *Guardian*, and one of those was quoting the other reference, in the *Daily Mail* (to demonstrate the universal approval since "even" the conservative tabloid agreed). In contrast there were 24 references to the right to protest in relation to the student protest, 10 of which were followed by "but" or otherwise conditionalised, five argued that the Millbank protesters had abused their right to protest (largely quoting London mayor, Boris Johnson), and two referred to the balance between the right to protest and protecting the public or imposing public order. This leaves just seven expressions of support for the right to protest that did not qualify that right in some way, including one criticism of those qualifications.

> Lip service was given to the idea of the right to demonstrate, but certainly, it seemed, there was no right to be angry; there was no possible justification for a broken window. (Amy Jenkins, *Independent* 13/11/10)

Indeed, it was consistently violence or property damage that was specified as lying outside the actions protected by the right to protest.

Perhaps more surprisingly, there were similar qualifications to the right to protest made in discussion of the Occupy movement's peaceful occupation at St Paul's Cathedral. The right to protest was frequently asserted – 52 times (11 times quoting Fraser) – but qualified 22 times to distinguish the right to protest in general (or abstract) from the right to protest by occupying public space, or that particular public space.

> In a free society, people have a right to demonstrate. They do not have a right to wreak havoc on one of the capital's most sacred spaces. (leader, *Telegraph* 25/10/11)

This suggests that the occupation as an intervention into a public space is chaotic and therefore uncivilised, or as an intervention into a religious space is unholy.

More to the point, this shifts the distinguishing line between *democratically protected* protest and illegitimate action to which they have *no right* – instead of violence or property damage, merely being considered a nuisance or an eyesore is judged to invalidate the right to protest.

> The Occupy tents are but the latest manifestation, taking full advantage of our precious right to freedom of expression. Such freedom, however, can be abused. Is it really a God-given right to turn the beautiful, historic space of St Paul's Churchyard enjoyed by millions into a squalid eyesore and a threat to public health. (Melanie Phillips, *Daily Mail* 24/10/11)

This suggests that the right to protest is in fact a privilege (of which they have taken "advantage"). She seems to start by referring to the legal right, but then shifts to a sense of 'natural' ("God-given") rights in order to suggest that some rights fall short of this essentialist boundary, and can therefore be rescinded. There are paternalistic overtones to the discourse of abusing the right to protest, that these privileges are granted only if the people prove themselves sufficiently responsible, and abuse by a minority can spoil it for everyone else.

Other critics cited the religious significance of the location as requiring a certain kind of behaviour to be culturally respectful, and in particular to respect the human right to freedom of religion. Occupiers were accused of having "denied" (Chris Roycroft-Davis, *Express* 25/10/11), "threatened" (George Carey, *Telegraph* 28/10/11), and "disrupted" (Giles Fraser, quoted in *Guardian* 28/10/11) this religious right. The *Daily Mail* quoted an aggrieved bystander who wished to worship at the cathedral and objected to the presence of the protesters.

> Marjorie Foyle told them: "I completely believe in your right to protest, but this is the wrong place to do it. You are stopping people from worshipping God. It is meant to be a public place for all people, not just for one group". (*Daily Mail* 24/10/11)

This bystander, standing in for the church-going public in general, suggests that the occupation's presence effectively privatised the public space around St Paul's Cathedral. This implies an understanding of 'public' in terms of accessibility, and political argumentation as *excluding* 'the public' (or rather those who want to use the space for a different purpose) rather than the political *as* public (as opposed to religion, which might be regarded as a matter of private faith).

The possibility that the cathedral would remain closed over Remembrance Sunday was framed as offensive not only to religious sensibilities but the symbols and rituals of civil religion underpinning national unity.

> That would be a grotesque insult to millions of brave men and women who gave their lives in the name of freedom but whose memory is defiled by a protest that mocks that precious right. (Chris Roycroft-Davis, *Express* 25/10/11)

This objection raises the rights of the dead (to be respectfully memorialised) above those of the occupiers on the basis that those who fought and died in WWII had *earned* the right to demand respect, whilst the protesters were not even discharging their basic social responsibilities, making a communitarian argument that rights are limited to those who fulfil their responsibilities.

Not only were protesters judged less deserving of rights than other users of the space, but accused of demanding *more* rights than others. Libby Purves in the *Times* (24/10/11) argued that the protesters' "anarchism [...] demands more special treatment than its normal users". Apart from implying that the occupiers are not "normal", she suggests that the rights claim involved in the right to protest is a particularistic (identity) right as opposed to a civil (political) right, and therefore related to minority values and culture rather than the democratic process.

These arguments were also appealed to by politicians who argued that public order law should be revised to outlaw such peaceful occupations, and therefore officially delegitimise them as unlawful.

> Of course we need the right to protest but these tents – whether in Parliament Square or whether in St Paul's – I don't think is the right way forward, and I do think we need to look at this whole area and I'm very keen that we do. (Cameron quoted in *Independent*, *Telegraph*, *Times* 29/10/11, paraphrased in *Sunday Times* 30/10/11)

A local councillor alluded to the claims of disruption and disapproval to exempt occupation as a protest repertoire from democratic and therefore legal protection.

> "This isn't an attack on their right to protest – it's about setting a precedent that will prevent anyone just camping wherever they like with no thought for other people or businesses", added Stuart Fraser, echoing similar comments made by David Cameron and Boris Johnson, London's mayor, last week. (*Sunday Times* 30/10/11)

Stuart Fraser suggests that those camping on the cold streets of London were being thoughtless and therefore selfish, rather than principled and sacrificing their comfort for a moral goal, discursively distinguishing the action from democratically legitimate protest.

In contrast, a *Guardian* commentator argued that protest was by its very nature a challenge to the status quo and therefore to the state, whilst the right to protest – as a legal right granted by the state – is by definition limited to action that is not a threat to the state:

> And, finally, there's the concept of the "right to protest" itself. We accept this right unthinkingly – without wondering whether it is, in fact, a paradox. Can a protest worthy of the name ever be entirely condoned and legitimised by the state? Or does it need to cross a line, to provoke, in order to have any effect? And if so, where does it stop? (Patrick Kingsley, *Guardian* 26/10/11)

Kingsley suggests that there is a moral basis for the right to protest that may go beyond the legal definition, but still needs to be delineated somehow. This dilemma was shared by conservative commentators, but they were more concerned with stability than democracy.

In relation to the student protest, there were contrasting accounts of the democratic significance of the right to protest in the *Daily Mail* that both made reference to the Prime Minister's visit to China. The first presented it as an important distinguishing characteristic of democratic countries.

> We should remember that peaceful student agitation is natural and – on a day when our Prime Minister was visiting China, which not so long ago crushed student protesters beneath tanks – a reminder of the difference between democracies and totalitarian regimes. (*Daily Mail* 11/11/10)

However, two days later, a *Daily Mail* columnist made a rather different assessment of the comparison between civil rights in China and Britain.

> THE irony was not lost on many people that while David Cameron was in Beijing telling Chinese students about the benefits of democracy, hordes of British students were running amok in the streets of London. Violent thugs, ineffective policing, wanton vandalism and innocent women bystanders terrorised – welcome to the West's treasured right to protest. Maybe sometimes you can have a little bit too much democracy. (Amanda Platell, *Daily Mail* 13/11/10)

Platell clearly suggests that stability and order are more important than democracy, and that civil liberties need to be tightly constrained by public order policing.

Another conservative commentator sought to frame positive "human rights" as a threat to negative "liberty".

> Public protest has become over-sanctified by human rights. Rioters now turn up with their own legal advisers filming and taking notes. It has become harder to get convictions against troublemakers for the ancient offence of "breach of the peace". Yet without that peace being kept, our great traditions of liberty don't work. (Charles Moore, *Telegraph* 13/11/10)

It seems odd that Moore believes that an increase in evidence of an incident should make justice less likely.[5] More to the point, however, keeping the peace suggests quiescence as much as a non-violent resolution of differences.

The student occupation of Millbank and the planned environmental occupation of Ratcliffe on Soar were contrasted in a *Guardian* leader column as exemplifying the "sensitivity" of "the proper line between legitimate and illegitimate action" (11/01/11). In the first "the dividing line is between the citizen's right to demonstrate and the crime of violent disorder" (specifically the thrown fire extinguisher), in the second "between the proper police role of preventing crime – an alleged attempt to shut the Ratcliffe-on-Soar power station – and the improper one of potential entrapment of peaceful protesters". The editorial suggested that the difference between the two cases is that the first involved protesters (or a protester) transgressing the boundaries of legitimate behaviour, whilst in the second it was the police who crossed the threshold, specifically by acting disproportionately to the 'crime' they intended to prevent.

Boundaries of legitimate public order policing: Surveillance and force

As with the legitimacy of dissent, the legitimacy of public order policing strategies and tactics is related to both legality and morality. The primary concern is usually the use of force in the policing of protest on the ground, with studies noting the failure of the news media to acknowledge the role of police aggression in precipitating violence (Ackerman 2000), or the virtue of policing by consent rather than a show of force (Joyce 2002, Reiner 1998). Whilst the student protest coverage did conform to type to a large degree, there was also explicit discussion of the balance between 'tough' and 'softly-softly' styles of public order policing. Furthermore, the coverage of police infiltration into environment activist groups was discussed in a wide range of newspapers in terms of the legality and morality of police surveillance of protesters.

Legitimacy of police use of force in the policing of protest

There was very little mention of police aggression in the coverage of the student anti-tuition fees protest – just one remark in the *Belfast Telegraph* (11/11/10) that "some of the protesters blamed the confrontation on police", and quoting

---

5   Since breach of the peace requires only that harm is *likely* to be done to person or property as a result of a disturbance, the subjective judgement of officers on the ground may well be flawed.

a protester alleging excessive use of batons. There were no other references to violence against protesters, only protesters' 'attacks' on the police (2,267 words, 18% of coverage of 'violence').

More interestingly, Mark Kennedy's allegations of being subject to police violence whilst attending protests in his undercover role were broadly ignored. Kennedy gave his account of the incident and resulting injuries in an interview with the *Mail on Sunday* (16/01/11), which implied criticism of police brutality in the phrase "savagely beat him up", and the *Independent on Sunday* on the same day described him as having been "badly beaten". But despite the choice of adverbs, the incident tended to be framed as a case of mistaken identity, or as ironic given it was Kennedy's intelligence that had alerted the police to the demonstration in the first place.

> He had tipped off the police about the demonstration, only to be mistaken for an anarchist by his colleagues and ending up with head wounds, a broken finger and a prolapsed disc. (*Daily Mail* 17/01/11)

This seems to imply the only error was "mistaken" identity, with no implication that the beating would have been wrong if he had, in fact, been an "anarchist".

In contrast, the Occupy protesters were portrayed as peaceful, and relations with police officers as on friendly and relaxed, or at least calm and low-key terms (18 times). Even on the global day of protest, when the peaceful London march that ended with the establishment of the occupation at St Paul's was paralleled by less orderly marches across the world, the coverage of violence did not follow the established pattern. Even the *Express* – the fiercest critic throughout – appeared to acknowledge the role of police tactics in sparking violence.

> In Rome, violence erupted on Saturday when police used teargas and water to stop attacks on property. (*Express* 17/10/11)

Instead of property crimes being referred to as 'violence', and as precipitating the legitimate use of 'force' as a response by police (Ackerman 2000), the passive construction of "violence erupted" removes agency and therefore blame on either party, and whilst the police are portrayed as responding, the connective "when" links the violence to the police use of teargas rather than the protesters' property damage.

The vast majority of the mentions of violence related to the potential for violence during a forced eviction. In contrast to traditional framing, the prospect of a violent confrontation between police and protesters was regarded as a PR disaster, not for the protesters, but for their opponents, although it is certainly significant that their opponents were defined primarily as the church rather than the police. The accidental involvement of the church led to an explicit moral and ethical framing, with less focus on interests than might have been the case in front of the Stock Exchange itself, especially due to the objections of Canon Giles Fraser to violence in the name of the church.

Fraser was instrumental in securing the dominant framing of the occupation as peaceful, and eviction (though legal) as violent, in two fairly widely quoted remarks.

> I feel that the church cannot answer peaceful protest with violence. (Quoted in *Daily Mail*, *Guardian*, and *Telegraph* 28/10/11)

> I resigned because I believe that the Chapter has set on a course of action that could mean that there will be violence in the name of the church. (Quoted in *Star*, *Sun*, and *Telegraph* 28/10/11, *Times* 29/10/11)

This framing, along with an awareness of media attention to violence, was picked up by sympathetic newspapers who framed potential conflict as likely to attract sympathy. This could be related to the US reaction to police brutality at Occupy Wall St in Zuchotti Park, which Castells (2012) argues had increased public sympathy.

Protesters and their supporters were quoted arguing that images of police aggression could be beneficial to their cause.

> Vaughn said he hoped the police would permit them to remain, but was aware that TV footage of protesters being dragged away could publicise the campaign: "We're not going there for a fight with the police. This is about legitimate concerns that we have". (*Guardian* 15/10/11)

> It would have been easy to opt for a line of action that would have led to images of police dragging away protesters, but they want to talk. (Shami Chakrabarti, quoted in *Observer* 30/10/11)

Interestingly, Chakrabarti suggests that peaceful obstruction and resistance *can* precipitate police aggression, but that police would have been blamed nonetheless. The low-key policing of the camp was significantly different from that in New York, and was reportedly approvingly in as far as it was noted at all, but this had not been the case in coverage of the student protest, and in particular the police's expectation that the march would be peaceful.

Policing by consent and preparedness for violence

Police numbers and preparedness for violence was a key angle in the student protest coverage, with a broad consensus that both were inadequate. The policing of the protest accounted for 13% of the overall word count, and was given particularly strong attention in the *Sun* (27%), *Telegraph* (24%), and *Daily Mail* (21%), although the largest amount of coverage was in the *Guardian* due to its greater overall coverage of the story.

Although the primary problem for the police had been their underestimation of the number of protesters, this was given surprisingly little attention. On the day of the protest, both the *Guardian* and the *Independent* (10/11/10) reported that over 24,000 students were expected to join the march, and that the police were expecting a lower number of 15,000. Following the march, 15 newspapers reported the protesters' estimate of around 50,000, with only the *Guardian* (12/11/10) and *Independent* (13/11/10) adding that the police estimated turnout at just 25,000. It is unusual for the press to report protesters' higher estimate, but the lower figure doesn't fit with the framing of an under-policing of the event.

Just a fifth of the references to the estimated turnout mentioned that the police had underestimated the numbers. Only the *Guardian* (11/11/10) noted that the Metropolitan police had briefed journalists that they thought that the NUS and UCU had "inflated their numbers", and challenged police sources on the underestimation. Just nine of the 19 newspapers that covered the story referred to the police's unpreparedness for the scale of the turnout, and two of these blamed the student organisers rather than the police.

> Police [...] said they had been told only about 12,000 students would be attending the march. (*Herald* 11/11/10)

> NUS organisers had met police officers on Tuesday and estimated that they would have 15,000 protesters. (*Times* 12/11/10)

Instead, the main focus of the criticism of the police was the failure to anticipate that there would be violence (1,229 words), often explained as excessive caution following previous criticisms of heavy-handed public order policing (722 words).

Metropolitan Police Commissioner, Sir Paul Stephens was quoted in three newspapers (*Belfast Telegraph, Daily Mail*, and *Western Mail* 11/11/10) arguing that there was "no real history of that level of violence" among student protesters. Somewhat surprisingly, only one commentator noted social class as a factor in police planning:

> Perhaps the police are like the rest of us and have bought the myth that all students are middle-class and the middle class don't do this. Perhaps they believe we have been so groomed for austerity that we will go quietly. Perhaps they did actually learn a lesson from the G20 protests when a man died after being struck by an officer. (Suzanne Moore, *Mail on Sunday* 14/11/10).

Moore was also unusual in maintaining that lessons learnt following the death of newspaper vendor, Ian Tomlinson at the G20 protests in London the previous year had been valuable. The conservative press more generally, however, argued that concerns about heavy-handed public order policing had resulted in excessive caution.

Five newspapers lamented a "softly softly" approach (*Sun, Telegraph* 11/11/10, *Daily Mail* 12/11/10, and *Observer* 14/11/10). The *Daily Mail, Express* and *Sun* (11/11/10) quoted unnamed police sources complaining that police were hampered by previous controversies and criticisms, especially the prosecution of officers following the G20 protests. A *Telegraph* editorial explicitly argued that the Millbank occupation vindicated those who defended a robust enforcement of public order against arguments for an emphasis on consensus policing and the facilitation of peaceful protest.

> Yesterday's march was also the first real test of the Metropolitan Police's new strategy for dealing with street protests. After last year's demonstrations in the capital during the G20, the Met faced widespread – and, we believe, totally misguided – criticism for being heavy-handed. In truth, it dealt firmly and effectively with a serious threat to public order. Yet a critical report by Sir Denis O'Connor, the chief inspector of constabulary, concluded that the police could be seen as having been "aggressive and unfair" during the demonstrations. Yesterday, we saw the fruits of the softly, softly approach proposed by Sir Denis: the besieging of a political party's headquarters, a baleful first for this country. No doubt the police will now face criticism for getting it wrong once again. Damned if they do, damned if they don't, they have every reason to feel hard done by. (leader, *Telegraph* 11/11/10)

Another conservative commentator similarly argued that the inconsistency of the criticisms invalidated them.

> Whatever the police do, they can never win. If officers had been out in force, in full riot gear, they would have been accused of being heavy handed and inciting violence. Instead, they're blamed because they weren't. They're damned if they do and they're damned if they don't. (Julia Hartley-Brewer, *Sunday Express* 14/11/10)

This rhetoric of "damned if they do, damned if they don't" suggests that the same sources are criticising the police in contradictory ways. It is likely that this is true of news stories in as far as dominant news values and routines, especially in relation to a 'watchdog'-oriented professional ideology, favour accusations of wrongdoing and blame. Neither commentator acknowledges the news media role, however, instead suggesting that it is the news *sources* that are being contradictory. However, it is also likely that the two arguments come from *different* sources in disagreement with one another, in which case Hartley-Brewer and the *Telegraph* leader-writer suggest that the police should ignore controversy about their methods.

The *Observer*, furthermore, quoted an anonymous police source arguing that the "student violence had helped police" to justify the use of force:

> To be frank, this will have done the commissioner a favour. In the past we've criticised for being too provocative. During the next demo, no one can say a

word. You cannot stand by and let people commit acts of vandalism, threaten public property, damage public property. We have a right to stop that and sometimes we have to do that by using the appropriate force, and we have to be allowed to do that. (anonymous police source quoted in *Observer* 14/11/10)

Several anonymous police sources cited the legality of their use of force as evidence of its legitimacy, and complaining of fearing being "hauled in front of a judge for doing our jobs" or being "reluctant to be filmed even lawfully striking at protesters" (unnamed officers quoted in *Daily Mail* 11/11/10).

The same officer also complained that "higher up there is a lack of political will to keep these sorts of protests tightly controlled by use of aggressive intelligence tactics" (*Daily Mail* 11/11/10). Cuts to the surveillance budget were also identified by the *Daily Mail* as a further constraint on policing.

Savage cuts to the police intelligence budgets are also said to have contributed to yesterday's demonstration getting out of hand. Budgets for the National Public Order Intelligence units have been cut by 20 per cent in recent months and the National Extremist Tactical Coordination Unit, based in Cambridge, was shut at the end of October. (11/11/10)

This news was claimed as a revelation by the *Sunday Telegraph* (14/11/10) in a lengthy interview with the departed head of the National Extremism Tactical Coordination Unit (NETCU), whose unit was merged into the National Public Order Intelligence Unit (NPOIU) – their description of its intelligence database included its role "watching groups such as the Campaign for Nuclear Disarmament, trade union activists and Left-wing journalists". To this end, the *Observer* reported moves to impose military-level control on dissent to ensure public order.

As police face continued criticism for failing to control the march, the Observer has learned that defence firms are working closely with the armed forces and contemplating a "militarisation" strategy to counter the threat of civil disorder [...] The move coincides with government attempts to introduce the use of unmanned spy drones, facilitating an expansion of covert surveillance that could provide intelligence on future demonstrations. (*Observer* 14/11/10)

This revelation was oddly played down, buried at the end of the article. However, following the Kennedy case a few months later, there was far greater concern voiced about police surveillance, and the *Daily Mail* was among the critics of the NPOIU and other unaccountable ACPO units.

Legality of police surveillance

In comparison with the rest of the coverage of the revelations of Mark Kennedy's lengthy and active infiltration of an environmental activist group, the *legal* questions focused on the *personal* conduct of Kennedy himself, and that of other officers, as opposed to the legitimacy of the police unit as a whole. In particular, the collapse of the court case was related to his participation in (2,784 words) and organisation of (1,935 words) various protests including the planned occupation of the Ratcliffe on Soar power station, and whether this constituted having acted as an agent provocateur (1,475 words).

> Legal documents suggest Kennedy's activities went beyond those of a passive spy, prompting activists to ask whether his role in organising and helping to fund protests meant he turned into an agent provocateur. (*Guardian* 10/01/11)

The *Guardian* and other left-leaning titles interpreted this as an issue of whether Kennedy had encouraged the defendants to take the actions of which they were accused, with implications for a potential miscarriage of justice. Instead, the more conservative newspapers framed it in terms of a failure to prevent the protest activity.

> Mr Kennedy refutes suggestions that he crossed the line, became an agent provocateur and played a central role in organising the very protests police wanted him to sabotage. (*Mail on Sunday* 16/01/11)

Similarly, sister paper the *Daily Mail* said he had "gone too far by organising and directing the very protests the police had hired him to help stamp out" (*Daily Mail* 11/01/11). This framing places blame on the individual officer, even though his activities were supervised and to some degree monitored, which suggests that he was *not* in fact exceeding his brief. It also reflects widespread uncertainty of the purpose of the undercover infiltration – to detect and prosecute criminal behaviour among otherwise legitimate protest or to disrupt (certain types of) protest activity, although the conservative press tended to assume the latter.

It also indicates the concern of the right-wing press about police officers engaging in illegal protest behaviour, rather than about the interference of police officers in legitimate (though occasionally unlawful) protest.

> Ultimately, a British police officer is sworn to uphold the law. The spy or the security agent has no such clear duty. Yet Mark Kennedy constantly witnessed breaches of the law, or was present at the planning of lawless actions. He can be accused – at the very least – of condoning lawlessness by failing to act against it. (editorial, *Mail on Sunday* 16/01/11)

This focus on illegal protest activity by police in the course of infiltration ignored the questionable legality of the infiltration itself, as indicated by the collapse of the court case.

An academic, in a letter to the editor in the *Guardian* (15/01/11) argued that such legal testing of undercover operations is rare precisely because the aim is not generally to bring prosecutions against illegal protest, but to disrupt it pre-emptively.

> [T]he major objective of covert "public order" policing is not to collect evidence leading to prosecution but "intelligence" facilitating disruption. Managerial control of what undercover police do can be relatively lax because their actions will not be tested in court. If the objective were prosecution, then greater controls would be required to ensure the legality of the process by which information was collected. (Peter Gill, University of Liverpool, letter to the editor, *Guardian* 15/01/11)

Whilst for Gill the measure of morality is still legally defined, his definition is not a binary framing of legal versus criminal, but of transparent legal decisions in public court versus covert and shadowy operations.

Democratic legitimacy of police surveillance

This question over the *legal* legitimacy of undercover units' operations was rare, but the issue of accountability was raised surprisingly extensively (3,578 words, 42% of police legitimacy). From the outset, Kennedy's unit, the National Public Order Intelligence Unit (NPOIU), and the National Domestic Extremism Unit (NDEU) of which is it part, were described as secretive. Simon Jenkins (*Guardian* 14/01/11) labelled them "securocrats", whilst a *Daily Mail* editorial (17/01/11) described the NDEU as "Orwellian-sounding". Later this developed into significant concerns about the Association of Chief Police Officers (ACPO), which runs the NDEU, being a private company, which even the *Daily Mail* objected to at some length (leader, 17/01/11). Three newspapers noted that ACPO's status as a private company means it is not subject to freedom of information law (*Guardian* 12/01/11 and 18/01/11; *Observer* 16/01/11; *Daily Mail* 17/01/11).

The democratic implications were most strongly questioned in the *Guardian*, in particular by the environmental writer George Monbiot.

> So who are the domestic extremists? Which body represents the real threat to society, to public order and the rule of law? A group of peaceful campaigners acting on "the highest possible motives"? Or a private corporation running a secret spy ring, which looks as if it's using police budgets to try to change the political character of the nation? (George Monbiot, *Guardian* 18/01/11)

Such concerns suggest an activist understanding of civil society, which includes protesters and excludes private corporate interests. ACPO describes its change of status from a professional association to a limited company as "a pragmatic step taken to maintain independence from Government while enabling ACPO to fulfil its support functions, such as the employment of secretariat staff, and allow for transparency in publishing accounts",[6] suggesting a more neo-liberal understanding that focuses on independence from the state, without concern for independence from corporate interests.

Monbiot explicitly suggested that ACPO's operations against activists served private commercial interests: "It looks to me like a state-sanctioned private militia, fighting public protest on behalf of corporations" (*Guardian* 18/01/11). The relationship of ACPO units with the energy industry was also raised by the *Daily Mail* (17/01/11) and *Mail on Sunday* (16/01/11), both of which remarked that the company sells information from the Police National Computer, and the *Telegraph* (15/01/11) and *Mail on Sunday* (16/01/11) reported that after resigning from the police, Kennedy worked for a private company that provides intelligence to corporations, including the owner of the power station targeted by the Nottingham protesters. Simon Jenkins in the *Guardian* (12/01/11) noted that "we do not know if E.ON UK, the operator of Ratcliffe-on-Soar power station, paid for security intelligence from Kennedy" (Simon Jenkins, *Guardian* 12/01/11), implying that ACPO may have sold the information he gathered, which suggests that the claimed public interest motive is contaminated by private gain.

One commentator voiced (somewhat vague) scepticism that ACPO's status as a private company did in fact guarantee independence from government.

> The police like to assist the politicians on whom they depend, and it cuts both ways. I'd like to know more about the rights and privileges enjoyed by ACPO, and how, precisely, a limited company controls undercover police agents. (Peter McKay, *Daily Mail* 17/01/11)

The only other comment on the relationship with government posited that police have a "vested interest in fear":

> The desire of police lobbyists is to frighten politicians from cutting their budgets, and, in the case of green protesters, to exaggerate the threat they pose to social order. (Simon Jenkins, *Guardian* 12/01/11)

Arguably this exaggeration of threat was precisely the aim of the anonymous police sources and sympathetic commentators arguing for "aggressive intelligence" tactics in response to student 'violence'.

Moral legitimacy and proportionate policing

The moral legitimacy of the police operation was primarily focused on the legitimacy of specific tactics (2,469 words, 29% of police legitimacy), of targeting environmental protesters (964 words, 11%) and the proportionality of using those

---

6   Available from the ACPO website at: http://www.acpo.police.uk/About/History. aspx.

tactics against those targets (744 words, 9%). Whilst there was far more attention given to the individual conduct of Kennedy and other undercover officers than to systemic or organisational police legitimacy – making up a full quarter of the total for the case study (17,977 words) – much of this was descriptive. Interestingly, despite the legal questions focusing on Kennedy personally, and the tendency of the press to personalise blame, there was more coverage of the police management of undercover officer's conduct (2,157 words) than blame on Kennedy as a 'rogue officer' (1,344 words). Inevitably, there was a great deal of fascination with Kennedy's sexual relationships whilst assuming a false identity (6,053 words, a third of coverage of officer conduct), though 29% of this queried whether this was sanctioned by his supervising officers. It is likely that the unusual focus on structures of governance is due to the lack of interest of the tabloids in the story, and, moreover, its dominance by the *Guardian*, which accounted for almost half of the coverage of police legitimacy.

Table 5.1   **Coverage of legitimacy of police surveillance: Level of scrutiny**

	Police Legitimacy	Legitimacy of Kennedy operation		Legitimacy of unit's operations		Legitimacy of general policing of protest	
	n	n	horiz %	n	horiz %	n	horiz %
Guardian	4,113	1,661	40.4%	2,195	53.4%	581	14.1%
Daily Mail	1,085	504	46.5%	934	86.1%	0	0%
Times	709	285	40.2%	258	36.4%	146	20.6%
Daily Telegraph	497	166	33.4%	314	63.2%	18	3.6%
Observer	488	284	58.2%	374	76.6%	0	0%
Mail on Sunday	447	252	56.4%	127	28.4%	128	28.6%
Independent	412	287	69.7%	135	32.8%	124	30.1%
Western Mail	215	215	100%	0	0%	0	0%
Independent on Sunday	167	25	15%	81	48.5%	0	0%
Express	166	166	100%	0	0%	0	0%
Sunday Express	50	0	0%	0	0%	50	100%
Sunday Times	49	49	100%	24	49%	0	0%
Herald	48	48	100%	0	0%	13	27.1%
Sunday Telegraph	17	0	0%	17	100%	0	0%
Belfast Telegraph	11	11	100%	0	0%	0	0%
Total	8,474	3,953	46.6%	4,459	52.6%	1,060	12.5%

In terms of the level of scrutiny of police legitimacy, there was extensive discussion not only of the Kennedy operation (47% of legitimacy coverage), but also the questions it raised regarding the unit as a whole (53%), though markedly less on overall policing of protest (13%).[7] However, the practice of "objectivity as strategic ritual" (Tuchman 1978) meant that these discussions were dominated by quotes from lawyers, politicians, and other sources calling for the police authorities to answer questions about the operation and tactics overall, rather than specific arguments about what defines legitimate or illegitimate conduct.

The validity of targeting environmental protesters in undercover operations, especially by a unit related to 'domestic extremism', was raised in 22 references, nine of which specified the protesters as non-violent or of no serious threat, four quoting Jenny Jones, Green MP and member of the Metropolitan Police Authority.

> We have state spies, embedded in a fairly fluffy … group that has no plans to
> kill anyone and that is trying to raise awareness of the potential lethal effects of
> climate change. (Jenny Jones, Green MP, quoted in *Guardian* 14/01/11)

Jones argues that coal-fired power generation is more harmful than the direct action protest planned by the protesters, connecting the illegitimacy of the operation with the legitimacy of civil disobedience. The description of eco-activists as "fluffy" was also reflected in the concluding remarks of an opinion writer in the Observer:

> Do we still employ undercover police officers to harass lonely homosexuals?
> Or do we only concentrate on the kinds of people who remember to turn off
> their lights and think that coal-burning power stations are a bit polluting? What
> next? People who want to save the whale? Who like cuddling kittens? Who think
> tuition fees are wrong? (Carole Cadwalladr, *Observer* 16/01/11)

The mixture of serious issues and frivolous pleasure ("who like cuddling kittens"), whilst somewhat belittling, is intended to suggest that concern for the environment is uncontroversial and reflective of an other-oriented personal disposition, and the example of "lonely homosexuals" serves to remind that law and legitimate policing are open to change.

These accounts of the protesters as harmless were intended less to argue that protest activity was not a legitimate subject for public order policing, but that the undercover operation was disproportionate to the threat posed. Kennedy's own remark that the scale of the operation in terms of number deployed was "like a hammer to crack a nut" was quoted in three newspapers (*Guardian*, *Independent*, and *Telegraph* 11/01/11), and elaborated on by Simon Jenkins in the *Guardian*.

> Whether tree-hugging and the occasional trespass constituted threats to national
> security is moot. A gilded sledgehammer was clearly being deployed to crack a

---

7   These categories were not mutually exclusive, and sometimes overlapped, which is why the sum is more than 100%.

few nuts. They were not a serious terrorist threat. The denouement was a costly fiasco. This is what happens when authority has too much money and no one in charge to impose a sense of proportion. (Simon Jenkins, *Guardian* 12/01/11)

One of the protesters argued that this was a conscious escalation by police, focusing on the seriousness of the intervention:

Political protest of the kind being planned that day presents no risk to the public, yet the police consistently resort to the most extreme tactics they can muster. (Danny Chivers, defendant in collapsed trial, quoted in *Independent* 11/01/11)

However, more concerns were expressed over the disproportionate extent of the operation (4,005 words) than the disproportionate seriousness of the tactics (2,469 words), 58% of which cited the scale of the operation in the numbers deployed and length of assignment (especially in the *Guardian*, *Times*, *Independent*, and *Independent on Sunday*), and 43% mentioned the cost of the operation (especially the conservative titles).

Where the legitimacy of tactics was raised, 44% specified particular tactics, 76% of which queried undercover deployment, and 24% challenged the use of surveillance altogether. The *Guardian* (14/01/11) quoted Jenny Jones calling police spying powers "anomalous", and questions were raised in editorials in the *Daily Mail* (17/01/11) and *Mail on Sunday* (16/01/11) as well as the *Observer* (16/01/11). A news report in the *Guardian* (14/01/11) highlighted the inclusion of peaceful protesters in police databases, including an 85-year-old man and his daughter. The article reports environmental protesters' allegations they had been targeted as an opportunistic replacement for violent animal rights activists, as the domestic extremism units "sought new targets to justify their budgets and existence".

Police dismiss the claims, insisting they only monitor the minority on the far left and right who might commit crimes such as damaging property or trespassing to promote their political aims. (*Guardian* 14/01/11)

The police framing of the tactics of civil disobedience as extremist ("far left and right") passes without comment, but the term "domestic extremism" is consistently used in sceptical quotes.

However, other newspapers defended the use of surveillance, and reproduced the police discourse of activists as domestic extremists.

Controlling dissent is thought to be central as is building up a database of information on activists and extremists, such as animal rights agitators. (*Express* 11/01/11)

Despite being unusually critical of the policing of protest, the *Daily Mail* did appear to assume that activism was illegitimate and warranting suspicion.

The Metropolitan Police will take charge of the unit for which Mr Kennedy worked, which also controls a database of *suspected activists*. (*Daily Mail* 19/01/11, my emphasis)

This reflects a broader tabloid assumption that strong political belief is, in itself, suspicious.

The most contentious element of the moral legitimacy of the police operation, however, was the sexual relationships conducted by undercover police officers under their false identity. Whilst significant attention was given to activists' objections that this was an abuse of power and intolerable invasion into their private lives (1,376 words, 21% of coverage of sexual relationships), sexual affairs were also seen as a mere self-indulgent distraction (446 words), a perk of the job, or even a legitimate part of a spy's duties (392 words).

Nine newspapers reported allegations and complaints that undercover officers' sexual relations with their targets were an abuse of power and invasion of privacy. The *Independent on Sunday* raised concerns about the contravention of a "duty of care" (16/01/11), the *Times* reported "allegations of gross abuse of his position" (*Times* 15/01/11), a German politician was quoted twice accusing Kennedy of "trespassing" into private lives. One activist who had slept with Kennedy was quoted 14 times objecting that she felt "violated", and another alleged that the deception amounted to sexual abuse.

> It is well known in the movement that Kennedy slept with a large number of women who didn't know he was a police officer, and he therefore had sex with them without their informed consent. (activist quoted in *Guardian* 13/01/11)

However, Both the *Belfast Telegraph* (leader, 19/01/11) and Caroline Callwalldr in the *Observer* (16/01/11) dismissed the suggestions of harm or violation, arguing that men often lie to get women into bed.

This was sometimes framed as a perk – "an extra-curricular fringe benefit" (*Sunday Times* 16/01/11), and part of Kennedy's decadent lifestyle funded by the taxpayer, spending £1.75million "frolicking around Europe and conducting affairs with female eco campaigners in the guise of Mark 'Flash' Stone" (*Telegraph* 15/01/11).

> Mark Stone, aka Kennedy, clearly had a good job. He could climb trees, buy drinks, sleep with girls, shout at the fuzz and chain himself to nuclear power stations, all on the taxpayer. (Simon Jenkins, *Guardian* 12/01/11)

It was also framed as simply part of the identity politics and lifestyle of activism:

> While undercover, Officer Kennedy was serially "the spy who shagged me", enjoying the fruits of an anarchist ethos that sees monogamy as just another

form of authority to be challenged. (Harry Browne, *Sunday Times* Irish edition 16/01/11)

However, it was also portrayed as a dereliction of duty on the part of a self-indulgent officer: "as his undercover operation progressed, far from being solely committed to the fight against possible crime, he was also interested in pleasing himself" (*Daily Mail* 15/01/11).

The *Daily Mail* was concerned Kennedy had exceeded his brief by indulging in sexual relationships when there was not tactical advantage:

> For it was aboard Tamarisk, as well as in private homes and hotels throughout Europe, that Kennedy indulged what police sources describe as his Achilles' heel: his penchant for sleeping with women, even when it was not necessary for his undercover role. (*Daily Mail* 15/01/11)

This assumes that there might be times when it *was* required as part of the job. Although the paper also fretted that "the reality is that Kennedy's tangled love life was making a difficult undercover operation more complicated." (*Daily Mail* 15/01/11), this suggests concern over effectiveness rather than principle.

In contrast, the *Guardian*, and to a lesser extent the *Independent on Sunday* and *Daily Telegraph*, questioned whether it was an authorised tactic to attribute responsibility for the abuse of power.

> Did PC Kennedy have sexual relations with Anna to obtain information for the British state? If so, then this looks like state-sponsored sex abuse. (*Guardian* 12/01/11)

Even the *Daily Mail* reported the concern of one of the women Kennedy had slept with about the principle of state invasion into private life: "It is not just his undercover role that disgusts her, it is the sexual exploitation by a paid agent of the State" (*Daily Mail* 15/01/11).

However, a *Belfast Telegraph* editorial portrayed this as moralistic squeamishness

> Alongside the James Bond antics, though, a weird kind of political correctness has been in evidence. Flash's cushy number came to an end when his employers discovered, to their profound horror, that he was sleeping with the enemy. What used to be part of a spy's duties now caused trills of moral outrage. (leader, *Belfast Telegraph* 19/01/11)

This portrays the criticisms of systematic deception in people's private lives as a prim disapproval, and seems to confuse James Bond fantasy with the oppressive reality of police surveillance.

These case studies highlight the inconsistencies and contradictions in the dominant news-framing of direct action, in particular, occupations designed to cause disruption.

> "There are so many complications in this area of protest – the police feel we cannot win," Mr Fahy said. If police stopped a major incident – using Mr Kennedy to halt the planned invasion of Ratcliffe-on-Soar power station in Nottinghamshire – they were accused of stifling peaceful protest. But if they did not gather intelligence, as happened with the student invasion of Millbank Tower in London in November, they were accused of failure. Mr Fahy said: "It is really about how does society view actions like a power station being closed down or an airport being seriously disrupted or a political party's building being invaded. Is that a victory for democracy, a victory for protest, or is it seen as a failure of policing?" (*Times* 11/01/11)

Whilst some newspapers have been fairly consistent in their attitude to the legitimate policing of protest (the *Guardian* at one end of the ideological spectrum and the *Express* at the other), others such as the *Daily Mail* have chosen the framing that justifies the most outrage and the most emphatic critique, whether at inadequate or over-zealous surveillance and control.

Summary

Whilst the dominant account of property damage framed it in traditional terms as criminal and illegitimate violence, and focused disproportionately on the spectacular, there were some subtle shifts in framing. The discourse of anarchist hijack has become an established news routine, used as an off-the-peg frame for any outbreaks of conflict or destruction in a planned peaceful march, regardless – as in the case of the Millbank action – of the evidence. It is possible that this was a response to past criticisms of the tendency to characterise whole protests by the actions of the violent minority, offering a neat distinction and further delegitimising the 'extremist' deviance of the minority in contrast to the moderate majority. This has echoes of Gitlin's (1980) "moderate alternative", but that was a specific reaction to the development of elite dissensus over the course of a long campaign, whereas student tuition fees were already a topic of legitimate debate, and the frame was deployed at the outset. Conversely, it may be intended, as several critics noted, to undermine the more broadly destabilising sense of a general mood of dissent that could erode the government's authority.

   Disruption is also an established news-frame related to instability, chaos, and inconvenience, but in the case of the peaceful and cooperative occupation at St Paul's critics struggled to portray it as a social threat. Instead minor inconveniences were framed as transgressions of people's right to go about their business unimpeded (a negative liberty). This could be considered the new ground of contemporary anti-protest discourse, and indicates that although recent protesters may have been successful to some extent in widening the criteria of legitimacy beyond the purely legal, their critics have also moved in to claim the moral high ground on the basis of moral (rather than legal) rights.

Nonetheless, the debate over the moral legitimacy of public order policing demonstrates that the line between legitimate dissent and legitimate social control continues to be contested. Whilst the policing of the student protests reflects the oscillation between facilitating protest through policing by consent and enforcing social control with tough public order tactics, as identified in previous research (della Porta and Reiter 1998), the line of contention is on surveillance. The strong criticisms, even in the conservative press, and not only of Mark Kennedy as a rogue officer, but also of the disproportionate operational strategy and unaccountable organisational structures, may have been partly driven by the adversarial instincts of the watchdog model of the press, with its appetite for scandal and wrongdoing, but it also represented a remarkable defence of environmental direct action.

Chapter 6

Representation and its Alternatives: Political Legitimacy

Political legitimacy is closely related to legal legitimacy, in that law-breakers are often not considered legitimate political actors, or their protest repertoires recognised as political actions. This is particularly true in relation to 'violence' as a criterion that excludes people, individually and collectively, from civil society. But in as far as some law-breaking action is judged within the bounds of legitimacy on the basis of moral motivation (as civil disobedience) or as at least ambiguous (as subject to challenge in civil rather than criminal law) it may be recognised as political. Yet even those strategies that are recognised as political address, whether legal or not, may not be considered politically legitimate.

The definition of political legitimacy is just as contested as other legitimising structures, especially in relation to appropriate forms of argumentation and address, but also the structures of decision-making within civil society organisations. Both of these aspects relate to the perception of political agents in civil society, and their orientation to the structures and processes of the political system, directly and via broader publics. In addition, there are other repertoires that do not seek to engage with the political system but to operate collectively outside of the state. This may be intended as an alternative to a state-mediated existence or to mainstream culture and society, or as an example for wider social change, but it does not seek political legitimacy on the same terms.

Structures of decision-making are contested between models of representative democracy and more direct, participatory, or deliberative models. Whilst the public sector unions are legally mandated to mirror the core political system with a formal membership, hierarchical leadership, and secret ballot – largely because of their traditional position as 'insider' groups who are engaged by the government in formal, corporatist negotiation – more informal and outsider associations and movements have rejected this model. The Occupy movement, like other iterations of the wider anti-global capital or alter-globalisation movement, were highly critical of the limited and periodic opportunities for political participation and substantive influence afforded by the current system of representative democracy, and instead conducted their own business through a system of direct democracy adapted to the specific conditions of occupation. This involved a series of hand gestures to indicate agreement, veto, the desire to speak and so on, as well as a form of committee organisation adapted from the "spokes and wheels" model of connected "affinity groups" developed during the 1990s summit sieges. Most importantly, it was determinedly leaderless and horizontal and hosted talks and discussions, which were not intended to expound a set point of view, but to debate issues in an open-minded way, in keeping with the Habermasian public sphere (although he is critical of direct democracy).

However, other kinds of political communication strategies were also in evidence, that could be regarded as coercive, manipulative, and illegitimate, or as pragmatic strategies in an increasingly competitive and dominated communication environment. Such reading could apply to the spectacular image events of the student occupation of Millbank, and in less confrontational terms, to the Occupy camp as performative spectacle, as well as the symbolic and rhetorical forms of communication within and from the camp.

Finally, Occupy throws up particular considerations about the role of cooperation, solidarity and political affect in such encampments, and the extent to which they have wider political implications. The potential interpretations range from a neo-Tocquevillian or communitarian notion of association producing civic virtue, to the dangers of an insurrectionary mood bred from lack of trust in representatives.

This chapter will address in turn the themes of decision-making structures, communicative strategies, and protest repertoires as an enactment of social alternatives. Firstly, however, it is worth noting that at the most basic level of access and voice, the protesters and strikers were accorded a much greater legitimacy than previous studies suggest (Glasgow University Media Group 1972; MacLoed and Hertog 1992).

Presence of civil society sources

Civil society sources had a very strong presence in all of these stories, and in all but the Mark Kennedy case, had a greater proportion of material attributed to them than either political or police sources. Coverage of Occupy LSX drew on civil society sources for as much as 40% of all quoted material on the story (15,935 words), 84% of which was from the movement, and they received significantly more attention than church sources and political sources. It is also striking that the over half of quotations from Occupy (7,203 words) were from individual occupiers rather than spokesmen or statements issued.

Coverage of the public sector strikes similarly drew on civil society sources for 42% of all quoted material (12,957 words), 83% of which were union sources (others being corporate associations, the headteachers' professional association, the Taxpayers Alliance and so on). By comparison politicians contributed less than a third of quoted material and public sources made up under a fifth. Student protesters had a slightly lesser presence at just under a third of quoted material (8,756 words), but were still more prominent than both political and police sources. What's more, student protesters themselves, individually or collectively, were quoted more than official NUS sources (40% to 36%). Interestingly, the Millbank protesters not only dominated the coverage in comparison with the peaceful marchers, but were also more often allowed to speak (81% of student quotes), albeit in a context framed and circumscribed by journalists.

Table 6.1 Proportion of attributed (quoted or paraphrased) material by source type in coverage of student protests, strike, and Occupy LSX

	Student protests				Public sector strikes			Occupy LSX				
	Civil society sources	Political sources	Public sources	Police sources	Civil society sources	Political sources	Public sources	Civil society sources	Church sources	Political sources	Public sources	Police sources
Belfast Telegraph	65.2%	24.7%	0%	10.1%	57.1%	13.4%	9.6%	65.7%	34.3%	0%	0%	0%
Daily Mail	15.3%	35.2%	0%	40.9%	34%	56.4%	0%	11.4%	53.1%	16.9%	12.5%	6%
Daily Telegraph	32.9%	20%	30.4%	10.7%	38.8%	33.5%	20.5%	34.5%	30.3%	18.2%	6.7%	4.1%
Express	19%	6.1%	50.8%	17.6%	28.5%	43.3%	24.2%	35.4%	11.5%	41.6%	3.6%	7.9%
Guardian	25.4%	26.1%	15%	12%	46.3%	30.7%	18.4%	38.1%	34.3%	8.1%	8.8%	3.6%
Herald	13.7%	3.8%	70.7%	7.4%	11.2%	18.6%	58.3%	69.4%	3.2%	15.2%	0%	12.1%
Independent	71.8%	14.7%	0%	13.5%	17.8%	25.9%	34%	34.2%	39.7%	8.7%	13%	4.7%
Indp't on Sunday	0%	0%	0%	0%	0%	0%	0%	48.7%	27.1%	6.2%	7.5%	0%
Mail on Sunday	10.1%	70.9%	8.2%	2.3%	0%	0%	0%	46.4%	42.5%	11.1%	0%	0%
Mirror	24.7%	17.4%	51.4%	5.6%	76.2%	20.2%	0%	56.8%	11.5%	26.3%	5.4%	0%
Observer	44.4%	20.7%	0%	16.9%	0%	0%	0%	67.5%	12.2%	11.6%	6.3%	1.3%
People	0%	0%	0%	0%	0%	0%	0%	0%	0%	0%	0%	0%
Star	25.9%	47.3%	0%	7.7%	31.9%	53.3%	6.1%	59.4%	22.9%	14.8%	0%	2.9%
Sun	40.3%	35.4%	0%	24.3%	19.9%	50.8%	28.3%	39.3%	48.8%	3.3%	0%	8.6%
Sunday Express	42.2%	0%	0%	44.6%	0%	0%	0%	0%	0%	0%	100%	0%
Sunday Mirror	0%	0%	100%	0%	0%	0%	0%	22.8%	77.2%	0%	0%	0%
Sunday Star	0%	0%	0%	0%	0%	0%	0%	0%	0%	0%	0%	0%
Sunday Telegraph	32.6%	24.3%	3.9%	34.6%	0%	0%	0%	0%	0%	0%	0%	0%
Sunday Times	16.4%	19.2%	46.1%	0%	61.1%	33.4%	12.6%	34.1%	8.1%	30%	11.5%	13.7%
Times	24.8%	21.4%	34.7%	12.9%	59.7%	26%	12.9%	32.2%	25.3%	19.1%	12.5%	3.8%
Western Mail	40.2%	41.4%	0%	18.4%	0%	0%	0%	29.8%	52.2%	8.4%	4.5%	3.5%
Total	31.9%	25.3%	19.5%	14%	41.6%	32.4%	19.1%	40.2%	29.4%	13.6%	8.4%	4.1%

Structures: Hierarchy and representation within civil society associations

Trade unions have the most formal structures of representation and accountability, with a hierarchical structure of elected representative leadership, and votes to agree collective action. However, these organisations are also the most consistently delegitimised in traditional news-frames, selectively challenging the legitimacy of mechanisms of representative democracy. The tendency to delegitimise movements by undermining their leaders has also been noted in news coverage of student protest (Gitlin 1980). However, the Occupy movement, as with previous anti-global capital movements, rejected such structures and employed horizontal structures and mechanisms of direct democracy in the agora. This has the potential to disrupt routine news-framing, although the networked organisation of summit sieges of the 1990s did not attract attention (Klein 2001).

The unions' use of strike ballots attracted a significant amount of coverage, but was rarely framed as a legitimating mechanism, and was instead largely understood as a legal constraint on the 'power' of the unions. Of 7,002 words on the legitimacy of union claims to represent their members (especially in the *Mirror* and *Times*), over half (3,857 words) examined the strength of member support for strike action, and 29% (2,024 words) specifically disputed and (just twice) defended the ballot mandate, especially the *Sun*, *Times*, and *Telegraph*, but also the *Guardian*. The vast majority of this coverage focused on the turnout, whilst only the *Independent* reported the proportions that voted in favour. The extent of members' participation in the strike was interpreted as evidence both for and against their support of the leadership and the strike decision (1,096 words on the number of strikers and 832 words on the turnout at marches), primarily in competing truth claims from union and government sources. Finally, union leaders were framed as unrepresentative of their more moderate membership (2,317 words) and delegitimised as self-serving 'fat cats' who were remote from their members' interests (286 words).

Whilst the mandate for strike action from balloted members was mentioned seven times, there were more than three times as many references to low turnouts in the public sector union ballots undermining the claim for a mandate.

> One big difference between the 20th-century Winter of Discontent and the 21st-century Summer of Discontent is that back then, the majority of union members voted in favour of strikes. Today the support within the unions is patchy at best and dismal at worst. (Chris Roycroft-Davis, *Express* 29/06/11)

The *Sun* asserted that "More than a million pupils and their hard-working families will be affected by the strike – even though just one in five sirs voted for it" (*Sun* 28/06/11), based on a calculation of the number of yes votes in the balloted unions as a proportion of all teachers in the country, whether balloted or not. Andrew Grice, the political editor of the *Independent*, noted a similar calculation by ministers in relation to the PCS turnout – the lowest of the three main unions taking part – as part of "their propaganda battle" (01/07/11).

The primary definer for this framing was Francis Maude, the Cabinet Office minister:

> The vast majority of hard-working public-sector employees do not support today's premature strike and have come into work. I am not at all surprised by the very low turnout for today's action – less than half of PCS's own members chose to take part. Very few civil servants wanted this strike at all – less than 10 per cent of them voted for it – and they are right. (Francis Maude quoted in *Independent* 01/07/11)

Various versions of this quote appeared in the *Times*, *Sun*, and *Western Mail* on the same day. Some of those papers also quoted the PSC leader's counter-assertions, claiming extensive participation.

> This is the best supported strike we've ever had. The Government made a lot of the fact that after the strike ballot it was clear civil servants didn't support strike action. But today we can see that they have voted with their feet and sent a clear message to the Government that they will not tolerate these attacks on their hard-earned pensions rights and will fight the cuts that threaten to devastate our communities and jobs. (Mark Serwotka, PCS general secretary, quoted in *Express, Sun*, and *Western Mail* 01/07/11)

Of course, as noted in the previous chapter, the conservative newspapers set up expectations of high participation based on the full membership numbers (despite arguing that most had not voted in favour of action), framing it as illegitimate power because of the disruption they could cause. Then following the strike, they declared it illegitimate on the basis of the *absence* of disruption: "described as a 'flop' by the Government after trade union threats proved hollow and the industrial action caused 'minimal disruption'" (*Telegraph* 01/07/11).

These various ways of delegitimising union action, meaning that no outcome would have been deemed politically legitimate, led to some contradictory reporting.

> One of the largest strikes in a generation by hundreds of thousands of teachers and civil servants had "minimal impact" on public services, despite the closure of more than 7,000 schools, No 10 said yesterday. Up to 300,000 teachers and at least 100,000 civil servants across Britain walked out in protest over "unfair and unjust" changes to their pensions. But with little disruption to airports, Jobcentres, or courts the action was dismissed as a damp squib by a Downing Street source. (*Times* 01/07/11)

Union leaders were also uncertain how they should frame their claims for success without jeopardising their claims for legitimacy, given the conflicting criteria of political and social legitimacy.

Serwotka's focus on countering government arguments that there was little impact (and therefore low support) was criticised as ill-judged by the *Guardian*'s political editor (01/07/11) on the basis of insensitivity to public disapproval (explored in more detail in the next chapter). Another union leader (Mary Bousted, ATL General Secretary quoted in *Mirror* 30/06/11), more conscious of this, argued that they had sought to minimise disruption, even though this seems to make a nonsense of the tactical power of strike action, and the TUC General Secretary argued that the level of disruption should not be taken as the measure of success: "The Government can say 'well it didn't have quite as much impact on services as it might have had,' but that's not what I see as the key measure" (Brendan Barber, quoted in *Independent* 01/07/11). More commonly, however, union sources acknowledged that widespread disruption was part of the pressures on government, but expressed regret for the inconvenience to the public.

> Kevin Courtney, deputy general secretary of the NUT, said the early indications were that "large numbers" of schools were affected by the action, around 80 per cent. "We realise that's very disruptive for parents and we do regret that," he added. "We had hoped to reach a settlement before the industrial action, but the Government isn't serious about talks." (*Express* 01/07/11)

These sources sought to shift responsibility for socially illegitimate disruption to the government, and less explicitly to defend the political legitimacy of strike action as a sanction for the government's non-cooperation in bargaining and negotiation (discussed in more detail under strategies, below).

Assertions and counter-assertions of conflicting truth claims evaluating the turnout of both ballot and strike action as measures of legitimacy and effectiveness were rarely contextualised. Only one commentator (Andrew Grice, *Independent* 01/07/11) compared the union ballots with the coalition's mandate from general election – noting the higher turnout in the general election, but lower vote in favour of either of the two parties in government – and just one source argued that the government's own mandate for cuts was wanting (letter to the editor, *Guardian* 30/06/11, see below). Otherwise, the legitimacy of government power went unchallenged, whilst the far more marginal collective power of workers was deemed so disproportionate that it should be curbed by legal constraints: "Now ministers are fighting back – demanding a majority of ALL members before strikes can go ahead" (Trevor Kavanagh, *Sun* 27/06/11).

A significant frame interpreting the claimed low turnouts (in ballots and/or strike action) was to suggest that union leaders were not representative of their members, especially in ideological terms, contrasting the "moderate" union membership with the "militant" leadership. Five newspapers described union leaders as "militant" (856 words), especially the *Sun* and *Express*. The *Telegraph*, *Sun*, *Daily Mail*, and *Times* argued described members as more moderate (214 words). Editorials in several conservative newspaper argued that most union members, like the rest of 'mainstream' public opinion, recognised that it was an unjust and unwinnable cause.

Indeed, the Mail firmly believes the silent majority of public sector workers are as aware of this as anyone else. (*Daily Mail* 30/06/11)

This is understood by most people in the country, which is why so many union members decided not to strike or declined to vote in the ballots that triggered the action. (*Telegraph* 01/07/11)

Today we call on parents and the majority of moderate teachers to keep schools open. (*Sun* 28/06/11)

The *Sun* even used a speech act in one news article, under the legitimating term "campaign", "urging the moderate majority of teachers to defy the strike" (*Sun* 28/06/11). A *Daily Mail* news article by Political Editor James Chapman attributed a similar imperative to Francis Maude: "SHOW 'DUNKIRK SPIRIT' AND WORK THROUGH MILITANT DAY OF ACTION, MINISTER URGES PUBLIC SECTOR STAFF" (sub-head, *Daily Mail* 30/06/11).

Even one union source (albeit an anonymous one) argued that the striking unions were led by an unrepresentatively militant leadership.

You have to remember the PCS goes out on strike every year and the best turnout has been about 140,000, and the numbers are often down at times to a 80,000 to 90,000 hardcore who always walk out. There is a weariness among the membership and there are issues around their hardleft leadership. (Anonymous union leader quoted in the *Times* 30/06/11)

This is connected to the distinction that was also made between more "hardline" or "militant" unions and more "moderate" unions. There were only four references to moderate unions (two in the *Times*, two in the *Western Mail*) and one to a moderate union leader (a sceptical reference in the *Sun* 27/06/11), but they suggested that *even* moderate unions may be drawn in to strike action.

This indicates the way in which striking was routinely assumed to be intrinsically "militant" behaviour (437 words), four newspapers also framed this particular militancy as unusual (394 words over 13 references, in the *Guardian*, *Mirror*, *Western Mail*, and *Times*).

Margaret Phelan, UCU Wales regional official, added: "Educators do not like taking strike action. Our chosen vocation is to change lives and transform life chances and we are unlikely militants. (*Western Mail* 29/06/11)

Yesterday's strikers are not natural militants. Teachers haven't staged industrial action on this scale for many years. They have been driven to it by deliberate government tactics. (*Mirror* 01/07/11)

This seems to attempt to distinguish these respectable, *reluctant* strikers from habitual radicals. We will come back to this notion of the 'professional protester' in the next chapter in relation to personal legitimacy.

Only the *Mirror* highlighted and challenged the discourse of militancy directly, and then still distinguished the public sector union strikers from the historical hate figures of the miners strike, rather than question the framing of industrial action as threatening the stability of the country.

> THE peddlers of hate said they were militants hell-bent on bringing the country to its knees. They caricatured them as the Sperm of Scargill, who would drag us back to the dark days of the 1980s. Yet rallies accompanying yesterday's public sector strike felt more like groups of worried parents protesting against mobile phone masts near their school than an enemy within trying to smash capitalism. (Brian Reade, news analysis, *Mirror* 01/07/11)

The implicit distinction between the legitimate protest of teachers resembling "worried parents" and the miners, drew on the inferred respectability of the middle class professions, though the *Independent* (01/07/11) suggested that it was also related to familiarity through social contact.

In addition to the framing of union leaders as not representing members' moderate views, there was also a more marginal frame of strike-happy leaders not representing members' *interests*. Commentators in the *Express, Mail, Sun*, and *Times* suggested that union leaders were motivated by justifying their own well-paid jobs.

> A SELFISH STRIKE: UNLIKE their members, union leaders have nothing to lose from the public sector strikes threatening to bring the country to its knees. Indeed, every day they look more isolated – not only from the general public but from those whose interests they claim to represent. (leader, *Daily Mail*, 28/06/11)

The editorial went on to ask, rhetorically, "Do they seriously want to do battle, on the orders of this privileged clique of commissars, in defence of what they know to be indefensible?" Members were framed as having been duped by these self-serving figures, and their claims to represent their best interests. Interestingly, this was a particularly prevalent view in the letter pages of the conservative tabloids.

> I was a union member for 30 years but realised they live off the backs of the workers they are supposed to represent and earn huge sums while workers survive on minimum wages. (letter to the editor, *Sun* 29/06/11)

> YESTERDAY'S strike and any future industrial action by public sector unions that claim only to have their members' interests at heart rings very hollow. What we are seeing are overpaid, militant union leaders leading their members into conflicts, the main aim of which is to hurt and inconvenience the public and damage Britain's infrastructure. (letter to the editor, *Express* 01/07/11)

The Dispatches documentary, *What's the Point of the Unions* (27/09/10), also suggested that leaders who favoured strike action were 'militant' and unrepresentative, with a focus on Bob Crow of the transport union RMT, who was described as "a former communist", and a former Conservative Transport Minister called him "one of the original class warriors, he really is rather antique these days".

The documentary also dedicated a section to union leader pay, with this voiceover playing over pictures of leaders waving hand-shaped placards at a media photo opportunity with members saying "all together for public services":

> "But many union leaders are also well-paid, on deals worth over £100,000 a year, and several have had large rises recently. That doesn't go down well with some of their members" (*Dispatches* 27/09/10)

A single vox pop interview was offered in support of this assertion:

> Interviewer: "You don't think they should get a rise?"
> Union member: "No, they get enough!"
> Interviewer: "So if I told you someone like Bob Crow has just got 12%, and two general secretaries of Unite have had something like 50–80% since '87"
> Union member: "It's bad. Me personally, I think it's bad. Same as the greedy bankers. I'm sorry, but it is." (*Dispatches* 27/09/10)

This comparison with bankers was also made in the press.

The *Daily Mail* found several sources to assert their claim that union leaders could not claim to represent underpaid workers when themselves generously paid. A representative of the Taxpayers Alliance, who produce an annual 'rich list' of union leaders, framed this as hypocrisy: "These union fat cats claim to speak for workers – but it looks hypocritical when they take home whopping salaries at the same time as they criticise high pay elsewhere" (quoted in *Daily Mail* 28/06/11). In strikingly similar terms, MP Dominic Raab suggested that members' sacrifices were not being shared by the leadership.

> Fat-cat union bosses are increasingly out of touch with financial reality. It is rank hypocrisy for them to be fleecing their members to pay for their six-figure salaries, and then instructing them to forfeit their own pay by participating in strikes the majority don't support. (quoted in *Daily Mail* 28/06/11)

Both of these sources turn the 'fat cat' label – a term used to delegitimise corporate CEOs, especially, following the banking crisis, those in the financial industry – back on some of its key proponents.

Unions defended themselves against the Taxpayers Alliance – a right-wing civil society organisation – by highlighting the comparative transparency and accountability of trade union structures.

A TUC spokesman dismissed the report. "This is a predictable attack from a shadowy right-wing pressure group who publish no information about who funds them," he said. "Trade unions are among the most democratic organisations in Britain. General secretaries are directly elected by members, and strike action has to be approved in a secret ballot." (*Daily Mail* 28/06/11)

Len McCluskey's personal legitimacy as an elected leader was also questioned, however, again on the basis of turnout: "Only 20 per cent bothered to vote in the leadership ballot. He won, with a derisory 6.7 per cent of Unite's members" (Trevor Kavanagh, *Sun* 27/06/11).

Attacks on "militants" in contrast with "moderates", polarising the trade union movement between the newsworthy and the legitimate, are long established news routines, as Gitlin (1980) identified in reporting of the New Left's opposition to the Vietnam War. Given the dominance of the student movement (Students for a Democratic Society) in the New Left, you would expect this to be at least as dominant a frame in the student protests against tuition fees. Certainly there was a strong distinction made between the minority who occupied Millbank and the majority who peacefully marched, with the former being more visible and the latter endorsed as more legitimate. However, the former were also depoliticised and the latter judged to have had their political cause damaged.

As we saw in the previous chapter, the Millbank protesters were initially dismissed as anarchists with an interest in violence for its own sake and no interest in the students' cause, before it became clear that the vast majority had been students. Even then, however, little attention was given to politically radical groups, and certainly not in terms of their objectives or arguments. There were seven references to the "National Campaign Against Fees and Cuts", all blandly reporting their call for a National Day of Action. The "Radical Workers' and Students' Bloc (RWSB)" were identified as militant (*Independent* 12/11/10), but quoted as such in their own terms, and only mentioned at all in support of claims that the Millbank action was planned not spontaneous.

The occupiers' 'violent' tactics were broadly denounced, not least by NUS leader Aaron Porter, but in as far as they were attributed political motivation, it was framed as an internal turf war within the student movement.

They [student left-wing cliques] are usually more interested in their own internal disputes than in the public good, and the violence was therefore aimed as much at undermining the moderate and impressive (though still wrong) NUS President Aaron Porter, as at changing the mind of the Government. (leader, *Times Scotland* 11/11/10)

This is a peculiar assessment, since the only voices using the militants to discredit the moderates were those of media commentators. The *Observer* noted that after the dust had settled "those urging moderation have not won the day" (*Observer* 14/11/10), and whilst acknowledging a "moderate majority", Martin Ivens

(*Sunday Times* 14/11/10) argued that their political case had been "muddied" by the Millbank protesters. The only justification of this was a concern that recognition of the political purposes of violence would 'send out a message' that it was legitimate (see below).

Unlike the trade unions (or the SDS in the sixties), there was little focus on discrediting the radical leaders, merely dismissing them. Richard Littlejohn (*Daily Mail* 12/11/10) called them "Toytown trots" and likened the Millbank action to "Trumpton Riots" – the reference to children's TV show *Trumpton* (by way of a Half Man Half Biscuit song) suggests an immature imitation of a *real* political riot. Clare Solomon of the London University Student Union got some attention for her appearance on Newsnight with Porter: "Alas, as is always the case, the firebrand made for better television than the moderate student union leader alongside her" (Martin Ivens, *Sunday Times* 14/11/10). Although Ivens seemed somewhat enamoured by her "leather gear and stroppy demeanour" that make her "a dead ringer for Lisbeth Salander, the punk heroine of Stieg Larsson's detective trilogy", the focus on her appearance was politically belittling. Mark Bergfeld was quoted 10 times defending the Millbank action and criticising Porter, but only the *Sunday Times* (14/11/10) associated him with the Education Activist Network, and again, only in terms of tactics. However, delegitimising the 'rioters' – perhaps because they were portrayed as apolitical thugs not political militants – did not depend on elevating the moderate leaders: "Even the spotty little twerps who run the National Union of Students have said that the vandals damaged their cause" (Simon Heffer, *Telegraph* 13/11/10).

As it turns out, the Times' backhanded compliment above, that Porter was "moderate and impressive (though still wrong)" was the warmest endorsement he got. In fact, the only comment passed on Porter's performance ridiculed him for his moderate respectability, accusing him of auditioning for a mainstream political career:

> Aaron Porter is 25; he stood for the office as an independent, but is a member of the Labour party, whose dress code – the Nick Robinson-esque glasses are a good example – rather suggests that he's destined for a career in mainstream politics. Certainly, if you fancy being a high-ranking Labour MP, clambering to the top of the NUS isn't a bad move at all. His predecessors have included Jack Straw, Charles Clarke, the current shadow defence secretary Jim Murphy, and Phil Woolas [...] – all of which highlights the fact that NUS presidents are not exactly renowned for being what the French call enrages. (John Harris, *Guardian* 12/11/10)

> I thought the young were expected to be angry, but even the NUS leader seemed to be a stranger to all outrage except outrage at the "hijackers" of the protest. Already a member of the establishment, he didn't think anything of prostrating himself before some imaginary middle England consensus of disapproval. (Amy Jenkins, *Independent* 13/11/10)

Another commentator in a left-leaning newspaper, the *Mirror*, called Porter "career-seeking" and aligned him with "the powers that be" (Paul Routledge, *Mirror* 12/11/10), but even the more conservative titles mocked his ambitions.

> Also on Newsnight – and anywhere else that would have him – was the NUS president, Aaron Porter, condemning extremists, agreeing to hand over his own members' names to police and generally parlaying his reasonableness into a parliamentary seat and/or media career like Jack Straw, Phil Woolas or our own dear David Aaronovitch before him. (Janice Turner, *Times* 13/11/10)

Turner seems to suggest that Porter was willing to betray members of his own movement to ingratiate himself with the authorities.

There was rather less antipathy toward the Catholic Church for its hierarchical organisational structures, but interesting, concerns about representation of and accountability to lay members of the church, came from Catholic writers.

> And we might ponder too on who the pope and his bishops are speaking for. If they claim to represent the 10% of us who are Catholics, then they should reflect what, in good faith, we believe. (Peter Stanford, *Observer* 19/09/10)

> I'm sure lots of Catholics ask themselves, as I do, how many rules and attitudes one can disagree with before one no longer qualifies for membership. I've always been of that school of thought that says the people are the Church. (Frank Skinner, *Times* 17/09/10)

Interestingly, whilst representations of Catholics were predominantly in the role of mass attendees and cheering well-wishers, and therefore as supporters of the Pope as the figurehead of their religion (5,274 words in total, especially in the *Sunday Telegraph*), generalisations of the *beliefs* of British Catholics were almost exclusively portrayed as dissenting on key issues such as sexual and reproductive rights and gender equality (2,313 words in eight newspapers, especially the *Times*, *Independent on Sunday*, and *Guardian*).

These arguments point to the potential, and desire in some quarters, for religious organisations to produce virtue through democratic means of (critical) personal conscience and participative association, but that would require a democratisation of the church hierarchy.[1]

> The structures of the church support an expensive bureaucracy which seems to assume a passive role for the laity, and particularly the female laity. [...] Sermons inform us of the views of the individual priest or the "church line",

---

1   Most frequently, however challenges to the church hierarchy were made in relation to the alleged efforts of the church to conceal child abuse allegations, including in Peter Tatchell's documentary, *The Trouble with the Pope* (13/09/10).

but we almost never have the opportunity to debate the most fundamental
challenges of daily living. [...] We would like to see the church reconfigure
itself, become less self obsessed, and give the people the opportunity to learn
about and share their faith more fully. We would like to go back to basics and
access opportunities for shared reflection and debate in which the clergy listen
rather than lead. (Five female lay members of the Catholic Church, letter to the
editor, *Guardian* 17/09/10)

This analysis interprets the legitimacy of church structures in the terms of
activist civil society, with an emphasis on internal democracy and public-minded
external engagement, rather than neo-liberal or postmodern negative liberty
or communitarian social expectation. It also defines religious conscience as
something more personal, more akin to moral sentiment, than the Pope's account
of it as discussed in Chapter 4. A contentious point of reference on both sides of
the argument was the Anglican covert, Cardinal Newman, who was to be beatified
during the state visit.

Frank Skinner, a (celebrity) lay Catholic (*Times* 17/09/10) and Paul Vallely,
a Catholic theologian (*Independent on Sunday*, 19/09/10) quoted Newman's
toast "to conscience first and the Pope afterwards". Eamon Duffy, a theologian
(*Guardian* 18/09/10), Geoffrey Rowell, an Anglican Bishop (*Times* 18/09/10),
and John Cornwell, a Newman biographer and writer on ethics (*Sunday Times*
19/09/10) all noted Newman's opposition to Pope Pius IX. Cornwell noted how
he "opposed the dogma of papal infallibility [...] and emphasised conscience over
papal teaching", and Duffy elaborated on his opposition to a Vatican that "made
unquestioning obedience to hyper-orthodoxy the sole test of Catholicism", and,
along with Powell, described his defence of intellectual freedom – "'Truth,' he
wrote, 'is wrought out by many minds, working together freely'".

At the same time, Skinner also acknowledged the contradictory pronouncement
that "Religion as mere sentiment is to me a dream and a mockery" (although it is
unclear whether by this he meant moral sentiment in the Enlightenment sense, or
simply a tribal, emotional attachment to Catholicism), and Rowell pointed out
that "he fought a battle against individualist religion, the relativising of truth"
(as reflected in Benedict's remarks discussed in Chapter 4). Cornwell (*Sunday
Times* 19/09/10), along with Stephen Bates (news analysis, *Guardian* 18/09/10),
argued that Newman is claimed by both the liberal and conservative wings of the
church, though Benedict swerved direct engagement with this dispute by limiting
his comments on Newman to brief and bland praise at Holyrood of his "goodness,
eloquence and action".

The Occupy movement had the most elaborate and visible decision-making
structures, and since they were also novel to journalists (though not to activists)
attracted a significant amount of coverage. The reactions varied from admiration,
through scepticism, to irritation. There was particular frustration with the
absence of leaders, with even supportive commentators yearning for charismatic
leadership – the *Herald* (17/10/11) nominated George Clooney for the role,

whilst the *Guardian* (18/10/11) identified a leader emerging from the Chilean movement – but especially among the more hostile newspapers.

> The extreme anti-capitalist views are complemented by the deliberate lack of leadership in the camp. I approach a young woman in a bobble hat who chaired one of the meetings. "Who is the leader?" I ask. "We don't have leaders," she replies angrily. "I'm a facilitator." (Iain Hollingshead, *Telegraph* 20/10/11)

Hollingshead seems exasperated by the notion that one would *deliberately* lack leadership, and then externalises that irritation onto his source. Melanie Philips in the *Daily Mail* (24/10/10) insisted that there must be "a high degree of co-ordination" because the various camps across the world were similar, and the *Sunday Times* (30/10/11) argued that Occupy LSX was taking on "the appearance of the kind of multinational company it claims to abhor" on the basis of having IT and finance teams.

Other columnists defended the unconventional structures as a rejection of an increasingly uncivil formal politics.

> The protesters shun formal leaders and hierarchies – and I also don't see why they should be criticised for this at a time when conventional leaders and hierarchies have been so conspicuously useless. (Andrew Rawnsley, *Observer* 30/10/11)

Rawnsley went on to give examples of personal insults and fist-fights on the global political stage, and argued that the protesters look "more grown-up" than their international statesmen.

One commentator identified the source of conservative irritation as the frustration of conventions of delegitimisation – that critics want leaders so that they can undermine them.

> No-one has been described as running this international show, or preaching to it, or drawing up rules of procedure. That makes it peculiarly hard to deal with: if a movement has a Leader you can run him in. (Elaine Morgan, *Western Mail* 21/10/11)

This accords with Gitlin's (1980) account of the way in which the SDS were undermined, and also reflects Naomi Klein's (2001) argument for the advantages of the networked form of contemporary protest movements, and the particular strength of Occupy in resisting co-option by established ideologues (neo-Marxists, anarcho-syndicalists, and so on) on the one hand and or formal politics on the other. Having said that, Klein was also reported to have "argued to protesters in New York, the movement will also need democratic structures and institutions if it's to put down roots rather than fizzle and burn out" (*Guardian* 20/10/11).

Similarly, the consensus-oriented decision-making processes were described, often in some detail – explaining the hand-gestures and the human microphone – but only in five newspapers, with two other titles (*Sun* and *Sunday Times*) describing decision-making only as by vote. In as far as a judgement was made on the effectiveness and legitimacy of the arrangements, the vast majority judged them difficult and laborious but worthwhile.

> Almost everyone's involved in something and, crucially, there's no hierarchy – or there's not supposed to be. The teams meet once a day and agree things by consensus, in a discussion "facilitated" (but not led) by a different member of the group each time. [...] At its best, the system is empowering. But facilitating's a tough job – and even though some of the more visible members of the camp constantly encourage newbies to get involved, sometimes the same people end up mediating discussion. (Patrick Kingsley, *Guardian* 21/10/11)

> Nobody votes for its leaders, because it doesn't have leaders – everyone is an equal participant in the process, and all voices are supposed to be heard equally. Unfortunately, it's a system that can often mean that the simplest housekeeping questions take ages to finalise. I've been to a meeting that took four hours to decide whether we should be allowed to smoke indoors. But it's miles better than the microcosmic Soviet Union that you seem, rather unimaginatively, to envisage as the end-point of all radical politics. (Laurie Penny, in debate with Joan Smith, *Independent on Sunday* 30/10/11)

Inevitably, not all commentators were so taken with the idealism and dedication, arguing that it was not more broadly applicable beyond the camp, that this "is not really what democracy looks like: or only in tiny simple communities" (Libby Purves, *Times* 24/10/11). However, commentators, especially but not exclusively in the left-leaning papers, recognised the camp as a legitimate critique of representative democracy, and in common with the related protests, as a response to a government policy of public sector cuts that had no formal mandate.

This was a particularly strong frame in relation to the student protests since the Liberal Democrats had signed an NUS pledge to vote against any rise in tuition fees, and had reneged on that promise in exchange for a place in coalition government. Issues of accountability and democratic legitimacy accounted for as much as 13% of the total coverage of the student protest (12,967 words), of which 40% was related to electoral mandate, 38% referring more generally to politicians' policy-making decisions, and 21% to the negotiations that established the coalition.

Even the *Express* recognised the democratic deficit in the electoral process in relation to the tuition fee policy:

> There are legitimate grounds for students and their parents to be angry at the coalition's handling of higher education finance. It can even be argued that the Government lacks a mandate for the changes it proposes given that

the Conservatives barely mentioned the issue in the election and the Liberal Democrats campaigned on the opposite policy to the one that is to be enacted. (leader, *Express* 11/11/10)

More predictably, John Harris in the *Guardian* (G2, 12/11/10) argued that it was not just the Lib Dems who have failed to deliver on their electoral mandate, but also the Conservatives, who had promised no cuts to frontline services – "And really: they wonder why some people are increasingly angry" – and Fiona McIntosh in the *Sunday Mirror* (14/11/10) asked "Tell me who voted for that? Where was this plan in the touchy-feely Tory manifesto?" The only defence was from Tim Farron, writing in the *Guardian* just before he was elected president of the Liberal Democrat party (12/11/10), who defended "negotiation and compromise", slightly patronisingly, as "grownup, pluralistic politics".

There was less attention to the democratic legitimacy of public spending cuts and bank bailouts in the Occupy coverage – 4% (5,539 words), although of that coverage a similar proportion to the student protest coverage of the topic (39%) related to politicians' policy-making and performance. In the conservative papers this tended to focus on politicians' threats to prevent future occupations, whilst the *Independent on Sunday* addressed potential policy resolutions to the protesters' critique of capitalist democracy, and the *Guardian* focused on the policy errors that caused the crisis. A further fifth addressed the relationship between politics and capitalism, especially in the *Observer* business pages (30/10/11), where Heather Stewart in the analysed the argument that much of what banks do is "socially useless", so don't deserve the kind of political deference they receive. A Guardian headline asserted that "Power has slipped from democratic institutions and is ever further from the people" (21/10/11), Anne Johnstone in the *Herald* argued that "There is a sense that capitalism is more powerful than democracy and that the odds are stacked against ordinary people, who feel controlled by events" (20/10/11), and even Libby Purves in the *Times* (24/10/11) acknowledged that the protesters had a point about "the overweening power of corporations and the kowtowing of governments to big money".

The public sector strike attracted far less coverage of accountability and democracy (2%, 2,487 words), and most of that (59%) addressed union structures and political proposals to reform them, and the relationship between the unions and the Labour Party (23%), with just one reference to the lack of mandate for public sector cuts.

The government has no democratic authority to impose these cuts; the Tories and the Lib Dems both pledged before the election to honour the existing indexing and accrued rights of pensioners. In the face of such ruthlessness, trade unions have a right and a duty to challenge this government. (retired NUT member, letter to the editor, *Guardian* 30/06/11)

In contrast, the *Express* asserted the general electoral mandate of representative government against undemocratic union power: "The militant and bombastic statements coming from trade union leaders suggest they are once again determined to challenge the legitimacy of an elected government" (leader, *Express* 28/06/11). The reason for this contrast with the other two protests that broadly opposed cuts is perhaps that the unions' hierarchical structures and majority vote system of decision-making *invite* comparisons with formal politics, and make it easier for their conservative critics to undermine them in contrast to the legitimate claims of representative government, drawing unfavourable comparisons between their claims for a mandate.

Disillusionment with formal politics was interpreted in either reformist or rejectionist terms. The former reading of Occupy's account of their protest as part of a "global movement for real democracy" (*Independent* and *Western Mail* 15/10/11) was that they sought to hold liberal democracy to its own ideals, "asking for democracy that does what it says on the tin" (Laurie Penny, *Independent on Sunday* 30/10/11), or to more radically reform politics to deliver "a new style of democracy" (occupier quoted in *Independent* 17/10/11). The *Guardian* was alone in connecting this with reformist stands of anti-capitalist thought, as "calling for a democratisation of the global finance system" (*Guardian* 15/10/11), and asking "how do you create economic democracy in an era of global financialisation?" (Katharine Ainger, *Guardian* 29/10/11).

The elitist assumptions of representative democracy were contrasted with the ideals for which people risked their lives across North Africa and the Middle East.

> The protesters are criticised for not having the answers, but neither does anyone else. They're in effect being asked to go home, shut up and leave the problem to the political elite. That won't do, especially from a country that backs and applauds the raw democracy emerging from the Arab spring and Egypt's Tahrir Square. Democracy in the 21st century has to mean more than a tick in a box once every five years. (Jenni Russell, *Sunday Times* 30/10/11)

However, other commentators drew slightly different conclusions from the expressions of solidarity with the Arab Spring, focusing on a belief that real change won't occur through the political system but outside it.

> But it's this year's drama in Tahrir Square (acknowledged with an Egyptian flag at the London camp) that has given it such evocative power. [...] What both [1990s anti-global capital and Occupy] movements now and then also share is an intense commitment to direct democracy and the influence of an "autonomist" opposition to engagement with mainstream politics – seen as a central part of the problem, rather than any solution. (Seamus Milne, *Guardian* 20/10/11)

The comparison with Tahir Square was not universally accepted, but where it was, it seemed to introduce a contextual framing in which revolution was democratising rather than a threat to stability, and to criticise Occupy for not being sufficiently revolutionary. The alternatives to the political process will be discussed below, but first we will turn to representation of the ways in which the protesters addressed the system.

Strategies: Discursive, rhetorical and spectacular strategies

Political argumentation was as often criticised for its form as its substance, and delegitimising an assertion for being inadequately rational, pragmatic, publicly-oriented, persuasive or effective is a common short-cut. Judgements on the legitimacy of advocacy (of arguments or demands reached in private) were particularly contradictory. However, the use of spectacle and performative dissent attracted less criticism than might be expected.

Deliberation, advocacy, and rhetoric

Although in principle, Occupy's participative decision-making was met with approval (if with some scepticism about the pragmatics), the actual practice of open-minded (Habermasian) deliberation was often criticised. In particular, as indicated above, the movement was criticised for opposing a problem without offering a solution. Iain Hollingshead, in the *Telegraph* (20/10/11) complained that it was an emotional response to "the unfairness of life", not "campaign with an achievable goal", and in as far as it had developed objectives they were an "amorphous mission to reform the global financial system, end tax injustice and bring about world peace", which seems to allude to a stereotype of the naïve politics of the beauty queen pageant.

There was a fairly common suggestion that the absence of a clear and detailed manifesto indicated a lack of political sophistication.

> But I wonder how many of the protesters have got involved in politics of any description before now. I suspect one of the reasons we're in this mess is that it's easier to exchange rants with like-minded people online, set up camps and issue manifestos than do the hard slog of politics – standing for election, knocking on doors, winning people over. (Joan Smith in debate with Laurie Penny, *Independent on Sunday* 30/10/11)

Smith assumes that proper politics is representative politics – that reaching out beyond "like-minded people" means rallying support to gain the authority to speak for others, and the 'failure' to do so makes them "weak and inarticulate" (James Harkin, *Independent* 18/10/11). The former Archbishop of Canterbury, George Carey, writing in the *Telegraph* (28/10/11) even suggested that the Habermasian ideal of deciding in the public sphere, rather than advocating predetermined *private* positions, was in itself illegitimate: "But it is making up its demands as it goes along – truly rebels without a cause".

Government sources tried to frame the problem as technical and the solutions as managerial, not ideological, and therefore beyond the competence of protesters. Foreign secretary William Hague implied that protesters were railing against economic forces over which they have no control, and should leave such things to the government to handle: "The answer is governments to control their debts and deficits. I'm afraid protesting on the streets is not going to solve the problem" (quoted in *Independent* and *Star* 17/10/11). This denies the ideological assumptions behind the government response to the financial crisis. In contrast more supportive commentators recognised the movement's analysis of the problem as related to power and social justice.

> The occupation movement is succeeding where conventional politics of both left and right have badly failed. It articulates a profound public resentment with over-mighty finance and the failure of government to do anything about it. (Andrew Rawnsley, *Observer* 30/10/11)

For Rawnsley the expression of this diagnosis is in itself a politically significant argument, regardless of solutions.

The Occupy movement, unlike previous protests against the unregulated power of global capitalism, assumed that the failures and injustices of unregulated capitalism had become visible to a broad public. This avoids a discourse of an unenlightened, duped or uncaring public who need to educated, which can be easily delegitimised as didactic and sanctimonious. Nonetheless, they were still criticised in some quarters for illegitimately imposing idealistic values through a rhetorical construction of consensus.

> The trouble with UK Uncut and the idealistic, self-righteous campers of Occupy London is that it is impossible to think of any clear, feasible action by an elected government that would satisfy and shift them. (Libby Purves, *Times* 24/10/11)

Idealism is set against feasibility, "self-righteous campers" against "elected government", staying against doing.

Even left-leaning opinion columnists emphasised pragmatism over political values.

> There's a well-meaning but self-congratulatory atmosphere about these protests that doesn't have much to do with real life – caring for elderly people, creating jobs, improving the outlook for the disabled and children in care. (Joan Smith in debate with Laurie Penny, *Independent on Sunday* 30/10/11)

Joan Smith doesn't deny a role for ideals, morals or ethical values, but seems to locate them in the communitarian, self-sufficient (and therefore neo-liberal) Big Society – rather than in politics.

Deliberation and particularistic values

Pope Benedict's central theme for his state visit was the role of religion in public life, which for the most part related to the role of Christianity in instilling civic virtue, as explored in Chapter 4, but there was also reference to religion as "a vital contributor to the national conversation" (quoted by *Mail*, *Express*, *Mirror*, *Observer*, *Times*, and *Western Mail*) and "the legitimate role for religion in the public square" (quoted by *Mail*, *Telegraph*, *Express*, *Herald*, *Observer*, *Sun*, *Times*, and *Western Mail*). His choice of "public square", suggesting the agora in republican terms, rather than the more Habermasian formulation of "public sphere" is interesting. Certainly Benedict was aware of his compatriot, since they had a debate in the Catholic Academy of Bavaria in January 2004 (or, more accurately, an exchange of speeches, followed by a debate unrecorded in the published version).

In this post-9/11 reflection, Habermas shifts his position slightly on state neutrality, from a Kantian version which would exclude particularistic beliefs and values as publicly acceptable reasons, to include secularism as a value position that should not be given a privileged position, though he argues that the contribution of views deriving from religious faith still need to be translated, as with interest politics arising from the lifeworld, into "a language that is accessible to the public as a whole" (Habermas 2005). For his part, the then Cardinal Ratzinger (he was not appointed as Pope until the following year), contrasted reason and faith, seeing "pathologies" in both, cast doubt on the universality of human rights in an international context, and argued that reason could look to religion for the value basis that would rationally underpin human rights (Ratzinger 2005). Indeed, the Westminster Hall speech echoed some of the concerns and phrases in this exchange with Habermas, including the "purifying" role of reason and religion in relation to one another.

There was relatively little direct interpretation of the Pope's Westminster Hall speech as calling for a place for religion in debate or deliberation, and it attracted only qualified support that distinguished the right to contribute arguments from the right to have those views accepted.

> Doubtless the Pope believed that he was applying "a corrective role" in claiming the UK Equality Act "violates natural law", in outlawing discrimination against gay people. Parliament disagreed with him. Nevertheless, the Pope is right to defend the right of the church to be heard in such public debates. (leader, *Herald* 18/09/10)

For the *Herald*, the failure of secular civil and political society to listen undermines the democratic tradition and strays toward imposed civic virtue, reflecting Benedict's concern about hubris: "Aggressive secularism that would banish religious faith from decision-making is as arrogant as the conviction that the church embodies moral rectitude"; however, it also argued that "it must be a conversation in which the Catholic Church is prepared to listen as well as speak" (leader, 18/09/11). Similarly, the *Guardian* called for "a little less preaching and more humility" (leader, 18/09/11), and a letter from a reverend asked whether the Pope "has come to Britain to learn or only to speak" (*Times*, 17/09/10).

Peter Stanford in the *Observer* similarly noted that Benedict sought to "restore religion's place in national debates" (19/09/10), but argued that religious leaders must therefore submit to the same democratic responsibilities as other participants.

> But if it is dialogue and respect he is demanding [...] then it cuts both ways. If religion – and the Catholic church – is going to make "a vital contribution to a national conversation", it is going to have to start listening as well as wanting to be heard. In particular, it will have to accept with better grace than hitherto that in a democracy other opinions will sometimes prevail, and that those opinions are not necessarily always wrong and/or evil. (Peter Stanford, *Observer* 19/09/11)

This reflects the stipulation of deliberative democracy that participants should accept the process as valid, even if disagreeing with the conclusions. However, faith in the process does also require that they feel that they have had a fair opportunity to inform the decision.

These critics argue that the Pope may participate on equal terms with other representatives of civil society, but cannot expect special treatment or rights (on the basis of a religious identity that doesn't accept the jurisdiction of the political system or legal human rights over questions of values and morality), and must accept the procedural legitimacy of decisions based on values he doesn't share. Where critics defended human rights against Benedict's criticisms, however, it is as a the product of *reason*, however, not as a product of procedure:

> Nowadays, we tend to get our moral values from great man-made documents like the Universal Declaration of Human Rights. These embody a morality based on reason rather than dogma. (Peter Tatchell, quoted in *Mirror* 17/09/11)

This suggests that value judgements can be based on reason alone and that once decided, they are proven true (see also Dworkin 2011). This does not allow for the revisability of law, which in the terms of procedural democracy would harm the prospects of the procedure for agreement being respected by those who disagree with the outcome. Of course Mill argued that even if an assertion *is* true or a perspective is sound, if it goes unchallenged it will be accepted as mere received wisdom, whilst a view that is challenged is defended on the basis of reasoned argumentation.

This suggests that publicly acceptable reasons are assumed to be intrinsically based on objective, scientific reason, as the Pope also suggests in his contrast between the political world of reason and religious world of moral and ethical value. However, values are arguably not especially susceptible to reason, and more easily asserted via rhetorical appeals (such as to emotions). This was also used to delegitimise the Pope's critics, as being "militant" (13 times, only one of which was critical of the framing), although interestingly, prominent critics of the Pope were predominantly delegitimised as personally disagreeable and offensive (which will be discussed in the next chapter).

A further problem with the Habermasian requirement that public reason should make reference to shared values and goals, is that on many issues they are dominated by neo-liberal assumptions (DeLuca 1999). This is especially clear in the (quasi-) Habermasian criticism of sectional interests working against the public interest.

Deliberation and interests

The public sphere, in its Habermasian definition, defines legitimate contributions to deliberation as appealing beyond the immediate interests of a particular group to something that could be identified as the public interest or common values. Both the public sector unions and the students (themselves organised by the National Union of Students) could be regarded as defending sectional interests, but made claims to be defending public services. In contrast, Occupy LSX pointedly resisted portrayal as an interest group making claims on the rest of society, or indeed an ideologically marginal social movement, with a prominent claim to speak for the interests of "the 99%" against a wealthy and culpable minority.

Accordingly, Occupy were not delegitimised in these terms, and in fact it was the banking sector that was occasionally framed as pursuing its own sectional interests against the public interest. In particular, critics questioned the acquiescence of politicians to demands from financial corporations. Politicians were accused of being afraid to challenge banks or markets more generally, not only by the *Guardian* (29/10/11) and *Observer* (30/10/11), but also the *Telegraph* (22/10/11) and *Daily Mail* (24/10/11). Business writers accused the government of "believing the mystique the financial sector wove around itself" as singularly crucial to the health of the economy (Heather Stewart, Business, *Observer* 30/10/11), and "the political elite and big bosses have pandered to the banking lobby." (Margareta Pagano, Business, *Independent on Sunday* 23/10/11). Even the *Times* published a letter that talked of the "disconcerting ties between the political and financial elite" (21/10/11), and columnist Stefanie Marsh argued that the US protesters' concerns about "the influence that corporations wield in politics" were gaining some political traction (29/10/11).

The students were largely assumed to be asserting their own interests, although the left-leaning newspapers did recognise that there were principles at stake (as explored in Chapter 4), but few noted that the students were protesting on behalf of others who would have to pay the higher fees (which they would not), and others affected by austerity policies more broadly.

> Now there may be something faintly ludicrous about these relatively privileged students calling for unity with the workers. But their moral outrage was sincere. Remember, most of those on the march will never have to pay the £9000 a year

fees that are being planned in England because they have already begun their courses. (Iain MacWhirter, *Herald* 11/11/10)

MacWhirter rather gently suggests that students are naïve to compare their plight with that of the genuinely poor and marginalised, but he argues that they are taking a principled stand in the defence of others' interests. Only MacWhirter and Joan Smith in the *Independent* (13/11/10) – who argued approvingly that "This is above all a class issue" – made this point, whilst a *Times* leader refused to believe that this was a conscious political stance: "Sadly, however, their true position is not one of generosity. It is one of naivety – that somehow the education will arrive without an invoice to pay" (leader, *Times* 11/11/10).

There was, as might be expected, substantial attention given to interest politics in the coverage of the public sector union strike, accounting for 9% of the total word-count (9,699 words). Only 535 words (6%) specifically argued that sectional interests were against the public interest (especially in the *Mail* and disproportionately in the *Express*), whilst 1,299 words (13%) argued that their claims were both reasonable and in the service of the public interest, largely quoting union members explaining the impact that the increase in contributions and later retirement age would have on their ability to get by and to do their job effectively (especially in the *Mirror*). However, the most extensively asserted interest was that of 'the public', for whom strikes were inconvenient and therefore assumed to be against their interests. For this reason it was broadly argued that the appropriate forum for resolving the dispute was at the negotiating table.

Negotiation was described as more legitimate than both strike action (953 words, 15% of reference to negotiation) and, less often, than government union-bashing, including threats to change industrial law (175 words, 3%), and both sides claimed to prefer negotiation and to appreciate that the public preference was also for settlement by negotiation (1,108 words, 17%). However, the government were accused of not being serious about talks to almost the same extent (1,538 words, 24%) as unions were blamed for striking whilst talks were still ongoing (2,015 words, 31%). There was also a certain amount of concern that by striking whilst the government was still at the table, the unions would give the *impression* that they were not willing to negotiate (518 words, 8%), assuming that they would be blamed by the public for the failure of talks, rather than the government.

The belief that strike action was illegitimate whilst talks were still ongoing was mostly stated as a general principle, almost as an article of faith. Some of the context of the assertion gave the impression that it had been divorced from any notion of negotiation as a process in which both sides are prepared to make some concessions.

The Prime Minister told public sector workers strikes were 'wrong' at a time when discussions were ongoing, pointing out that their retirement funds are costing every household in the country £1,000 a year and must be reformed. (*Daily Mail* 29/06/11)

The *Daily Mail* suggests that unions are obliged to negotiate, but that they are also obliged to accept the government's position, whilst the *Express* (29/06/11) was more explicit about this interpretation: "The walk-out is set to go ahead despite the Prime Minister's call on unions to halt the action and accept that pension packages are unsustainable". This framing was mostly contributed by politicians (1,042 words), especially Francis Maude and David Cameron, but also opposition leader Ed Miliband. The latter argued that the unions that *were* continuing to talk had the right strategy, to avoid "giving the government the fight for which, too often, it seems to be spoiling" (*Guardian* 29/06/11), though he and his the shadow justice secretary, Sadiq Khan, were also quoted arguing that strikes represented a failure on both sides.

The *Mirror*, too, called for both sides to take the negotiations seriously, and make a real attempt to resolve differences, in two separate leader columns.

> The speed with which Whitehall issued a detailed statement condemning the unions suggested ministers never expected the meeting to succeed. And nor, in truth, did most of the union leaders present. Yet both parties sitting back down around the table to thrash out disagreements is the only realistic way forward if more stoppages are to be averted. (leader, *Mirror* 28/06/11)

> Both sides should, in the national interest, resume meaningful talks instead of shouting insults at each other. (leader, *Mirror* 01/07/11)

There were 38 references (1,231 words) to concessions or compromise, 12 of which (315 words) referred to the government's "concession" to hold separate talks on the local government pension scheme, because of specific concerns about it, and four references in one *Times* article (28/06/11) referred to the unions' willingness to concede the move to a career average pension scheme as a revelation from a "leaked" document, although it was already public knowledge. Interestingly, though, the newspaper framed the union's willingness to concede an issue as a potential "betrayal of key principles".

Despite the government "concession", union leaders argued that the government was only willing to negotiate and compromise on peripheral issues and not those that the unions contested.

> And Mark Serwotka, leader of the civil servants Public and Commercial Services union, said: "It was a farce. Again the Government has shown no interest in actually negotiating on any of the key principles at the heart of this dispute." (*Mirror* 28/06/11)

Serwotka was also paraphrased as "hoping that a strong show of support in today's strikes would strengthen the PCS's hand in the talks" (*Telegraph* 30/06/11), but equally, after the strike the *Times* (01/07/11) reported that "Ministers will now use the higher than expected turnout at work by civil servants to strengthen their hand when they resume negotiations with the TUC next week".

However, there was little sense of union negotiation as collective bargaining that aims to counter the structural power of employers, and industrial action as a sanction on the exertion of power against workers' subordinated interests. Beyond the abstract notion of talks aimed at reaching agreement, neo-corporatist bargaining was seen as the illegitimate pursuit of interests. The *Express* described favourable public sector conditions as a "racket" suggesting that collective bargaining is anti-competitive and even dishonest (Leo McKinstry, news analysis, *Express* 01/07/11). There were also four references to strike action as aimed at forcing the government to back down, suggesting a bullying strategy by powerful interests.

There was also comparatively marginal but significant focus on the need for unions to communicate publicly acceptable reasons for their position in a more deliberative sense, especially as regards winning over public support.

> I understand why teachers are so angry with the Government but I urge them to think about whether causing disruption in the classroom will help people understand their arguments. (Ed Miliband's blog, quoted in *Independent* and *Mirror* 29/06/11)

However, there was no such argument for the government to justify its position. In fact both a *Daily Mail* editorial and *Express* letter-writer (30/06/11) called for the government refuse to compromise, and instead to impose its will.

Union appeals to the public interest – claims to be defending public services, preventing a drain of talent from the teaching profession and so on – did attract some coverage, though not a great deal. More unexpectedly, however, framing of the unions as sectional interests working against the public interest were also fairly few, with just one explicit reference:

> They are not in the public interest, or even about the public interest. They are simply a call for other people, no better off than them, to have smaller incomes so that their members can have larger ones. [...] The attempt to resist this reform is the assertion of sectional interest over the public interest. And it is wildly unfair to taxpayers. (leader, *Times* 30/06/11)

Not only does this conflate taxpayers with private sector workers, and exclude public sector workers from that implicit signifier of the 'legitimate' or 'deserving' public, but it also implies those taxpayers would lose out as a direct consequence of the defence of public sector pensions.

More oddly, the *Daily Mail* acknowledged both the hardship caused by cuts to public services, and that the unions were "fighting spending cuts", but still described them as "acting against the public interest" with no explanation other than the disruptive nature of the strike *tactics*.

> The disclosure has sparked outrage that local authorities are squandering millions on union activists acting against the public interest. It comes at a time

cash-strapped families are struggling to meet rising bills while local services, such as libraries, are axed. [...] Emma Boon, of the TaxPayers' Alliance, said: "Trade unions are fighting spending cuts and planning disruptive strikes, but many people don't realise they're getting organised to do this on taxpayers' time. There's nothing wrong with union reps getting time off to do union work, but it's grossly unfair that taxpayers are funding that time, especially when it's spent acting against the public interest." (*Daily Mail* 27/06/11)

Others accepted the argument that cuts were inevitable and necessary and argued that everyone needs to do their bit, therefore the union opposition was not very public spirited: "All in all, they seem a little bit selfish. In these tough times, everyone's accepting the cuts; they just need to accept them too" (letter to the editor, *Independent* 29/06/11).

Most commonly, then, the legitimacy of interests was framed in the discourse of 'fairness' identified in Chapter 4, arbitrating between public and private sector workers, resting principally on assertions and counter-assertions about who gets paid more, or has better working conditions, or is more 'hard-working' or 'productive', and (less commonly) on assertions and counter-assertions about whether the cuts were necessary for – or perilous to – recovery, growth and jobs. This is not an appeal to the public interest but shared values – 'fairness' as the retreat of the state (fair to the taxpayer), and progress as growth (whatever benefits corporate interests). These values are assumed and asserted, but not rationally argued for.

For this reason, Kevin DeLuca (2005, DeLuca, Sun, and Peeples 2011) argues that social movements need to use spectacular image events to disrupt those assumptions with powerful 'mind-bombs'. Both the short-lived and destructive Millbank occupation by student protesters and the much longer and less confrontational occupation of the steps of St Paul's by the Occupy movement can be understood as image events.

Spectacular image events: The political effectiveness of violence

As outlined in Chapter 5, beyond the legal legitimacy, in political terms the broken windows and flaming placards of the Millbank occupation were argued both to have attracted attention to the protest, and to have distracted from or undermined the cause. Either way, there was a surprising amount of attention to 'violence' as potentially political. Five newspapers made comparisons between the student occupation of Millbank and the 'poll tax riots' as a measure of its political significance, with three referring specifically to the damaging implications for the government or formal politics as a whole. The recognition that some confrontational forms of protest are political, and politically effective, certainly does not in itself imply that political violence is legitimate, but it is a significant distinction from the purely criminal framing.

The disorder was described in political terms more often than might be expected. Although descriptions of the action as "resistance" was limited to direct quotes from the protesters themselves (in the tweeted statement from the roof quoted in *Belfast Telegraph, Independent, Star*, and *Times* 11/11/10, *Mirror* 13/11/10), journalists did refer to it as "unrest" 12 times (as often in right-leaning titles as the more sympathetic left-leaning ones[2]), and the *Telegraph* referred to an "uprising",[3] albeit a "hostile and violent uprising" (11/11/10). A handful of commentators did, however, seem to suggest that the motivation and the ends could justify the means.

> The anger of the young can be a force for good. It rid us of the hated poll tax after the Trafalgar Square riots of 1990. And it would have averted our involvement in the Iraq war, if Tony Blair had listened. (Paul Routledge, *Mirror* 12/11/10)

Routledge suggests that politicians need to be more heedful of citizens' judgements on their policies, regardless of the way in which it is expressed.

He doesn't make a distinction between the violent and peaceful repertoires of these two protests, only between the political outcomes, but other commentators contrasted them to make a point about their relative effectiveness.

> THE suffragettes chained themselves to railings, were arrested and force-fed to get the votes for women. The poll tax riots helped stop the regressive tax. In both cases it was a struggle for our rights. I marched peacefully in February 2003 against the Iraq War, along with millions of others, and nothing happened. But if you break a few windows people listen. I support the students. (letter to the editor, *Mirror* 15/11/10)

Although the Iraq war protests didn't stop the UK's involvement in the invasion, Will Hutton (*Observer* 14/11/10) argued that Blair did eventually pay, like Thatcher over the poll tax, by losing office.

There were different evaluations, however, of the effectiveness of political unrest. Martin Ivens in the *Sunday Times* (14/11/10) disputed the lesson of the poll tax riots, arguing that the unpopularity of the policy was more effectively expressed through the normal channels of representative government, whilst John Harris (*Guardian* 10/11/10) portrayed it as an exception. Where even the critics tended to agree, however, was that political violence *can* be effective if it creates the impression that the government is struggling to exert its authority.

> If a rash of violent disputes were to become a settled pattern, the coalition government might look as if it is no longer in control; its agenda of early cuts too confrontational; its narrative of national salvation challenged. Public opinion is the prize. Who runs the country, asked Ted Heath in 1974? If a prime

---

2   The *Guardian* three times, *Sunday Telegraph* three times, and once each in *Sun*, *Telegraph, Belfast Telegraph, Independent, Mirror*, and *Mail on Sunday*.

3   This predates the beginning of the Arab Spring by a month.

minister has to ask then it's clearly not you, replied the voters. (Martin Ivens, *Sunday Times* 14/11/10)

He concluded that "A government can only survive so much excitement". However, his advice to David Cameron is not to reconsider public spending cuts, or even to persuade people of the case for austerity, but to ensure tougher policing of the next protest. Matthew D'Ancona in the *Sunday Telegraph* made a strikingly similar point.

Always casting a cold shadow over every prime minister is a simple question: who governs? Who is in charge round here? Last week's riots framed that question in vicious microcosm; and, as a portent of greater struggles to come, reminded Cameron that the answer must never be in doubt. (Matthew D'Ancona, *Sunday Telegraph* 14/11/10)

Social control via the suppression of protest is therefore seen as a pragmatic necessity for the retention of power, rather than a question of legitimacy.

Indeed, one critic, despite acknowledging that it was possible the student protesters might have a just cause, argued that acquiescing to violent protest would reward such behaviour and encourage further violence.

I would rather the Government stuck with a bad policy than send out a signal that violent law-breaking can have any effect on democratic law-making. (Julia Hartley-Brewer, *Sunday Express* 14/11/10)

Whilst there was some criticisms of "the very suggestion that violent cuts might engender violent protest would send us all rioting up the streets in copycat fashion" (Amy Jenkins, *Independent* 13/11/10), the more common belief was that "political violence can never prevail over rational debate" (Baroness Warsi, *Mail on Sunday* 14/11/10) and that "as a civilised country we must show anarchy can't be tolerated" (letter to the editor, *Mirror* 15/11/10).

Dear old bourgeois society tends to comfort itself too easily at these times that the wreckers are "a tiny minority". They always are. But the task for civil society is to make sure that this minority does not gain the leverage it seeks. (Charles Moore, *Telegraph* 13/11/10).

The conclusion drawn is that the government should demonstrate their moral condemnation of violent *behaviour* by resisting their political *demands*, regardless of their validity. This demonstrates that confrontational forms of direct action enable conservative commentators to portray protesters as a minority illegitimate insurrection that must be quashed by strong government in the interests of social control, regardless of the effect on peaceful protest.

Spectacular image events: Performative politics

The Occupy camp was *in itself* a spectacle – even the conservative press acknowledged that they had attracted tourists and curious visitors – but it also included some performative aspects of dissent, using performing arts and symbolic challenges such as the satirical Monopoly board attributed to the famous street artist Banksy. The left-leaning press saw these performative elements as a way of reaching out to outsiders – even opponents:

> Other locals get involved in more surprising ways. Round the north side of St Paul's, five men kick about a football. This is Occupy FC, Occupy London's official football team, and they were founded late on Monday. The funny thing is, the players aren't all occupiers. Two of them are wearing suits, businessmen on their way back from lunch. "It's like that football game they played in no man's land during the first world war," muses one suit, Ian, a management consultant who won't give his surname. "We were just on our way back from our gentlemen's club, the ball rolled in our path, and we thought we'd have a quick match." Twenty-three-year-old Tom Rodriguez Perez, the club's co-founder, is ecstatic. "This is what it's about," he says. "We're not saying football's going to change everything – but it's starting a conversation, it's bringing people in." (Patrick Kingsley, G2, *Guardian* 21/10/11)

> For some, the charm offensive was a bit too much. "I was just offered a hug," said a male investment banker on his way to work. "I thought about it, but he was a man and he'd spent a couple of nights in a tent, and I've just had a shower, so I decided maybe not." (*Guardian* 18/10/11)

The *Guardian* places emphasis on the cooperative and outward-facing aspects of the activities that contrast with the more confrontational uses of the carnivalesque in summit siege protests, such as Jeffrey Juris' (2011) account of Prague protests against the IMF and World Bank.

However, in the conservative papers these elements were described as "entertainment" and described to provide 'colour', not interpreted as itself political.

> The protest, which is also on the doorstep of the London Stock Exchange, has the middle-class, hippy atmosphere of a music festival. Campaigners sit in circles, sharing biscuits and tins of Cadbury's Heroes, playing music and listening earnestly to one another. [...] There is no shortage of entertainment, with poets, singers and street theatre galore as well as debates with titles such as 'Where did all the money go?' and free haircuts offered by 'the radical barber'. (*Mail on Sunday* 23/10/11)

> In fact, the only action seemed to be a young man performing t'ai chi in his dressing gown. Frankly, you would be forgiven for thinking you'd stumbled into Glastonbury, not a protest camp. (*Sunday Times* 23/10/11)

There were five comparisons to Glastonbury among 12 references to hippy culture and alternative community. Given that Glastonbury has become a mainstream, middle class, middle-aged event, this is hardly portraying the occupiers as a lunatic fringe, but it does suggest boho posturing and frivolousness – protest as fashion.

Not only was pleasure seen as suspicious, but also in-group solidarity:

> For them, the protests are as much a social gathering as a serious political encounter. Most of the activists post regularly on Twitter. They talk about each other's activities and whereabouts as part of a club with its own rules and behaviour. (Stephen Pollard, *Express* 18/10/11)

There is an assumption that any kind of counter-cultural identification is not only exclusive (in contrast to the above) but also a greater motivation than the claimed political objectives – this will be explored in more detail in the next chapter. Interestingly though, this also applies to the mainstream media interpretation of participation in "wild public screens" (DeLuca, Sun and Peeples 2011) via social media, seeing it as a medium of communication within closed groups rather than infinitely interconnected networks.

Rather more damningly, however, a similar criticism was made by Žižek.

> In a San Francisco echo of the Wall Street occupation this week, a man addressed the crowd with an invitation to participate as if it was a happening in the hippy style of the 60s: "They are asking us what is our programme. We have no programme. We are here to have a good time." Carnivals come cheap – the true test of their worth is what remains the day after, how our normal daily life will be changed. (Slavoj Žižek, *Guardian* 27/10/11)

He suggests that spectacle can focus too much on solidarity in communal sense, whilst losing sight of political communication beyond the group. However, some sought not to change mainstream society or politics, though, but rather to reject it and create an alternative.

Alternatives: Solidarity, community and regulation outside formal politics

Hardt and Negri are far more sanguine than Žižek about the comparison with 1960s counter-culture: "An occupation is a kind of happening, a performance piece that generates political affects" (2012: 18).

> For professional politicians, and indeed anyone who has not spent time in the encampments, it is difficult if not impossible to understand how much these constituent experiences are animated and permeated by flows of affects and indeed great joy. Physical proximity, of course, facilitates the common education of the affects, but also essential are the intense experiences of cooperation, the creation of mutual security in a situation of extreme vulnerability, and the collective deliberation and decision-making processes. The encampments are a great factory for the production of social and democratic affects. (Hardt and Negri 2012: 56)

This is related to Juris' account of "affective solidarity" through "free-form direct action" (2011: 99), but that Hardt and Negri optimistically argue that it points toward radical change driven by a new political solidarity, through which citizens will constitute themselves in an alternative system, following "a kind of exodus from the existing political structures" (2012: 46–7).

Solidarity and political affect

To some degree the emotional basis of solidarity was reflected in the press coverage by journalists who visited the camp, and particularly those who stayed overnight.

> It is easy to dismiss the demonstration as a stage set rather than revolution – except it is impossible to disagree with the protesters' views and their excitement is infectious. (John Walsh, news analysis, *Independent* 28/10/11)

Even the harshest critics recognised the solidarity that emerges through the lived experience of an alternative way of living, describing the energy as part "camaraderie that comes from trying to live together in an inhospitable environment", in the "strange little Eden they've created for themselves" (Iain Hollinshead, *Telegraph* 20/10/11), but he clearly regards it as apolitical and rather self-indulgent. This is the hazard of separatist or opt-out responses to mainstream society.

Sympathetic commentators saw it as a functioning alternative if only on the scale on which it operates.

> If anything, the camp itself is their demand, and their solution: the stab at an alternative society that at least aims to operate without hierarchy, and with full, participatory democracy. And to be fair, in its small way, it kind of works. (Patrick Kingsley, *Guardian* 21/10/11)

However, it was less obvious how many of the occupiers would be prepared to live in this way on a long-term basis beyond the novelty and political prominence, and given the dual commitment balanced between the camp and a mainstream existence (as evidenced in the empty tent controversy explored in the next chapter) it seems unlikely to be the majority.

Just one commentator, a writer involved with the anti-capitalist movement, gave a convincing account of how this kind of politics could translate into socially transformative action.

> These local assemblies have broken out of the activist ghetto. Full of ordinary citizens, they organise against emergency ward closures, occupy university departments against cuts and prevent evictions of those who cannot keep up mortgage repayments. This has kept the movement plural and grounded, because people of all political persuasions understand the language of solidarity.
>
> To take a recent example in Barcelona, a local assembly working with homeless associations occupied a vacant block of flats that had been repossessed by a

bank five years before and moved eight homeless families in. The public
assemblies held in the square outside are a moving and respectful interchange
between activists, the homeless families and neighbours. Donated mattresses
pile up on the pavement outside, and debates about the ethics of a bank holding
repossessed property empty for years during a social housing crisis go on into
the night. (Katharine Ainger, *Guardian* 29/10/11)

These socially transformative goals distinguish the protesters' shared identity as
what Castells (2010) calls a "project identity", as opposed to simply a defensive
"resistance identity" rooted in countercultural attachments.

Criticisms of rejection of political system as dangerous

Inevitably, right-wing commentators were critical of this disengagement from the
political system, and interpreted it as a loss of trust in representatives, which must
be restored.

What they appear to mean is that they support any protests against bankers
and rich people – and also because the demonstrations by-pass the established
political process. The immediate reason for that is the widespread and dangerous
disillusionment with the entire political class, which has given rise to a kind
of insurrectionary enthusiasm for direct action. (Melanie Phillips, *Daily Mail*
24/10/11)

This was reflected in concern across the protest coverage, about 'anarchists'
seeking to destroy the state although they were far fewer in relation to the Occupy
coverage (10 references, excluding protests in European cities on the day of
action), and although conservative commentators such as Melanie Phillips (*Daily
Mail* 24/10/11) lamented "extreme left-wing agitators", others such as Andrew
Rawnsley in the *Observer* (30/10/11) rather mildly called them "niave [...]
muddled or utopian".

In apparent contrast, one commentator suggested that the camp was an outlet
that *prevented* a serious threat to public order and stability, and therefore eviction
was the more dangerous option.

I'd like to ask the government, the church and the City a question: what kind
of protests would they rather see at a time of crisis? The polite, thoughtful,
questioning approach of the Occupy London movement? Or the stonethrowing,
store-torching, inarticulate anger of the summer riots? I'm afraid that if they shut
down the safety valve of the civilised option, they won't be going back to normal.
They'll just be laying themselves open to more expressions of incoherent rage.
(Jenni Russell, opinion, *Sunday Times* 30/10/11)

Russell defends the right to protest, not as a moral claim to agitate for change,
but rather as accommodating an instinctive emotional reaction to feelings of
oppression and powerlessness, as a "safety valve" until the "crisis" is over.

But even the left-wing were wary of the rejectionist stance:

> Much of the Occupy movement's rank-and-file understandably wish to bypass a political process that seems either irrelevant or part of the problem. But the stakes are far higher than they were during the heyday of the anti-globalisation movement. (Owen Jones, *Independent* 21/10/11)

Owen goes on to argue that without an engagement with formal politics, the 1% will not be dislodged from power, and the resulting anger and desperation will "erupt in ugly, directionless ways".

But for Žižek, the problem is not that something disagreeable might happen, but that *nothing* might happen.

> While it is thrilling to enjoy the pleasures of the "horizontal organization" of protesting crowds with egalitarian solidarity and open-ended free debates, we should also bear in mind what GK Chesterton wrote: "Merely having an open mind is nothing; the object of opening the mind, as of opening the mouth, is to shut it again on something solid." (Slavoj Žižek, *Guardian* 27/11/10)

Even the great provocateur, better known for critique than an identifiable political project, argues that clear objectives must emerge for the movement to be effective.

Summary

There does not appear to be one dominant model of political legitimacy, and news media instead accommodates criteria of political legitimacy from a range of models. However, those criteria are often strategically selected to support a prior judgement on the legitimacy of the subject. Subordinated interests are rejected on the basis of the criteria of deliberative democracy (the failure to appeal to generalisable interests), whilst embattled identities are accorded a legitimate claim to assert particularistic values, and genuinely open-ended discussion is rejected as politically naïve. Habermas regarded civil society as bringing problems from the lifeworld and translating them into wider social and public concerns (the antenna or signal function), which is typically the dominant role attributed to 'the public' by news media – that of "affected individuals" (Birks 2010), yet when those affected individuals become political agents they are delegitimised as not proposing concrete solutions. The relationship between these two statuses, as affected individuals and political collectives, is a particularly common referent in determining the personal and social legitimacy of civil society actors.

Chapter 7
Civility in the Public Realm: Social and Personal Legitimacy

The previous two chapters covered the construction of legitimacy in civil society in legal and political terms. This chapter will deal with two further aspects – in *social* terms as (un)acceptable to 'the public', and in *personal* terms as (il)legitimate public participants. It will start with an analysis of the construction of 'public opinion' as bestowing social legitimacy through social consensus. Secondly, the appeal to dominant social norms will be explored, in terms of manners and shame in social space. Finally, it will turn to personal legitimacy as defined in terms of political sincerity and emotional authenticity.

To some extent, the Occupy movement successfully resisted many of the traditional delegitimising news-frames that would depict them as marginal outsiders. Despite the long tradition of occupation as part of protest repertoire, this particular form of occupation was seen as novel, and as more socially acceptable than disruptive forms of occupation aimed at directly preventing the activities they oppose (despite a handful of commentators assuming that this *was* the aim, as noted in Chapter 5). And unlike the summit-siege protesters, and other prior forms of protest against global capital, they maintained a long-term presence in public space that facilitated unmediated communication. As discussed in the previous chapters, they were not violent or confrontational, or even especially declarative, but playful and, crucially, welcoming and discursive, inviting bystanders in for discussion. Nonetheless, the extent to which the Occupy movement was judged to have broad public support is remarkable, albeit there was significantly *less* discussion of public opinion and use of public sources in the reporting of Occupy than the other protests, where 'the public' was assumed to be rather less supportive.

Protesters are traditionally depicted as alienating to mainstream society through the transgression of dominant social norms. McLeod and Hertog's (1992) account of mainstream news representation of public opinion on protest indicated that social norms were a common point of reference. They highlighted references to "the 'abusive' behavior, 'obscene' language and 'eccentric' appearance of the protesters" (1992: 265). In addition, lifestyle and appearance, mainstream social responsibilities, and cultural expectations were raised in relation to all of the protest stories.

Finally, the previous chapters have noted the ways in which repertoires and communicative strategies have been judged either legitimate or illegitimate, but the use of them is also used to delegitimise individuals personally, not only to reject their contribution, but to judge them unworthy of a hearing. In particular this framing hinges on constructions of identity, political sincerity, and emotional authenticity.

Public opinion: Social legitimacy and social consensus

There are four main ways in which the news media typically represent 'the public' or 'public opinion'. The most obvious is opinion polling, although this is used less often than might be supposed (Lewis et al. 2005). Secondly, remarks from bystanders are used to stand in for public reaction to protest (McLeod and Hertog 1992), and other vox pops are used in an unrepresentative way to illustrate a range of public opinion or reaction of a particular (affected) group. Thirdly, there is the traditional form of feedback in the press – the letters to the editor page[1] where individuals can contribute their opinion unbidden on issues about which they feel especially strongly, avoiding the false production of public opinion of polling (Bourdieu 1979) but subject to editorial gatekeeping (Wahl-Jorgensen 2002a, 2002b). Finally, a very common form of construction of public opinion (Lewis et al. 2005) is unsupported claims made by journalists and their sources, ventriloquising the public.

Representations of public opinion appeared more commonly in coverage of the public sector strikes (4% of total coverage) than the other protest stories. Over half (54%) made abstract claims about the public in general, but almost a third (31%) was backed up by reference to opinion polls. Public sources accounted for almost a quarter of quoted material (24%, 7% of total coverage) – mostly in the form of letters to the editor (63%,) and vox pop interviews with people affected by the strike, especially parents inconvenienced by the closure of their children's school.

Claims about public opinion most commonly asserted that the public did not support the strike (25%) in comparison with 17% judging that they did support it. Conversely, 19% claimed that the public did not support *government policy*, to 13% claiming that they did. Opinion polls suggested that people were slightly more inclined to oppose than support the strike, though they also indicated higher support for the cause than the for the protest tactic. Quotes from members of the public were rather more evenly split between those voicing either outright support (33%) or outright opposition (32%), with a further tenth who were broadly supportive of the cause but not of the strike tactic.

---

1   Of course there are other ways in which readers can now respond to stories, especially the comments section underneath the online versions of many (mostly comment) articles. However, there is mixed evidence on the extent to which these comments are read, especially by journalists or politicians (Bivens 2008), and they are, in any case beyond the scope of this particular study.

Table 7.1   Representations of 'public opinion' in coverage of the student protests, public sector strike, and Occupy LSX

	Public sector strikes				Students protest				Occupy LSX			
	Public opinion	Public opinion – poll	Public opinion – claims	Public as affected individuals	Public opinion	Public opinion – poll	Public opinion – claims	Public feeling or mood – claims	Public opinion	Public opinion – poll	Public opinion – claims	Public feeling or mood – claims
	words	% public opinion	% public opinion	% public opinion	words	% public opinion	% public opinion	% public opinion	words	% public opinion	% public opinion	% public opinion
Belfast Telegraph	35	0%	100%	0%	0	-	-	-	15	0%	0%	0%
Daily Mail	180	41.7%	58.3%	13.3%	51	0%	41.2%	58.8%	25	0%	0%	0%
Daily Telegraph	183	70.5%	47.5%	12.6%	69	53.6%	46.4%	0%	139	0.0%	0.0%	69.1%
Express	261	36.8%	52.5%	0%	0	-	-	-	210	0%	72.4%	0%
Guardian	1501	11.5%	58%	0%	458	51.7%	71.4%	15.3%	818	27.5%	20.7%	21.5%
Herald	90	70%	30%	30%	0	-	-	-	94	29.8%	0%	39.4%
Independent	716	53.1%	38.3%	5.2%	273	0%	42.5%	13.2%	55	0%	47.3%	52.7%
Independent on Sunday	0	-	-	-	0	-	-	-	272	0%	0%	41.9%
Mail on Sunday	213	33.8%	39.9%	14.6%	84	0%	54.8%	0%	0	-	-	-
Mirror	0	-	-	-	32	0%	0%	100%	41	0%	0%	0%
Observer	0	-	-	-	23	0%	0%	100%	192	0%	25.5%	32.3%
People	0	-	-	-	0	-	-	-	0	-	-	-
Star	41	26.8%	73.2%	0%	23	100%	0%	0%	0	-	-	-
Sun	191	68.1%	40.3%	21.5%	18	0%	100%	0%	0	-	-	-
Sunday Mirror	0	-	-	-	26	0%	0%	100%	0	-	-	-

	Public sector strikes				Students protest				Occupy LSX			
	Public opinion	Public opinion – poll	Public opinion – claims	Public as affected individuals	Public opinion	Public opinion – poll	Public opinion – claims	Public feeling or mood – claims	Public opinion	Public opinion – poll	Public opinion – claims	Public feeling or mood – claims
	words	% public opinion	% public opinion	% public opinion	words	% public opinion	% public opinion	% public opinion	words	% public opinion	% public opinion	% public opinion
Sunday Telegraph	0	-	-	-	121	0%	71.9%	0%	0	-	-	-
Sunday Times	0	-	-	-	137	0%	27%	0%	26	100%	0%	0%
Times	113	0%	100%	0%	74	0%	54.1%	45.9%	115	35.7%	49.6%	0%
Western Mail	112	0%	100%	0%	26	0%	100%	0%	44	0%	0%	0%
Total	3,636	31.1%	53.7%	5%	1,415	21%	53%	17.7%	2,046	15.6%	22.1%	25.1%

Table 7.2 **Public sources in coverage of the student protests, public sector strike, and Occupy LSX**

	Public sector strikes				Students protest			Occupy LSX			
	Public Sources	Letter writers	Bystanders	Vox pops with affected individuals	Public Sources	Letter writers	Bystanders	Public Sources	Letter writers	Bystanders	Visitors to camp
	words	% public sources	% public sources	% public sources	words	% public sources	% public sources	words	% public sources	% public sources	% public sources
Belfast Telegraph	103	100%	0%	0%	0	-	-	0	-	-	-
Daily Mail	0	-	-	-	0	-	-	222	0%	74.8%	25.2%
Daily Telegraph	789	91.1%	8.9%	0%	894	64.8%	19.5%	256	0%	16%	84%
Express	774	67.3%	0%	0%	418	100%	0%	69	205.8%	100%	0%

	Public sector strikes				Students protest			Occupy LSX			
	Public Sources	Letter writers	Bystanders	Vox pops with affected individuals	Public Sources	Letter writers	Bystanders	Public Sources	Letter writers	Bystanders	Visitors to camp
	words	% public sources	% public sources	% public sources	words	% public sources	% public sources	words	% public sources	% public sources	% public sources
Guardian	957	87.4%	3.1%	0%	928	92.2%	7.8%	957	97.1%	72.5%	27.5%
Herald	664	100%	0%	0%	998	100%	0%	0	-	-	-
Independent	2,109	0%	0%	100%	0	-	-	490	0%	89.4%	5.3%
Independent on Sunday	0	-	-	-	0	-	-	187	0%	27.3%	18.7%
Mail on Sunday	0	-	-	-	103	0%	0%	0	-	-	-
Mirror	421	100%	0%	0%	642	67.9%	32.1%	26	0%	100%	0%
Observer	0	-	-	-	0	-	-	258	0%	22.5%	77.5%
People	0	-	-	-	0	-	-	0	-	-	-
Star	31	0%	100%	0%	0	-	-	0	-	-	-
Sun	557	100%	0%	0%	0	-	-	0	-	-	-
Sunday Express	0	-	-	-	0	-	-	105	0%	35.2%	0%
Sunday Mirror	0	-	-	-	26	0%	0%	0	-	-	-
Sunday Star	0	-	-	-	0	-	-	0	-	-	-
Sunday Telegraph	0	-	-	-	28	0%	0%	0	-	-	-
Sunday Times	0	-	-	-	199	100%	0%	120	0%	68.3%	0%
Times	247	100%	0%	0%	1105	93%	0%	571	57.4%	73.7%	6.5%
Western Mail	676	77.1%	0%	22.9%	0	-	-	88	0%	100%	0%
Total	7,328	62.6%	1.8%	30.9%	5,341	84.5%	8.5%	3,349	42.1%	39.2%	24.8%

Public comment was disproportionately oppositional in the *Express* (100%), *Sun* (84%), *Daily Telegraph* (56%), and – more surprisingly, given the strong Welsh Labour tradition – the *Western Mail* (53%). Conversely, the *Guardian* disproportionately published supportive public views (75%), as did the *Times* (77%, due to a letter from a union leader) and *Belfast Telegraph* (100%, but from only one source). Letter writers were slightly more oppositional (37% to 33% voicing support), and vox pops slightly more supportive (38% to 19%) but more likely to sympathise with the cause but not the strike (18%) and to be otherwise ambivalent (14%).

Turning to the student protest, claims about public opinion on the anti-tuition fees march and Millbank occupation were far lower than on the strikes – just 1.4% (1,415 words). Again, over half (53%) made unsupported claims about public opinion, but a further 18% made unsupported claims about public 'feeling' or 'the public mood'. Over a fifth (21%) of claims about public opinion were supported by opinion polls, though this only amounted to four references (297 words). Public sources were slightly less prominent than in reporting on the strikes (5,341 words, 20% of quoted material, 6% of the total coverage), and the vast majority (85%) of public sources were in the form of letter-writers, with relatively few bystanders.

Public opinion was most commonly described as contradictory or ambivalent, although this was made up by just three articles in the *Guardian* and *Independent*. On the one hand, commentators in the conservative newspapers claimed that the public supported government policy (18%) and opposed violence (14%); on the other hand, others (including in the *Sunday Telegraph* and *Times*) claimed that the protests reflected a growing mood of anger and dissent (9%) and increasing opposition to fees and cuts (8%). Unsupported claims about public opinion were fairly broadly split in their substance, though the greatest amounts judged the public to see government austerity as necessary or fair to taxpayers (27%) and oppose violence (23%). Opinion polls were primarily interpreted as indicating contradictory or mixed public opinion (41%), thanks to the *Guardian*'s analysis (12/11/10), but otherwise more as showing support for public spending cuts (32%) than opposition to tuition fees (19%). Over half of the letters (20 of 37) were broadly supportive, and less than a quarter critical (9). Interestingly, all the bystander remarks were critical – Occupy offered a stark contrast in this regard.

Claims about public opinion on Occupy, meanwhile, were rather less common (2,046 words, 1.6% of overall coverage), and only appeared in 13 of the 20 newspapers that covered the story. A quarter described a public feeling or mood, disproportionately in the *Telegraph* and *Independent on Sunday*, and 22% made other unsupported claims about public opinion. Claims about public opinion on Occupy were half as likely to be supported by reference to opinion polls as such claims in the public sector strike coverage (320 words, 16%). Public sources were also far less extensively used than in coverage of the other protests (3,349 words – just 8% of all quoted sources), and more evenly spread among types of public source than the other two protests – 42% in letters to the editor, 39% quoting bystanders, and a further quarter words quoting visitors to the camp.

In as far as public opinion was discussed, it was predominantly as entirely supportive, with five of the 13 newspapers (*Herald, Independent, Sunday Times, Daily Mail,* and *Belfast Telegraph*) consistently portraying it as such. However, the three (*Express, Times,* and *Mirror*) who gave *no* such assessment brought the average down to 59%. On the other hand, even those critics generally hesitated to decisively claim public opposition, limited to quotes from fringe or aspiring politicians in the *Express* and *Times,* who also portrayed the public as ambivalent or split. More often, critics were reduced to expressing scepticism about the claims for public support, or portraying it as contingent or waning, at the very least acknowledging the dominant assessment.

Public sources were 38% supportive overall, with 39% of comment from bystanders expressing support, and even 22% from city and finance workers (although they were also less ambivalent, so two-thirds were critical), but all of those described as visitors to the camp expressed support (and indeed could possibly be more accurately described as supporters, or even non-camping protesters). Interestingly, neither the distribution of types of public source nor the opinions expressed were aligned with the editorial position of the newspaper title. Both the *Observer* and *Telegraph* disproportionately quoted visitors or supporters, and whilst the *Independent* had the greatest *volume* of quotes from supportive city workers, the *Telegraph*'s quotes from city workers were surprisingly more skewed towards supportive comment.

Opinion polling as representative of public opinion

Opinion polling was most broadly used in relation to public sector union strikes – almost a third of claims about public opinion were supported by reference to public opinion polls. However, the same ComRes opinion poll was interpreted by different newspapers as indicating public support for *and* opposition to the strike and strikers. Newspaper coverage of the other protests cited far fewer opinion polls, the student protest because its significance had not been anticipated, but the shortage of polls on the Occupy camp is more baffling.

The ComRes strike poll was commissioned by the *Independent* (28/06/11), and also reported in five other newspapers on the same day. It included a slightly peculiar question measuring public opinion about public opinion – 55% of the public don't believe that the public will support future strikes (if they hold co-ordinated strikes). This finding was reported accurately by the *Guardian* and *Independent* (28/06/11), but without caveat by *Express* (and repeated by a letter-writer in the following issue). The poll did not give an actual measure of public opinion by asking people whether they did support the strike, but did ask whether they thought the unions had a legitimate reason for striking – with which 49% agreed (to 35% disagreeing), but this was only reported by the *Independent* and *Mirror*. The *Mirror* also selected a similar finding from a YouGov poll for the *Sun* the following day: "SOME 48% of people have sympathy for the teachers' strike tomorrow but 54% support breaking it to keep schools open".

The minimum turnout rule proposed by some Conservatives was given support in the ComRes poll, though no more resounding than support for the strikers' cause (50% to 32%) – reported by *Express*, *Daily Mail*, and *Herald* as agreement. This was also the headline for the *Independent* (28/06/11), who had commissioned the poll – reported as "Public supports anti-strike law". The *Independent* (29/06/11) reiterated this figure the following day in support of their assessment that "Public opinion does not appear to be on the side of the strikers", in the context of political debate over whether strike action was justified. Interestingly, only the *Guardian* and *Mirror* reported the opinion poll question on which there was the most agreement – that 78% agree that "it is unfair for low paid public employees to pay the price for mistakes made by bankers before the financial crisis". Despite paying for the question to be asked, the *Independent* didn't report the finding.

The *Sun* commissioned a YouGov poll that was also reported in the *Guardian* and *Mirror* (29/06/11). The finding that 49% opposed and 40% supported the strike action was reported by the Sun in an article headlined "WE DON'T BACK IT", arguing that "MORE Brits oppose tomorrow's teachers strike than back it". The *Guardian*'s take, that "the country is split over the industrial action" more closely reflected YouGov's own interpretation.[2]

Conservative MP Dominic Raab, writing in the *Telegraph* (28/06/11) cherry-picked the most supportive figure for the minimum turnout proposal, and misrepresented the ComRes figure for sympathy to support his contention that "Union leaders are out of touch with public opinion": "according to YouGov, 59 per cent of the public support the measure, while a recent ComRes poll found that 63 per cent did not sympathise with strike action". Presumably, Raab has removed the 'don't know' answers to reach the 63% figure, and also presented it as a measure for support for the current strike, rather than a judgement on public opinion on a hypothetical future strike.

In contrast, Mark Serwotka of the PCS union, writing in the *Guardian* (30/06/11) concluded that "Polls show that public support for our campaign has grown, perhaps because the media has for once examined the issues in depth", without any reference to specific polls. A *Guardian* commentator gave a more nuanced summary of the poll data.

> But public opinion is volatile about this dispute. It is currently on the unions' side, albeit narrowly, over maintaining existing pensions rights – but against them, again narrowly, over striking on the issue. That could change if either side overplays its hand. (Martin Kettle, *Guardian* 01/07/11)

It is more typical for polls to be reported in unambiguous terms, with the majority seen as decisive, however slight. However, it still regards the polling as a

---

2   Available on their website: http://yougov.co.uk/news/2011/06/30/strikes-divide-opinion/.

meaningful measure of public opinion as an extant entity, rather than something that exists only as the product of polling (Bourdieu 1979).

There were no specific opinion polls run on the student protest itself, just one very unrepresentative quick poll which invited readers of the *Daily Star* to text a response. The result was rather interesting though, and probably not what the Star had been expecting, given the framing of the question.

> DAILY Star readers remained split last night over whether the students were right to riot, with 54% saying yes and 46% saying no. (*Star* 12/11/10)

It seems surprising that a majority – however small – would be in favour of a "riot", especially in a newspaper that was consistently negative about the protest. Otherwise, the only reference to polling was in reference to support for or opposition to government austerity in general, with John Harris in the *Guardian* (12/11/10) citing three polls on the topic, and Charles Moore in the *Telegraph* (13/11/10) referred to a *Channel 4 News* poll. The latter suggested that even liberal or left-leaning news media had to accept that there was public support for the cuts, whilst the former challenged this assumption and argued that various poll questions indicated that public opinion "is as contorted and contradictory as ever".

There were a handful of references to opinion polls in relation to the Occupy movement, but primarily citing US polls on Occupy Wall Street.

> Even in America, riven between Tea Party and Obama Democrat politics, a Time poll found 54% of people view the Occupy Wall Street protest favourably and 25% "very positively". The raw nerve of populism is with these protests. (Polly Toynbee, *Guardian* 18/10/11)

The *Time* poll was also cited in the *Herald* (20/10/11), and a similar *New York Times*/*CBS News* poll was cited in the *Sunday Times* (30/10/11). However, the one article citing two polls on the London Stock Exchange occupation appears to refer to unrepresentative quick polls on the newspapers' own websites.

> I have watched the encampment grow; listened to all sides; noted the Telegraph poll saying more than 80 per cent think the demonstrators should leave, and the Guardian one where 82 per cent back them. (Libby Purves, *Times* 24/10/11)

Whilst these figures don't seem to appear anywhere in either newspaper, a *Guardian* online poll dated 17th October[3] returned a result of 88% in support of the protest, and a poll on the Telegraph website[4] registered 47% agreement with the statement "I don't support the protest and think the protesters should be force to leave the site".

---

3   http://www.guardian.co.uk/commentisfree/poll/2011/oct/17/occupy-london-poll.
4   http://www.telegraph.co.uk/travel/destinations/europe/uk/london/8846935/Do-you-support-the-St-Pauls-protesters.html.

Oddly, both the *Guardian* and *Sunday Times* added a question on Occupy to their professional polling on the European Union, but the findings didn't make it into either newspaper's Occupy coverage. The ICM poll for the *Guardian*[5] found that 51% agreed with the statement "The protesters are right to want to call time on a system that puts profit before people", especially 18–24 year olds (57%), Labour voters (62%) and 'other' voting intentions (66%), against 38% agreeing that "The protesters are naïve; there is no practical alternative to capitalism – the point is to get it moving again", especially men (48%), AB social classes (46%) and Tory voters (67%) – and also, more surprisingly, northerners (43%). The top-line result was briefly mentioned toward the end of a lengthy article on the EU (24/10/11, not part of the sample). The YouGov poll for the *Sunday Times*[6] focused more on the Cathedral's response to the protest, finding a majority critical of the cathedral's decision to close (53% to 31%), but in favour of legal action to evict the occupation (47% to 39%), yet supporting the aims of the protesters even if not necessarily the form of protest (39% to 26%), but over a third (35%) said they weren't sure, possibly because they weren't sure what the aims were. Only the questions on the EU were reported in the newspaper (30/10/11, not part of the sample). In both cases it may be that the findings were not as conclusive as they had hoped.

Bystanders as representative of public opinion

Bystanders were particularly commonly present in the Occupy coverage, mostly portrayed as curious and intrigued by the protest, often as having made the trip to St Paul's specifically to see the camp.

> A straw poll of visitors suggested that more than three-quarters believe the Occupy camp complemented the lure of St Paul's. (*Observer* 23/10/11)

> Strikingly, however, public reaction to this encampment has been largely sympathetic. Passers-by actually say they think it adds to the significance of the cathedral. (Melanie Phillips, *Daily Mail* 24/10/11)

Whilst this often suggests a superficial (and presumably temporary) attraction to the camp as a novelty (and Philips went on to argue that sympathy for the occupiers was an irrational emotional reaction), there were also some accounts that portrayed visitors as engaging with the issues raised by the movement.

> For now, people are listening: a middle-aged Australian woman stops to read the initial nine-point statement, which also calls for regulators to be independent of

---

5   Results available from the ICM website: http://www.icmresearch.com/ pdfs/2010_oct_guardian_poll.pdf.

6   Results available from YouGov's website: http://yougov.co.uk/news/2011/11/11/ occupy-london-protests/.

the industries they oversee and for more money to be spent on social care than on wars. "It just seems so logical," she says. (*Independent on Sunday* 23/10/11)

This is in stark contrast to the confused and hostile reaction of bystanders described in McLeod and Hertog's (1992) account of news reporting on a more confrontationally performative anti-globalisation protest. In part this is due to the longevity of the protest as an established feature of the London cityscape, but also the product of a sophisticated media strategy, not only of self-mediation, as Castells (2012: 177) notes of Occupy Wall Street, but of engagement with the mainstream media, with a dedicated media tent, and the participation of various communication professionals.

Support for the camp was occasionally found in unexpected places. Both the *Independent* (18/10/11) and *Telegraph* (20/10/11) described some supporters or participants they encountered as "incongruous".

> Surrounded by an appreciative crowd, chartered accountant Tim Sanders cut an incongruous figure as he railed against the financial "gambling houses which have bankrupted the world". "I want to show it's not the non-suits against the suits," he said, decrying an economic system that had produced a "lost generation". (*Independent* 18/10/11)

Iain Hollingshead in the *Telegraph*, reported, with some consternation, the participation of a gentleman described as both "a Telegraph subscriber" and a stockbroker "handing out a sober sheet of A4 about the iniquities of investment banking, commodity trading, short selling and derivatives". Interestingly, there was often a fuzzy distinction between incidental passersby, purposeful visitors, and supporters who were there to express solidarity with the occupiers without actually camping overnight, but who could nevertheless be considered engaging in protest.

Of course, city workers were far more commonly critical, but even then, it is notable that they were found stopping by the camp and engaging with the protesters to some degree, rather than barricading themselves in their offices through fear of confrontation, or openly hostile to the protesters.

> Financiers were seen hovering on the fringe of the protest camp, reading their placards and trying to understand their demands. The bolder among them, such as financial recruitment company director Matthew Clapp, wandered through the occupation engaging the demonstrators in what he called "healthy debate". "There's a lot of protest, but there doesn't seem to be much of a solution," he said. "What are we going to do, barter cows and donkeys again? They say capitalism is bad: okay, what do they want to do about it?" (*Independent* 18/10/11)

There was only one account of anything approaching hostilities, when a city worker jogging through the camp at dawn shouts "wake up and get a job", and calls the journalist (Patrick Kingsley, *Guardian* 21/10/11) a "twat" (assuming him to be a protester), but then called on for his opinion, only criticises the occupiers (apart from for laziness and unemployment) for "vague thinking". In response to a bystander's declaration that they were all students or "benefit-scroungers", the same journalist in a later article (26/10/11) commented, "In order to delegitimize the camp, lots of passersby I met wanted to pigeonhole the protesters as either unrealistic youngsters, or lazy layabouts". It is notable that the *Guardian*, despite being the most supportive newspaper title in general, was more likely than average to acknowledge negative reactions, but did tend to pass comment on them, in this case on the tendency to delegitimise protesters in relation to dominant social norms (see below).

Other than passing city workers, critical or ambivalent bystanders tended to be churchgoers or tourists affected by the cathedral closure, and were therefore more critical of occupation as a form of protest, or of the cathedral as the location of the occupation, than the message of the protesters.

> Sybil Worsley, 58, of Cumbria, said: "It was great to have St Paul's open again. I sympathise with what the protestors are saying but perhaps not with the lengths they went to." (*Express* 29/10/11)

This seems to suggest, with the use of the past tense, that the cathedral had reopened because the protesters had ceased to go to 'such lengths', although by common consent very little had changed. The *Express* was the most uncompromisingly critical newspaper, yet apparently had struggled to get a less sympathetic vox pop from a passing worshipper.

There were a handful of vox pop interviews with bystanders affected by the public sector strikes, all describing the absence of disruption and delays at various airports. In the conservative papers (*Daily Star* and *Telegraph* 01/07/11) this was intended to demonstrate the failure of the strikes, whilst in the *Guardian* (01/07/11) it seemed to suggest that unions have been especially weakened in Britain: "In South Africa our strikes are more efficient. You would still be standing there". There were also four references *about* bystanders, two of which were in quotes from marching strikers reporting a supportive response from passersby (*Mirror* and *Express* 01/07/11).

Predominantly, however, the vox pop interviews that appeared in strike coverage were with parents affected by school closures. Although these sources might be expected to appear in the conservative papers and be critical of the disruption, they almost exclusively appeared in the *Independent* (28, 29 and 30/06/11, otherwise *Western Mail* 29/06/11 and *Guardian* 01/07/11) and were slightly more positive than letters to the editor on the topic and far more so than journalists' claims about public opinion.

> The way this has been done makes things awkward for me. But even though it is an inconvenience, I support the right to strike of my children's teachers because they should have a fair deal.

I trust my children's teachers. They are striking for a good cause and we need good, professional conditions for teaching in the future. They don't take decisions like this lightly, so I support the action and I am willing to live with the inconvenience in the short term. (quoted in *Independent* 28/06/11)

The personal contact and trusting relationship between parents and their children's teachers appears to have, or be perceived to have, a significant impact on solidarity and support, which may be pertinent in relation to dominant social norms and legitimacy.

In coverage of the student protests there was only one account of bystander reaction to the peaceful march: "Shoppers, bemused tourists and non-graduate building workers in hard hats showed little hostility", but little sympathy either – "an irate bus driver confessed: 'I was sympathetic until they blocked my bus. Where are the police?'" (*Guardian* 11/11/10). Bystander comments on the Millbank occupation mostly gave descriptive accounts, including their own and other bystanders' fearful reactions. The *Mirror* quoted a "shocked onlooker" remarking that they were "like animals" (11/11/10), and an "eyewitness" contributed an article in the same edition, giving his account of the "violence" as "sudden and terrifying". Charles Moore in the *Telegraph* quoted a Kosovan refugee hairdresser reacting to the TV news coverage: "You are so tolerant here", he said. "Nowhere else would they allow this." This is far more consistent with McLeod and Hertog's (1992) account from two decades previous, although the more desk-bound journalists of the 21st century more frequently quoted Twitter posts, such as "Police shouldn't have much trouble nicking the rioter wearing the YELLOW tiger outfit" (*Times* 12/11/10).

Letters to the editor

Nine newspapers published letters to the editor on the topic of public sector strikes, with four (*Telegraph*, *Herald*, *Sun*, and *Mirror*) giving over the bulk of the day's page to the topic. Many of the letters in the *Herald* and *Telegraph* framed their comment as pragmatically addressing the technicalities of pension reform, whilst making ideological judgements on what is "reasonable" (as explored in Chapter 4). Four letters argued that public sector final salary pensions were unrealistic, and three blamed the government and/or the previous Labour government for failing to bite the bullet earlier. However, one *Telegraph* letter (01/07/11) raised the argument that there was only shortfall because the government had spent pension contributions rather than investing them.

Letters in the *Express* were particularly likely to define public sector pensions as unfair in comparison with (their own) private sector provision, and blame the Labour government. In contrast, three of five letters in the *Guardian* criticised Ed Miliband for failing to support the strikes (although one also one accused the party of still being in the pocket of the unions). In the *Mirror* (30/06/11), there were six letters criticising Gove's 'mum's army', mostly as impractical or dangerous due to the need for a CRB check, and arguing that "being a parent doesn't automatically mean that you are fit to work [in a school]", but with a strong strain of hostility to the Conservative party, describing Gove as a "Tory twit" and the coalition as the 'ConDems', and remarking "we all know the Conservatives' record on the vulnerable". Some even framed the political argument in terms of gender politics.

> THE cheek of this Coalition beggars belief. It steals pensions from women and then asks them to act as teachers. Get stuffed comes to mind, Mr Gove. (letter to the editor, *Mirror* 30/06/11)

Again, of the published eight letters, just one – the final one – took a contrary position, being critical of the strikers.

Sun letter-writers (all 29/06/11) faithfully reproduced the *Sun's* discourse, including a rhetorical discourse of pragmatism ("Get into the real world", "when will trade union members wake up?", "When will these strikers realise that the only people to benefit from industrial action are the union bosses?"), of trade unions having anachronistic ambitions ("This is a blast from the past – an attempt to go back to the bad old days of the Seventies", "I CAN'T believe union bosses want to return us to the bad old days"), and of unions as a powerful threat against the mainstream ("IT cannot be right for one group of workers to hold the whole country to ransom", "ONCE again public sector workers are trying to hold taxpayers to ransom").

Letters to the editor on the student anti-tuition fee protests appeared in seven of the nineteen newspapers. A surprising proportion of letters (54%) expressed some support for the students – variously for the anti-tuition fee and/or anti-cuts message and rejecting the notion that the destructiveness of the Millbank action invalidated the cause, criticising the media coverage for tarring all the protesters with the same brush or giving too much emphasis to the direct action, or even occasionally expressly backing the Millbank protesters. As might be expected, *Guardian* letters were predominantly supportive (72%), as were those in the *Mirror*, although the newspaper was notably less supportive of the students than the unions. Three of six letters in the *Mirror* on one day (15/11/10) argued that the students' hand was forced by the democratic deficit of representative democracy, and just one distinguished the "admirable" marchers from the Millbank occupiers. Rather less predictably, letters published in the *Times* were the most skewed toward sympathy to the protest – five of the nine letters (12 nad 13/11/10) explicitly criticised the disparaging tone of the newspaper's leading article "Politics and Pantomime" (11/11/10), and three argued for the public benefits of an educated workforce and socially mobile citizenry. Only one very brief letter accused the students of having "reverted to type", and another praised police restraint.

On the other hand, half of those in the *Telegraph* were critical, and *all* of the letters in the *Express*. Those in the *Telegraph* took a droll tone that seems somewhat characteristic of the paper's letters page:

SIR – You report that Tanzil Choudhury, 22, a law student from Manchester University, brandishing a cricket bat which he had stolen from inside 30 Millbank, said that if the Government knew that they were willing to take this sort of action it would take them more seriously. Exactly what kind of law course is this student taking? (letter to the editor, *Telegraph* 12/11/10)

Of the three letters in the *Express*, two made extensive use of rhetorical questions ("How can acts of sheer vandalism achieve anything? Do these young people know how hard it was some years ago even to contemplate going to university?", 11/11/10), and two stereotyped young people as feckless and spoiled, with a sense of entitlement. Letters on both these topics suggest that letter writers reproduce the public idiom that the newspaper uses in editorials to synthesise a version of readers' tone of conversations with friends (Fowler 1991: 208–11) and perhaps not only in the tabloids.

Whilst there were 46 letters on the strikes and 37 on the student protest, there were just 11 on Occupy, five of which were in the *Guardian*. This despite the sample for Occupy covering 16 days in comparison with six days of coverage of the student protest and five days for the strikes. This perhaps supports Galtung and Ruge's (1965) notion that those events that coincide with the frequency of the news cycle are deemed more newsworthy than those processes that occur over longer periods of time and whose meaning is not immediately apparent.

In the first week, the only letters were two in the *Guardian* from activists (17/10/11 and 21/10/11) and three in the *Times* (21/10/11), of which only one directly addressed the protest, objecting to the characterisation of the movement as "anti-capitalist", whilst the others related to the cathedral's commercial activities and decision to close. Quite remarkably, given that the *Express* built up to a similar level of outrage about Occupy as about the other protests – even starting a campaign for their eviction – the only letter that the paper published on the topic (25/10/11) related to St Paul's admission charges. Even the letters in the *Guardian* were all from activists or from church figures, with none from members of the public who had not participated.

Ventriloquising the public

Claims about 'the public', 'public opinion' and 'public feeling' differed substantially in overall tone between the three protests, but also featured significant similarities in that it was principally assumed to be based on self-interested concerns. There was some indication, in the 11 months between the student tuition fees protest and Occupy LSX, of a shift from assumed support for the cuts agenda to anger and resentment, though uncertainty about the extent to which this extended to tolerance of disruption.

In reporting of the student protests seven of 11 references to the public *feeling* or *mood* interpreted the protests as *reflecting* public opinion, rather than reporting public opinion on the protest. They referred to sympathetic public anger, including a reflection that the British reaction had previously been "remarkably mild" in comparison with unrest in many European cities (*Independent* 11/11/10), government concern that the mood is shifting to "emulate" the continental response (*Times* 11/11/10), and suggesting that the "political and chattering classes have seriously underestimated the public mood" for dissent (Bob Crow, RMT union General Secretary quoted in *Guardian* 13/11/10). Two left-leaning Sunday newspapers painted a picture of growing outrage, arguing that the destruction at Millbank "reflected palpable rage that is simmering across the country" (anonymous diary of a civil servant, *Observer* 14/11/10) and that "there's enough boiling anger out there to drive many more people into the streets" (Fiona McIntosh, *Mirror* 14/11/10). However, a further three remarks on public feeling referred to distaste for violence (*Guardian* and *Mirror* 11/11/10, *Daily Mail* 13/11/10).

Most of the 23 references to public *opinion* and public *support* either argued that there was little support for violence or that there was widespread support for the anti-cuts cause (apart from Charles Moore in the *Telegraph* 13/11/10), with the main point of disagreement being over whether the violence had discredited the students' cause (seven references), as discussed in Chapter 5.

In contrast, there was just one reference to public anger about cuts in relation to the public sector strikes (one in the *Independent*, attributed to Mervyn King, 28/06/11). However, the unsupported claims about public opinion more often asserted opposition to public sector cuts than other sources of or claims about public opinion on the strikes, reporting union leaders claims that "the Government would have to make concessions to avoid alienating the general public" (*Independent* 01/07/11). There were, however, claims that public supported the cuts, again in the *Telegraph* (01/07/11), and also *Daily Mail* (28/06/11).

Assumptions that the public would not be sympathetic tended to be based on self-interested concerns. The Economics Editor of the *Independent* pointed out that private sector workers, for whom the pensions fight is already lost, greatly outnumber public sector workers – suggesting that the unions were losing the argument on the numbers as calculated by bare self-interest (Sean O'Grady, *Independent* 29/06/11). More emphatically and rhetorically, an *Express* commentator argued that the unions were "living on a different planet" if they thought that the public would sympathise with their attempt to defend more generous pensions (Chris Roycroft-Davis, *Express* 29/06/11).

More often, however, the claims of public opposition to the strike were on the basis of objection to the personal inconvenience of disruption to public services, especially school closures. This was led by government ministers, and picked up by a letter-writer in the *Sun* (29/06/11) and an opinion column in the *Herald* (Iain MacWhirter, 30/06/11). Cabinet Office Minister, Francis Maude "claimed there would be low public support for inflicting strike misery on hard-pressed taxpayers" (*Star* 28/06/11) and Education Secretary, Michael Gove argued that "The public have a very low tolerance for anything that disrupts their hard-working lifestyles" (quoted in *Guardian* 27/06/11), and "suggested the public might demand changes to prevent future "militancy" disrupting family life"

(*Sun* 27/06/11). The wording of "disrupting family life" is unusual, and recalls the human right to family life, inferring that the public are asserting rights that conflict with the right to protest, as examined in Chapter 5. The "hard-working" members of the public are presumably also considered more deserving of rights than the "militants". However, Ed Miliband, only recently elected to the Labour leadership at the time, with substantial support from the affiliated unions (though those involved in the strike were not), also argued that public sympathy would be diminished by disruption, though framed as friendly advice on good PR.

In as far as commentators argued that there was greater public favourability toward the strike than past disputes, this was judged to be based on the middle class respectability and social proximity of the public sector workers involved.

> But unions have a strength they did not have in their heyday, in that the social gap between their members and the rest of the public has closed. In 1926, middle-class people were frightened of the black-faced miners emerging to man picket lines, because they knew nothing about them and imagined the worst. Now, those on picket lines are the sort most of us encounter regularly – teachers, government office staff and so on. (Andy McSmith, news analysis, *Independent* 01/07/11)

Similarly, the *Mirror* argued that "The Government is right to be worried it could suffer a public backlash, because yesterday's strikes had the air of a Middle Britain rebellion, a revolt by people who work hard and pay taxes but feel unfairly treated" (leader, *Mirror* 01/07/11), although the paper went on to warn that further strikes could "alienate the general public".

Union efforts to appeal to public opinion related the action to the broader public interest through the connection to the quality of public services.

> Northern Ireland regional chairman Barney Loan urged the public to be sympathetic.
> "This action is about more than pensions," he said. "It is about jobs and services and the protection of those jobs and services." (*Belfast Telegraph* 29/06/11)

However, two commentators in the *Guardian* pointed to union claims of widespread participation in the strike as PR failures.

> But as well as the more clueless aspects of their tactics (witness Unison's Dave Prentis making a deeply clever appeal to middle Britain by citing such great popular touchstones as the general strike of 1926), the unions are held back by a bigger difficulty: the failure of the watershed moment into which we're being pushed to find any expression in the wider culture. (John Harris, *Guardian* 29/06/11)

> Serwotka – the Daily Mail's idea of a foaming union militant – who rattled off the 999 calls disrupted, juries sent home and driving tests postponed, as if the public would be grateful. (Michael White, *Guardian* 01/07/11)

Of course, the unions were countering the tabloid claims that the strike was a failure due to the lack of disruption – caught in a double bind whereby they are judged illegitimate if they succeed in causing disruption, due to public opposition, and also as illegitimate if they fail to cause disruption, due to lack of union member support.

Another common frame, then, defined the dispute as a battle for public opinion between unions and the government, which typically portrayed neither side as enjoying a great deal of public support.

> Leftwing heavies may want to bring down the government, while rightwing heavies may want to break the unions as they did in the 1980s. But the great mass of lights [those less attentive to politics] want, above all, for this dispute to be solved on reasonable terms, so that they don't have to think too much about it. (*Guardian* 01/07/11)

Much of the claims about the greater political legitimacy of talks over strike action discussed in the previous chapter made reference to public preference for negotiation. A former trade union leader wrote to the *Western Mail* (29/06/11) arguing that they should focus their argument to "concentrate their efforts on gathering public support for much higher taxation of the rich and a cautious approach to job losses particularly in the emergencies services", and to do so through protests, not strikes. This was broadly the approach taken up by the Occupy movement.

Initially, the reaction to Occupy LSX was interpreted as indicative of a change in 'public mood' – as an emotional response to economic conditions, but also to social injustice.

> They are the tip of the iceberg of public feeling about the injustice of a financial collapse that was caused by the most prosperous and greedy, and whose price is now being paid by the middle class and poor. (leader, *Guardian* 17/10/11)

This could be interpreted either as the majority of 'ordinary' people asserting their interests against those of bankers and other social elites – in Occupy's own terms, as the 99% – or as an increasing social concern for social justice in principle, regardless of personal self-interest.

Most assessments were ambiguous, describing the public mood as a general sense of unease, anger or resentment: reflecting "an inchoate sense that something is wrong", and "distrust" in institutions (George Carey, *Telegraph* 28/10/11), that "the sense that something is profoundly not right now covers a very broad range of opinion" (David Randall, special report, *Independent on Sunday* 30/10/11), "a clear sense of reflecting the common sense of the age" and being "in tune with millions" in terms of the problems, whilst there was no clear agreement on solutions (Seamus Milne, *Guardian* 20/10/11). Some commentators were unclear about whether the movement was claiming to represent majority support or majority interests, possibly conflating the two: "The protesters over-claim when they say they speak for "the 99%", but some of their themes do resonate very potently with mainstream voters" (Andrew Rawnsley, *Observer* 30/10/11).

Where there was explicit reference to the political principles behind this feeling of outrage and injustice (albeit mostly in the more sympathetic titles), it was accompanied by Occupy's reinterpretation of class conflict in terms that align the middle class with the poor rather than with the wealthy.

> The motivation of the protesters – that inequality has grown grotesquely, and that there are powerful groups not sharing the pain of recession – has many more sympathisers than activists. (Joan Smith, *Independent on Sunday* 30/10/11)

Giles Fraser's account suggested that the crisis had punctured the neo-liberal myth that corporate interests are identical with the public interest because they create economic growth to the benefit of all.

> I think there is a very clear question here to be addressed, [...] and the reason that the protesters have captured some of the public imagination is because a great many people think that something has gone wrong in the City of London and that the wealth generated by the City does not exist for the benefit of us all. (Dr Giles Fraser quoted in *Guardian* interview 28/10/11)

It was the protesters themselves who most explicitly framed these concerns as based in values and beliefs, citing Fraser as "an example of someone who's standing up for his principles – principles that we share, clearly, and that a wide section of society shares" (occupier quoted in *Guardian* 28/10/11).

Seamus Milne argued that this view was being seen as a real threat by the establishment, as indicated by efforts to co-opt the movement and placate it with more moderate reforms.

> In a climate where plutocrats like Warren Buffett are meanwhile begging to pay higher taxes, it's a clear sign of elite anxiety at the extent of popular anger and an attempt to co-opt the movement before demands for more fundamental change get traction. Something similar seems to be going on in Britain where – against a steady drumbeat of lobbying scandal and escalating unemployment – police and the conservative Daily Mail have so far both given the City occupation outside St Paul's Cathedral a notably easy ride. (Seamus Milne, *Guardian* 20/10/11)

There was also a concern within the church about "a growing feeling that the church was appearing out of touch" (anonymous insider, quoted in *Independent* 27/10/11).

This is an unusual focus on public opinion on the substance of the protest (even if largely unsubstantiated), and especially on positive assessments of that opinion, as opposed to the typical focus on the social acceptability of the protest repertoires and the protesters personally. As time went on, however, and especially following the closure of the cathedral, critics were emboldened to pour cold water on the strange emergence of hope (or at least partial suspension of cynicism) inspired by the camp. However, only the *Express* asserted a critical or hostile public reaction to the camp, and then only as an erosion of sympathy, which implies an acceptance of the dominant view that there at least initially been widespread support for the occupation.

> There is a growing public backlash against the anti-capitalist campaigners who have closed the historic building for the first time since the Second World War and are threatening religious services marking events such as Remembrance Sunday and Christmas. (*Express* 26/10/11)

However, the only source that they quoted in support of this assertion was the UKIP party leader, Nigel Farage, who predicted that "Public opinion will start to turn against those in the camp" if the Remembrance Sunday service were to be cancelled (quoted in *Express* 25/10/11). The *Express* later resorted to quoting a "former Tory candidate" (29/10/11) to justify negative assessments of public opinion through the strategic "use of quotations to remove the reporter's presence from the story" (Tuchman 1972: 688).

Other newspapers were more ambivalent about the public response to the occupation, including the Scottish edition of the Express, who judged that locals were "accepting, if reluctantly" the camp in Glasgow's George Square (*Scottish Express* 27/10/11), and an economics writer in the *Times*:

> In Britain, the general public is not sure how to react. Is this merely "British eccentricity"? The critics say the tents are an eyesore and "sucking the life out of the City". (Stefanie Marsh, *Times* 29/10/11)

She does not directly claim that these "critics" are among the public rather than the establishment. However, prominent activists argued that Occupy had effected a real shift in public assessments of occupation as a protest repertoire.

> He believed yesterday's protest represented a shift in the way the public views demonstrations. "I think the attitude coming out of protests here and on Wall Street has been incredibly positive," he said. "It's a desire to build, rather than smash things up." (Billy Bragg quoted in *Independent on Sunday* 16/10/11)

In other words, it was the inclusive, cooperative, and ultimately deliberative nature of the camp that has won the public over.

Dominant social norms: Manners and shame in social space

The behaviour of protesters is therefore presented as having a key role in the social legitimacy of their action and their cause. However, this was not limited to, or even focused on, the political behaviour, but their manners, appearance, and orientation to the social and cultural mainstream.

Behaviour

Beyond the *legality* of protest behaviour discussed in Chapter 5, judgements were made on the *social* acceptability of that behaviour. In coverage of the student protest, even though the march was described as peaceful (82 times) to distinguish it from the Millbank action, only the Goldsmiths statement (quoted in *Telegraph* 12/11/10) called it "good-natured" without going on to say that it "turned" nasty. Only the left-leaning *Guardian* and *Mirror* described the strike marches as "good-natured" (01/07/11), whilst the *Sun* reluctantly accepted that "most [were] good humoured" though it added that "some were poorly attended" (01/07/11). There were also a couple of accounts of a celebratory atmosphere – the *Mirror* also described a march in Brighton as having a "carnival feel", and the *Western Mail* (01/07/11) remarked that it was "almost as if a festival had broken out" (although elsewhere the festival analogy was more of a mixed judgement).

However, Occupy also received more praise, and was attributed more elaborate social virtues, for having created a civilised social and political arrangement.

> The protesters have largely been very decorously behaved. They have thus far displayed no propensity to riot or to loot. Their tents are erected in rather neat rows. They hold laboriously consensus-seeking meetings at which they keep minutes and take votes. Their spokespeople are polite and articulate. (Andrew Rawnsley, *Observer* 30/10/11)

In part, this is related to the democratic virtues of their decision making, as discussed in the previous chapter, but it is also about manners in public space, being "neat" and "polite". The closest that the coverage of the other protests got to this was the *Guardian's* observation that the main strike march in London "was very good about it's litter" (01/07/11) as part of a wry comment about teachers' concern with good behaviour.

There were 45 references to the occupiers being accommodating or amenable (1,730 words), especially in the *Guardian* (789 words), but also disproportionately in the *Daily Telegraph* and *Sunday Times*. Simon Jenkins remarked that the Wall St camp "seem meticulously concerned about being clean, quiet and of good community behaviour" (*Guardian* 21/11/10), and the London camp were similarly described as "at pains to be welcoming":

> While the language of the placards festooned across the camp occasionally sounds aggressive, with its talk of crisis and revolution, the activists are at pains to be welcoming and, in particular, not to alienate their ecclesiastical hosts. Noisy meetings have been rescheduled to avoid clashing with church services, with participants issuing self-imposed bans on taping posters to the cathedral

walls – it could damage the stone – or loitering on the main steps lest they
impede worshippers or tour groups. (*Guardian* 18/10/11)

They also reported that police had allowed organisers to chalk a boundary to the
encampment rather than be fenced in, demonstrating a cooperative relationship
with police that contrasts with the hostility associated with anti-capitalist summit
sieges or even the anti-environmental protests.

Whilst the *Guardian* gave the warmest and most lengthy endorsements of
these efforts, the conservative press were also won over by the camp's efforts.

> The camp established a media tent, a recycling zone, a library, a "tent university"
> and a first-aid stall. They've banned alcohol, chat happily with the police and
> use their megaphone only when people aren't praying quietly inside. (*Telegraph*
> 20/10/11)

It may be significant that the media tent is mentioned first, though in his analysis
of Occupy Wall Street, Castells (2012: 173–4) quoted a journalist reporting that it
was not the media strategy of the movement that convinced her to cover the story,
but a Tumblr account hosting personal narratives (recalling Wahl-Jorgensen's
[2001] account of the selection criteria of letters page editors).

Nonetheless, once established as a story, the message about their painstaking
efforts to comply with regulations was apparently effectively communicated.

> In the media tent a young man explained how anxious the protesters were to
> co-operate. When the church authorities had announced that they were closing
> the cathedral for health and safety reasons, the bewildered campers had called
> in the London Fire Brigade for an assessment and had been cleared. They had
> rearranged the tents in order not to block the highways, and had moved all the
> tents away from St Paul's to allow a 10-yard space between the encampment and
> the walls. (*Sunday Times* 30/10/11)

Occupiers' accounts of their effort to cooperate with fire authorities and health
and safety regulations were quoted or reported in several of the more sceptical
conservative newspapers (*Belfast Telegraph* 22/10/11, *Telegraph* 24/10/11, and
Daily Mail and *Express* 25/10/11), and even the most vociferous critics accepted
that the protesters had been cooperative and amenable to addressing safety concerns.

> By the time I reached St Paul's on Thursday, those "dwelling in the tents of the
> wicked" (Psalm 84) had politely moved to one side. There was far more risk of
> being run down by a bus in the nearby street than of tripping over a Left-wing
> guy-rope. (Charles Moore, *Telegraph* 29/10/11)

However, some aspects of the traditional delegitimising frames survived, especially
the stereotyping of occupiers' countercultural appearance and personal hygiene.

Appearance and hygiene

Despite the courteous behaviour of the occupiers, however, their appearance could still be judged uncivil.

> Though their tents are arranged in impeccable rows, the countenances of some of these new inhabitants – dreadlocks, nose rings, trainers – tend to offend the smart, besuited workers who usually dominate this quarter. They want them to leave with immediate effect. (Stefanie Marsh, *Times* 29/10/11)

Marsh suggests that signifiers of counter-cultural lifestyle and appearance (including a very common form of footwear) are anti-social and offensive to bankers, and that this personal reaction constitutes a harm, although not in Mill's terms since he rejected the claimed right to be shielded from that of which they disapprove, but rather as communitarian responsibilities to the community. Furthermore, it suggests that the City of London is governed by the social mores of the businessmen who work there, and not by more general expectations of acceptable public appearance, defining it as a private rather than public space.

In all there were 36 references to the counter-cultural appearance or lifestyle of the protesters, five references to cannabis, four to long hair, dreadlocks, tattoos and piercings, and four to 'Swampy', the accidental celebrity of the mid-nineties anti-roads protests who has come to stand for the paradigmatic protester. Conservative newspapers, the *Express*, *Sunday Times*, *Mail on Sunday*, and *Sunday Express* disproportionately referred to the occupiers' lifestyle and appearance.

One *Express* commentator objected to Occupy's claim to represent "the 99%" (misinterpreting this – perhaps wilfully – as a claim that "99 per cent of us agree with them"):

> You have to admire the cheek. It's difficult to imagine a group more unrepresentative of the general population. On the one hand are the trustafarians, ever-present at such events – languid, deliberately unemployed layabouts with inherited money who were at the back of the queue when brains and getup-and-go were handed out. Alongside them are the professional protesters, whose sole source of income is the benefits funded by those of us who work in the system they want to destroy. Dreadlocks are common to both groups. (Stephen Pollard, *Express* 18/10/11)

Pollard stereotypes the protesters largely, it seems, on their choice of hairstyle, and infers that their politics are simply a part of the lifestyle of the "trustafarian" or "professional protester". This denial of political sincerity is addressed in detail below, but the salient point here is that aspects of personal appearance are used to characterise them as both socially and politically marginal. Similarly, Cristina Odone in the *Telegraph* (17/10/11) judged the protesters to "look a motley bunch from what I've seen: angry youngsters, bearded Trotskyists and Israelbashers", extrapolating their politics from their facial hair.

However, not all of the judgements on appearance were entirely negative. One *Telegraph* columnist characterised them as "usual", but not the traditional characterisation of the 'usual suspects' – but rather an updated version of the stereotype for the "internet age":

> They were the usual protest mixture that the internet age produces – pretty young women with Red Indian hairstyles and expensive educations; friendly, slightly moth-eaten, unemployed, graduate thirtysomethings; and rather tougher, more politicallyminded public sector workers enjoying the ample leisure that their careers afford. (Charles Moore, *Telegraph*, 29/10/11)

This suggests a popular perception (perhaps with greater awareness since the Arab Spring) that the internet is understood to broaden engagement with protest, with digital mobilisation reaching beyond the established networks and removing barriers to participation (Rheingold 2002, Castells 2012).

Notably, the stereotype of the typical protester was accepted even by those who argued that it was not applicable in this instance, distinguishing the middle class occupiers from "the usual rentamob of Swampy lookalikes"[7] (Iain Hollingshead, *Telegraph* 20/10/11); even Polly Toynbee remarked that the "Swampy count is pretty low" (*Guardian* 18/10/11). However, there was a strong vein of criticism in the right-wing tabloids:

> The authorities should stop hiding behind health and safety as an excuse for inactivity. A fire risk? Outside the stone cathedral that survived the Blitz unscathed? That's pathetic. The only real risk to health is that a passerby might catch something from the great unwashed. If the risk is to the protesters' health because of their insanitary conditions they should be allowed to get on with it. Anyone going to lose sleep because Swampy's pals have got the runs? No, me neither. (Chris Roycroft-Davis, *Express* 25/10/11)

Although critical of the health and safety concerns, this account portrays the occupiers as breaking the codes and conventions of public behaviour by bringing private activities (especially defecation) into a public space, breaking the boundary of "shame" (Elshtain 1997).

There were 35 references in all to the camp as dirty – including to "the great unwashed" and "soap-dodgers" (*Sunday Express* 23/10/11), but mostly to the camp as squalid (4 times) and an "eyesore" (twice).

---

7   Daniel 'Swampy' Hooper was a tunnelling protester who came to prominence during the Fairmile road protest in 1996–7, when he was one of the last to end his underground occupation. Polite, middle class and photogenic, he became a media darling, but then retreated from the public eye. As a signifier, however, his name has come to refer to unemployed protesters with itinerant lifestyles, and also has connotations of a scruffy and unwashed appearance.

> Is it really a God-given right to turn the beautiful, historic space of St Paul's Churchyard enjoyed by millions into a squalid eyesore and a threat to public health? (Melanie Phillips, *Daily Mail* 24/10/11).

> I had decided to join hundreds of demonstrators laying siege to one of the capital's most treasured landmarks but lasted just two days before the filth and foul smell forced me to quit camp. (Sarah Cox, *Express* 29/10/11)

The metaphor of "siege" – used seven times by the *Daily Mail*, *Express*, *Star*, *Mirror*, and *Times* – evokes medieval imagery, reinforced by the anachronistic-sounding reference to "filth and foul smell". A similar analogy was with the squalor of poverty-stricken countries: "St Paul's is a UNESCO World Heritage site and they have turned it into a Third World shanty town" (Mark Field, Conservative MP, quoted in *Daily Mail*, *Express*, and *Sun* 25/10/11). These critics are concerned with the social standing of London and St Pauls on the basis of the status of their tourist attractions, and suggest that untidy political participation is showing the city up in front of the foreign sightseers, aligning public space with the commercial.

Social responsibilities and moral duties

Accordingly, the principle duty that protesters were accused of failing to meet was a responsibility to be productive for the capitalist economy. Occupiers were stigmatised as unemployed benefits scroungers 14 times, mostly delegitimising the poor and marginalised rather than recognising that the lack of job opportunities, job security, and career prospects were among the issues being protested. In one case, even where unemployment was recognised as a motivation, protest was not regarded as a constructive response – one opinion column was headlined "Don't whine about poverty – go out and create wealth" (Stephen Pollard, *Express* 18/10/11). However, six of these references – four in the *Guardian* and two in the *Mirror* – challenged the delegitimising framing, including Patrick Kingsley's account of bystanders who "wanted to pigeonhole the protesters" discussed above (*Guardian* 26/10/11), and a leader column in the *Mirror* pointing out that critics "who claim the unemployed don't want to work condemn protesters for leaving their vigil to hold down jobs" (29/10/11).

In the coverage of the public sector strikes, *both* sides of the debate appealed to the popular construction of 'hard-working' taxpayers or families as a legitimating signifier, to indicate deservingness.

> Don't tell low- and medium-paid workers on strike today in defence of their modest pensions that they are being unfair on the "hard-working taxpayer" – as if public sector workers are not in that category too. (PCS leader Mark Serwotka, writing in *Guardian* 30/06/11)

The six references were evenly split between politicians and union representatives asserting the deservingness of private sector and public sector workers' interests, although no-one accused teachers or public servants of not being hard-working.

Of five references to 'hardworking taxpayers' in the student protest three referred to taxpayers subsidising the public services and benefits of the more feckless, and just one to students and their (middle class) families (the other challenged David Cameron and George Osbourne's notion of themselves as part of this "club of hard-working people who pay their taxes, do their best to rear their children and find it desperately hard to make ends meet" – John Harris, *Guardian* 12/11/10). A further three remarks related to industriousness more generally, suggesting that students are "workshy" and have a sense of "entitlement" (letter to the editor, *Express* 11/11/10; Lorraine Kelly, *Scottish Sun* 13/11/10), with just one referring to them as "conscientious" (letter to the editor, *Mirror* 15/11/10).

Cultural sensitivity to the mainstream: National symbols as civil religion

As well as a social obligation to the nation as capitalist economy, there was a cultural obligation to the nation as symbolically constructed entity. In particular, this was asserted in relation to symbols and rituals that commemorate the two World Wars as historical signifiers of national pride and unity. St Paul's Cathedral was therefore accorded special status as a national monument that survived Nazi bombing (12 times, 591 words, mostly in the *Daily Mail*, *Express*, and *Times*). Two-thirds of the references to the historical significance of St Paul's made reference to the Blitz, which was raised by the Dean when he announced that the cathedral would close its doors for the first time since the war. More particularly, it was attributed continuing social significance as a symbol of the British character – the *Daily Mail* referred to the cathedral three times as a symbolising or representing "the nation's Blitz Spirit" (22/11/10 and 24/11/10) and columnist Melanie Philips called it "this soaring emblem of British stoicism" (*Daily Mail* 24/11/10). David Cameron called it "a key national site and key tourist site, important to the history and psyche of the country" (quoted in *Express* 29/10/11 and *Sunday Times* 30/10/11).

Some commentators even argued that it symbolised Britain's moral leadership and inspired the people to support the war.

> THE shining cross and dome of St Paul's stand out amid the inferno of the Blitz in one of the most iconic photographs ever taken. At a defining moment in British history, as Wren's great cathedral defied Hitler's bombs, that picture taken in December 1940 captured for all time our indomitable wartime spirit. London's greatest monument symbolised why we were fighting – the desire for good to triumph over the evil of the Nazis. At the height of that air raid, Winston Churchill ordered all fire-fighting resources be sent to St Paul's. The cathedral must be saved, he said, or it would sap the morale of the country. (Chris Roycroft-Davis, *Express* 25/10/11)

An elderly woman reported to have berated the occupiers for disrupting her right to worship also described the cathedral's survival as symbolic of, even as divine confirmation of, the rectitude of the nation in that conflict: "There was complete destruction and smoke all around the cathedral, but somehow it was almost completely untouched. It was as if the hand of God had been on it" (bystander, quoted in *Daily Mail* and *Times* 24/10/11).

Apart from the significance of the cathedral itself, its role hosting a Remembrance Sunday service was mentioned thirteen times, most emphatically in Express titles where the prospect of its cancellation was described as a "travesty" by Nigel Farage of UKIP (*Express* 25/10/11), and a city councillor said "it is important people are allowed to pay respects to those who lost their lives in conflict" (*Star* 25/10/11). The significance of the service was elaborated as "for our war dead" (*Express* 25/10/11), "to honour Brit servicemen and women who died for their country" (*Star* 25/10/11). This banal nationalism functions to reinforce values related to sacrifice for one's country, mutual respect, and national pride (and arguably also deference to governing authorities), but used against the protesters it suggests a vaguely nationalistic discourse of offence to national sensibilities or sentiment, which is as close as British media come to the accusation (more common in the US) of being unpatriotic.

In contrast, supporters – though limited to the pages of the *Guardian* – argued that the protest brought new meaning and significance to the cathedral as a national monument, appealing to an alternative notion of the cultural role of a monument such as St Paul's:

> It is one of those rare occasions that leaders in the contemporary church long for: to be at the heart of the action. In a society with little interest in organised Christianity, suddenly St Paul's Cathedral finds itself at the epicentre of the Occupy London movement (St Paul's may seek injunction to move activists, 24 October). Rather than serving as a museum to the past, it has become a site of public contestation. (letter to the editor, *Guardian* 25/10/11)

The newspaper took up this theme in a leader column the following day, arguing that the cathedral would "a whited sepulchre" if the protesters were "evicted to make room for empty pomp" (*Guardian* 26/10/11).

Political sincerity and emotional authenticity

Although Occupy broadly succeeded in resisting the typical tropes of social delegitimisation, apart from some critique of their personal appearance and employment status, critics also attempted to delegitimise the protesters personally by questioning their sincerity and authenticity, with a particular focus on the emotional and identity-based motivation of the protesters as individuals, again often drawing on countercultural stereotypes.

Political sincerity and commitment

Given that there were low expectations for Occupy LSX it is perhaps surprising that the scale and persistence of the camp wasn't portrayed as a remarkable achievement. At the outset the *Sunday Mirror* described the occupation attempt as having "fizzled out" and reduced to a "hardcore of activists" determined to stay "until tomorrow" (16/10/11). The *Independent* referred to "hardcore remnants of a global anti-capitalist movement" (18/10/11), and the *Telegraph* "an apparently dwindling number of hardcore pavement dwellers" (20/10/11). The term hardcore has a range of associations, including musical sub-genres, pornography, and colloquially to mean "intense, relentless",[8] in all cases meaning extreme, though with differing value connotations – it is therefore difficult to determine whether in these cases the intended meaning is 'determined' or 'marginal', much less how it is interpreted by newspaper readers.

There were 48 explicit references, however, to the occupiers' determination to remain as long as possible, and the apparent permanence of the camp. This was portrayed variously as an intention (22), capability (10), promise (2), warning (1), or threat (1). Melanie Phillips framed the determination to remain as bloody-mindedness rather than political commitment to the occupation: "The gathering announced that it intended to take up permanent residence on the cathedral steps and made clear that the interests of anyone else or society in general could go hang" (Melanie Phillips, *Daily Mail* 24/10/11).

Surprisingly, then, given that the willingness to dedicate time and brave discomfort to register their support was not thought particularly remarkable or significant, the most common delegitimsing frame was the empty tent controversy. There were 3,828 words dedicated to this angle, across 59 references. The *Daily Mail*, *Telegraph*, and *Times* reported that police thermal imaging had indicated that 90% of tents were unoccupied overnight (reported as a fact by the *Mail* and *Telegraph*), and the story was picked up by eight other newspapers. However, the greatest volume of coverage in terms of word count was in the *Guardian*, which dedicated 1,401 words overall to the issue, largely questioning or challenging whether the reports were accurate, including the original source of the claims (an overheard conversation), and the accuracy of the infra-red cameras used by the *Telegraph* to verify the claims (unable to penetrate canvas). In addition, the *Independent* reported from the camp that almost all the tents were occupied by 1am, and the *Times* cited occupiers' claims that many stayed up in a large communal tent until 3am.

Even among the Occupy movement, people took different positions on the significance of overnight occupation. Occupiers quoted in the *Guardian* and *Times* (26/10/11) argued that day-time participation was more important than overnight presence, and that the tents symbolised the scale of support whether occupied at night or not.

---

8   Urban Dictionary: http://www.urbandictionary.com/define.php?term=hardcore.

As Gearing says: "If people aren't sleeping between the hours of six and 12, it makes not one jot of difference. The most important thing is that they're there during the day so that they can take part in the debate." (Patrick Kingsley, *Guardian* 26/10/11)

Mr Phillips said: "Each tent represents a person, even if they are not here at night. We have jobs and homes and responsibilities too." (*Times* 26/10/11)

Another member of Occupy suggested that their integrity and commitment was signalled by cold and discomfort, and therefore undermined by occupiers' absence:

We try to keep vacancy to a minimum. The fact that we are camping out here shows how seriously we take our right to participate and be heard. (occupier quoted in *Times* 26/10/11).

Certainly the newspapers that were more hostile to the occupation took this to be the measure against which to judge the seriousness of the protest. Critics in the *Sunday Times*, *Daily Mail*, *Times*, *Express*, and *Sun* dismissed it as a "part-time protest".

Seven newspapers did give some room (12 references, 567 words) to occupiers' assertions that they had mainstream responsibilities to attend to – jobs, families, pets – that prevented them from full-time occupation. The vast majority of these are quotes from occupiers explaining their absences, one of which even appeared in the *Express* (26/10/11). As noted above, the *Mirror* also argued that critics were inconsistent for criticising protesters for leaving the camp to go to work whilst claiming that "the unemployed don't want to work" (leader, 29/10/12), although the more obvious inconsistency is that critics dismiss protesters as lazy militant outsiders, and then condemn their absence due to mainstream responsibilities. However, even those who acknowledged these responsibilities speculated whether such mainstream demographic was compatible with the occupation in the long term.

The bulk of the occupiers are not the protesters-for-hire of the far left, and the realities of life would suggest that Tent City may soon lose some of its occupants. (Mark Leftly, *Independent on Sunday* 23/10/11)

Furthermore, even supportive newspapers found the rationale for absence unconvincing – the *Independent* (27/10/11) argued in an editorial that "while it may be true that those with personal and professional obligations cannot devote 24 hours a day to their cause, it must be said that a part-time occupation detracts somewhat from its credibility."

More broadly, critical coverage of occupiers' overnight absence was illustrative of two key characterisations. Firstly, that they were comfortable (and comfort-loving) middle classes with no experience of hardship and therefore no authentic emotional basis for left-wing politics. For instance, Lord Carey, the former Archbishop of Canterbury, writing in the *Telegraph* (28/10/11) called them "cynical and opportunistic" and argued that "The emerging picture of spoilt middle-class children returning home at night for a shower and a warm bed begged questions about their commitment to their cause". Secondly, that they were inauthentic 'professional protesters' – counter-cultural outsiders who reject mainstream society and who protest as an end in itself – according to (among others) a local councillor who called the occupation a "charade":

> It just shows that most of the people don't have the courage of their convictions and are just here to make trouble. (Matthew Richardson, Corporation of London councillor quoted in *Daily Mail*, *Telegraph*, and *Times* 25/10/11)

In relation to the overnight absences, it was the latter argument that was most commonly challenged – on the basis that they *were* middle class and mainstream, but less frequently or explicitly claimed a legitimate emotional authenticity.

Authenticity of feeling and 'professional protesters'

In Aristotlean terms, anger can be a positive political emotion where it is part of a virtuous disposition that motivates just action. There were just a handful of references that explicitly framed anger in these terms: "righteous anger" (*Mirror* 29/10/11), "indignance" (twice) – all in supportive papers. Three of these were framed in terms of authenticity, with reference to heart and passion; not only that "their anger is heartfelt" (Heather Stewart, business opinion, *Observer* 30/10/11), but also their commitment to change.

> Mum Rachel Mariner, from Cambridge, was on her fifth visit. She said: "I want my kids to see people standing up for a better world, people who speak from the heart." (*Mirror* 29/10/11)

> Political discourse in the UK is often sterile and remote from people's lives. So let's hear it for the passion and energy of these protests. (Anne Johnstone, *Herald* 20/10/11)

This recognises the basis of all protest in anger against injustice and then enthusiasm for the cause in overcoming the fear (and apathy) that prevents engagement in protest (Castells 2012: 14–5).

Rather more often, however, moral outrage was portrayed as "self-righteous" (six times) or "self-indulgent" five times (including Lord Carey writing in the *Telegraph* 28/10/11, quoted in *Times* 29/10/11 and *Observer* 30/10/11), and smug, self-congratulatory, "naïve, pious and moralistic" (Hugo Rifkind, *Times* 28/10/11). Charles Moore compared the protesters, Giles Fraser, and the cathedral authorities to "the Pharisees attacked by Jesus shortly before he overturned the tables of the moneychangers. They are those who 'trusted in themselves that they were righteous, and despised others'" *Telegraph* 29/10/11).

One commentator in the *Independent* explicitly connected this with the role of emotion in bonding solidarity, in that it *excludes*:

> As Anthony Painter wrote on Labour List: "The way you change things is by getting people behind you, not by huddling together in a righteous and self-congratulatory embrace". (Andreas Whittam Smith, *Independent* 20/10/11)

There is also a suggestion that political solidarity risks sliding into identity politics, or a resistance identity (Castells 2010), which is not deemed legitimate in the Habermasian public sphere because it refers inwards to particularistic values, rather than outward to publicly shared or commonly acceptable values. But rather than recognise the potential for socially transformative project identities to emerge from such resistance identities, Whittam Smith sees them as mutually exclusive.

In complete contrast to the depiction of victims as emotionally authentic, *political* emotion was rejected as inappropriate to political discussion, and indeed as indicative of the lack of political capabilities – as childish and petulant. This is even the case when they are attributed some form of victimhood: a "generalised squeal of pain about the unfairness of life" (Iain Hollingshead, *Telegraph* 20/10/11), which suggests the well-worn parental response: 'well tough, life's *not* fair'. Even the perpetually outraged columnist, Melanie Phillips invoked the liberal democratic ideals of the rationalist public sphere:

> Such sentimentality entails the eclipse of rational and principled thinking by a spasm of emotion that disconnects people from true moral judgments and prevents them from holding the right people to account for their behaviour. (Melanie Philips, *Daily Mail* 24/10/11)

Philips detaches the substantive (principles, morals) from the affective (sentiment, emotion), and attaches it to the rational ("true moral judgements"). This would suggest that she believes her own judgement that protesters are "spoiled children" is "rational and principled thinking" and objectively "true".

The inauthenticity of political emotion was explained firstly as manipulative rhetoric but more often as a superficial pose. In terms of the first, a common objection, especially in the *Express*, was that the occupiers did not limit their arguments to the issue on which it was agreed that there was public sympathy – greedy bankers – but expressed other political concerns. Commentators suggested that the camp had attracted a range of activists seeking to publicise their own hobby horse issues – a political instrumentalisation of the camp.

> Ask them what they are protesting about and out spews an all-purpose list of objects of their anger. (Stephen Pollard, *Express* 18/10/11)

> Elsewhere, people perform plays about Palestine. Strange. I thought this was about the banks? (Sarah Cox, *Express* 29/10/11)

This range of political commitment was interpreted as evidence of a lack of *any* genuine political point.

> The campers have been criticised for sending out mixed messages about their purpose, with many accused of protesting just for the sake of it. (*Express* 26/10/11)

This suggests that protesters simply sign up to every emerging cause simply to have something to protest about, though it doesn't give a motivation for doing so.

In terms of the second, Damian Thompson in the *Telegraph* (29/10/11) pilloried the role of new media, in a lengthy critique of bloggers (despite himself blogging for the *Telegraph*).

> When you've finished screaming and screaming until you are sick, Violet Elizabeth Bott-style, boredom sets in. Goodness, is that the time? (Damian Thompson, *Telegraph* 30/10/11)

This suggests that moral outrage is a fashionable pose, and that protest is a form of identity-politics or lifestyle-based subculture, populated by shallow young people for whom protest is the equivalent of an edgy hairstyle choice.

Protesters were portrayed as not politically committed, but pathologically oppositional, regardless of the cause. There were five references to typical activists as habitual or "professional protesters", (Stephen Pollard, *Express* 18/10/11) whose identity is defined by demonstrating, often connected with the assumption of being unemployed counter-cultural drop-outs.

> Silly question but don't they have jobs? Or are they professional agitators funded by welfare handouts? (Chris Roycroft-Davis, *Express* 25/10/11)

Jan Moir in the *Daily Mail* (21/10/11) distinguished them from 'authentically' committed protesters, but arguing that the latter are undermined by the former:

> Yes, there are genuine and heartfelt protesters out there – but too often they are drowned out by the rent-a-cause activists, who are a plague of boils on the face of British public life today […] If the travellers ever had a case – and I don't believe they did – the anarchist daytrippers ruined it for them. (Jan Moir, *Daily Mail* 21/10/11)

She adds, "They are grief tourists who can walk away when the protest ends, unlike those directly affected by the outcome", suggesting that authenticity is defined by their emotional response to being personally affected, not by having political views. Therefore the occupiers are either dismissed as emotionally *authentic* but irrational and politically illegitimate, or as emotionally *in*authentic and protesting as a superficial pose.

Hatred and offence

Furthermore, the emotional motivation for action was also interpreted not as anger, but hatred, and therefore as raw, uncivilised and offensive.

> Today, this has given rise to an ugly scapegoating of bankers and the wealthy – with precious little difference between this seething hatred and what extreme Left-wing agitators have been declaring for decades. (Melanie Phillips, *Daily Mail* 24/10/11)

This was also presented as a prejudicial dislike borne of ideological oppositionalism.

> By tribal inclination and habit, they are state-hating, government-bashing, cuts-opposing Tory loathers. [...] They hate the establishment. [...] How I loathe them all and their urban guerrilla pretensions. (Jan Moir, *Daily Mail* 21/10/11)

Moir's delegitimisation of all protesters on the basis of their uncivil hate and loathing on the one hand, is contradicted by her own loathing of "them", in equally generalising and othering terms.

This was far more common, however, in reporting of the public sector strike, and of opponents to the Pope's state visit. The *Sun* labelled strike action as in itself hateful, billing the ongoing dispute as the "Summer of Hate" (28/06/11), and demonised two union leaders as "hate-filled women" (30/06/11). Trevor Kavanagh (*Sun* 27/06/11) summarised the criticisms of the "militant" leaders into pithy personal insults, describing Mark Serwotka as a "loudmouth Welsh leftie" (without explaining the significance of his being Welsh), denounced "Snarling lefties Bob Crow and Len McCluskey", and referred to Labour leader Ed Miliband as "Red Ed" three times in rapid succession. Christine Blower of the NUT was singled out for a particularly protracted character assassination in the *Sun*, *Mail*, and *Express*, including accusation of "using her own daughter as a pawn to further her Left-wing ambitions" (*Daily Mail* 30/06/11). Blower's response to the insults was wrly reported in the Guardian.

> Christine Blower of the NUT, appalled yet delighted at being dubbed a "Scar-Girl" by the Sun, said the proper response was one applied to children squabbling in the playground: "That isn't really appropriate, is it?" (Michael White, Political Editor, *Guardian* 01/07/11)

Her response serves to highlight the incivility of the newspaper discourse, but also to subtly undermine their attempt to apply the 1970s filter on the story by emphasising her identity as a respectable teacher.

Protesters against the Pope's state visit were accused of being "shrill" (Jonanthan Wynne-Jones, *Sunday Telegraph* 19/09/11), "unpleasant" (*Telegraph* 18/09/11), "sneering" and "pompous" (leader, *Telegraph* 18/09/11), and of spouting "venomous hatred" (*Daily Mail* 17/09/11) and an "astonishing variety and force of invective" (*Guardian* 17/09/11). Dawkins in particular was accused of "abusive" comments (Dominic Lawson, *Sunday Times* 19/09/11) and "coarse insults" (letter to the editor, *Times* 17/09/10).

Some objected to the absence of deference to an individual commanding or deserving respect: "stunned by the lack of tolerance, respect and regard for his position as an elderly, learned religious leader and head of state" (Eamonn Holmes, *People* 19/09/11) – this is a curious combination of demand for respect due to authority ("head of state") and vulnerability ("elderly"). Others argued that the significant distinction was between disagreement and personal vilification, that, like the Rev. Ian Paisley, they "don't just believe the Pope is wrong, they believe he's evil" (Brian Appleyard, *Sunday Times*). Finally, Hugo Rifkind, writing in the *Times* (also quoted in the *Sunday Times*) framed it as a self-defeating approach: "Personally, if I were desperately keen to convince the world that faith wasn't required to be a benevolent moral agent, I'd be at pains not to act like a nasty, bilious oaf". Even critics of the Pope argued that discretion may be the greater part of valour: "it does not follow from the fact that you feel strongly about something and have a right to speak about it, that you therefore should always make as much noise as possible" (Julian Baggini, *Guardian* 18/09/11).

However, also in the *Sunday Times* (19/09/10), Brenda Power argued that the church's definition of aggression and intolerance is lack of forgiveness, regardless of contrition for the offence, and therefore delegitimises criticism and challenge – "equating a lack of forgiveness with aggression, impatience and intolerance makes it a shamefully unacceptable stance".

Summary

Interestingly, despite including elements of anarchism and the carnivalesque, Occupy largely escaped the typical stereotyping and othering of protesters, perhaps because of its high profile visibility, including through self-mediation, but also in a geographical sense. In *Seeing and Believing*, Greg Philo (1990) argues that personal experience is a significant resource for audiences, enabling them to challenge the framing of picket lines as mostly characterised by violence on the basis on passing them daily and seeing none. The Occupy LSX encampment was in central London, where the presence of bystanders and visitors would be visible to journalists, perhaps limiting the extent to which they felt partial accounts and misrepresentations were tenable. Obviously, the new media landscape is likely to also have had an effect on reports that could be so easily challenged by these many witnesses. Further research addressing the account and perspective of the journalists involved in reporting the story would be valuable, as would audience research, to give a more full picture of the social and cultural context of news judgements on public opinion and anticipated audience reception.

Despite efforts to define civil society in terms of civility – as the manners and social conventions in public space instilled by the civilising process – the occupiers were relatively successful at defining it in activist terms. The space in front of St Paul's not only became public in the political sense rather than merely the social sense, but was broadly accepted as such – as a space for contestation rather than peaceful coexistence. Although Occupy included anarchists of various stripes (libertarian anarchists, anarcho-syndicalists, and so on) who are typically used to delegitimise a protest (as we have seen in the discourse of hijack in Chapter 5), attention was given to those occupiers who conceived of the camp not as counter-cultural in a rejectionist sense, but in more positive terms as a miniature version of their notion of 'the good society', including the forms of direct and participative democracy discussed in the previous chapter.

Since the social legitimacy of the occupation at St Paul's Cathedral as a form of public protest was generally positive, critics attempted to undercut this with a neo-liberal discourse of inauthenticity that gave a contradictory account of the role of emotion in political debate. Typically, emotion is used by the press as an authentication of the deservingness of interests, newsmaking convention demanding that a just cause requires a credible victim with whose experience others can empathise (Birks 2011), and this authenticity of emotional responses to experience is contrasted with political beliefs as manipulative rhetoric (Wahl-Jorgensen 2001). The attractive thing about victims, especially for the British press with its tradition of campaigning advocacy, is that they are passive and vulnerable and in need of the newspaper to step in as 'the people's champion' (Birks 2011). The occupiers, by contrast, were not depicted as afraid or devastated, quite often worried or concerned, but mostly they were angry. Much of this coverage reported protesters', and indeed *public,* anger as a fact, often without comment on the political significance or otherwise of this anger, but some of the sympathetic left-leaning press did frame it as a *political* emotion – as moral outrage at injustice.

The fact that those newspapers that opposed the occupation felt that they had to resort to arguments about personal authenticity demonstrates the extent of their success. After all, this is increasingly – rightly or wrongly – the legitimising criteria applied to conventional political actors (Langer 2010). Nonetheless, the right wing press associated the occupation with *community* (and especially identity-based attachments) and therefore with communitarian obligations or insular and defensive notions of identity, rather than the liberal democratic notion of voluntary association, as well as a level of value consensus not found.

The critical coverage of the empty tent controversy highlights two connected implications about political legitimacy in civil society. On the one hand the framing measured the behaviour of protesters against a stereotype that likely (though not explicitly) drew on past occupations such as Greenham Common – that it was a full time commitment and alternative lifestyle. That Occupy LSX protesters had mainstream commitments that limited their ability to stay overnight on a permanent basis was used against them to suggest that they were not the sincere activists that they presented themselves as but mere tourists. Of course on the other hand any suggestion that they did live up to that stereotype was also taken as evidence of their insincerity, as professional protesters who actually take pleasure in counter-cultural protest as an end in itself, regardless of the apparent cause.

Because they were not passively affected, but politically active, the occupiers were regarded as suspect. Legitimate political views, for much of the press, are based on emotion, but only in the role of victimhood, not principles.

Chapter 8

Conclusion

There is much to be optimistic about in this analysis of the news representation of civil society, especially as regards the activist model. Whilst many of the traditional delegitimising frames can still be detected, there is also evidence of more sympathetic framing of even relatively radical repertoires of dissent, especially in the case of the Occupy movement. Much of this was split along ideological lines, with more favourable coverage in the left-leaning newspaper titles and more hostile framing in the conservative press, but Occupy did seem to destabilise news routines even in the latter – if only, in some cases, as a temporary discombobulation, followed by strenuous efforts to find sources to support the established frame.

Some of the shifts identified here are part of a larger trend toward a more diverse circulation of meaning as discussed by scholars such as Simon Cottle (2011), especially in terms of a shift away from a delegitimising law and order frame. Nonetheless, Occupy does seem to represent a step shift, certainly in terms of coverage of the anti-capitalist or alter-globalisation movement. That is not to say, however, that the shift is necessarily led by a change in the status of protest groups as sources – as Cottle acknowledges (2011: 23), the legitimacy attributed to dissent in civil society is part of the media 'indexing' of elite dissensus. In other words, the tone of coverage of the Occupy movement could be attributed to a shift in the opinion of elite sources and primary definers, in much the same way as growing elite dissensus over the Vietnam war shifted it into the sphere of legitimate controversy in Hallin's (1989) analysis.

The banking crisis could be read as analogous to the Tet Offensive – a prominent trigger (albeit, in both cases, part of a gradually escalating crisis) that challenged the dominant consensus. In this case, the crisis undermined assumptions that the public interest was defined by overall growth, not the distribution of its benefits, that the UK economy was heavily dependent for that growth on the finance industry so the industry's interests were the public interest, and that those interests were best served by freedom from regulation. Evidence for this includes (mildly) sympathetic noises from billionaire financier George Soros, "Bill Clinton, [Federal Reserve Chairman] Ben Bernanke, and at least one member of the Buffet family" (Malone 2011). This was reflected in specialist sections of the media such as *The Economist* and *Financial Times*, followed by the specialist correspondents of some of the more sympathetic papers.

Correspondingly, 'anti-capitalist' protesters, who had previously been located in the sphere of deviance, were also relocated to the sphere of legitimate controversy. But again, this occurred through a slight of hand by which Occupy were framed as somehow distinct, as the 'moderate alternative', as Gitlin (1980) identified, again in relation to the Vietnam war. Then, it was the apparent emergence of a mainstream anti-war movement that allowed the press to present their shift in position as a response to a change in moderate opinion, whilst continuing to delegitimise the SDS and broader New Left as a counter-cultural and increasingly confrontational 'radical' fringe, even as they conceded some of their arguments. Now, the 1990s 'anti-globalisation' movement would be analogous to the SDS, with Occupy representing the 'respectable' middle classes.

More particularly, in relation to the Occupy LSX camp at St Paul's Cathedral, the role of the Canon Chancellor, Dr Giles Fraser was almost certainly pivotal in the early framing of the story. In asking the police to leave, he signalled to the press that there would be no confrontation between host and occupiers (although this changed over time, the Dean's later statement was framed in relation to that initial welcome), and also offered a novel angle, with 'unexpectedness' as a news value replacing 'consonance' (or 'expectedness'), where news is framed via established routines. Similarly, in coverage of the Mark Kennedy scandal, the judge who presided over the trial of the protesters who admitted conspiring to break into the Ratcliffe on Soar power station was key to framing the planned direct action as civil disobedience, motivated by moral principle.

However, this study suggests cause only for *cautious* optimism for a number of reasons. Firstly, the shift away from a law and order framing in criminal terms has been to some extent simply replaced with a civil law framing that relies instead on a discourse of conflicting rights. Secondly, the shift away from a framing of violence and illegality should not necessarily be read as indicative of an increase in political legitimacy. In particular, whilst attention is drawn to the issues in contention, and protesters have a much greater voice than has previously been supposed, the protesters' framing of the issues does not dominate the news framing. Thirdly, and connectedly, protesters are still delegitimised (in the conservative press) in personal and social terms, especially as too emotional to be rationally dispassionate, and simultaneously but contradictorily as insufficiently authentic as legitimate victims. Finally, the role of values in political debate is portrayed in a confused and contradictory manner that serves more often to close down debate than to open it up to an interrogation of our aspirations for the good society.

From legal delegitimisation to a discourse of conflicting rights

Despite the persistent presence of moral outrage at 'violent' protest involving property damage, there was enough support for the Millbank occupiers to provoke a discourse of 'condemning' versus 'condoning' violence in sections of the conservative press, but the most notable shift in the representation of protest repertoires was toward a more subtle delimitation of the right to protest. This was particularly aimed at the growing social acceptability of occupation as a central part of protest repertoires, with political leaders complaining that the right to protest did not include the right to disrupt other people's right to go about their daily lives, or even to impinge on their consciousness. The counter-assertion of rights claims is increasingly commonly pursued through the courts.

The shift toward civil action against protest is an insidious move, and one that looks set to escalate. More recently, power company EDF has threatened to sue direct action protesters No Dash For Gas for damages for their occupation of West Burton power station. This is intended as a deterrent to dissent, but it also asserts corporate rights to act as they wish (within the letter of the law), with corporate social responsibility impinging only on their PR budgets. Of course this is not entirely new, and the *McLibel* case may be a cautionary tale for corporations threatening civil action. Conversely, the civil case brought by UK UnCut Legal Action against Her Majesty's Revenue and Customs (HMRC) to challenge an alleged tax deal made with Goldman Sachs suggests a new initiative by protest organisations to turn the tables and challenge the behaviour of the powerful in legal terms.[1]

The discourse of rights was less frequently or broadly mobilised *in favour of* protesters. In the Mark Kennedy story, environmental activists' right to a private life was only taken seriously by the left-leaning press, with other commentators transfixed by a notion of spying informed more by popular culture than politics. The broader democratic legitimacy of this kind of police surveillance *was*, however, taken very seriously, even in the right-wing papers, but the disproportionality of long-term infiltration was based on the protesters being 'fluffy', which does not suggest political seriousness.

Political legitimacy and definitional power

It is significant that commentators did address the issues raised by the protesters, in that there was a surprising amount of discussion of equality and social justice. Occupy LSX, in particular, prompted significant discussion of deregulation as a cause of the economic crisis and the disproportionate impact on the least wealthy. However, the coverage was rather more focused on the banking bailout – the point on which there had been greatest elite dissensus – and framed more in terms of punishment of greedy individuals than any kind of structural challenge to unconstrained capitalism. Furthermore, it was the public sector union strike that generated the greatest volume of discussion on equality, justice and fairness, and in that case 'the 99%' were firmly turned against one another. The pensions issue defined fairness in terms of utilitarian cost and reward, and predominantly (though far from exclusively) as a squabble between taxpayers working in the private sector and public sector workers making demands on them.

---

1   Although ultimately unsuccessful in those terms, since they lost the case, and claimed a PR victory instead: http://ukuncutlegalaction.org.uk/2013/05/uk-uncut-legal-case-exposes-political-embarrassment-behind-goldmans-tax-deal/.

Protesters' inability to define the terms of the debate was related to the limited political legitimacy they were accorded. For the most part, they were not portrayed as politically competent in the analysis of the problem and its solutions. Inevitably, the student protesters were portrayed as politically naïve and not engaging with economic reality, but they were also patronised and belittled as merely playing at politics and political violence. Occupy LSX were criticised for refusing to coalesce around a single agenda, which was framed as a failure to advocate solutions rather than as part of a legitimate process of open-minded deliberative debate. In contrast, the clear agenda advanced by the public sector unions through a conventional structure of leadership and accountability was delegitimised as the manipulative and unrepresentative advancement of sectional interests. At the same time, the Pope's political objections to human rights law on the basis of injured identity were treated more sympathetically than not. Models of political legitimacy are therefore selectively and strategically used to delegitimise and dismiss protesters' specific agenda, even where they are accommodated as exercising a legally legitimate protest repertoire.

Personal and social legitimacy as the emotional authenticity of the passive victim

The delegitimisation of protesters in personal terms should be understood in the context of the personalisation of politics more broadly, as part of a shift towards political leaders establishing their ability to represent the interests and priorities of the people with reference to their private life experience and emotional responses (Langer 2010). Where political elites need to establish that they are not remote from the experience of 'ordinary people', those on the political periphery need to establish that they are not remote from mainstream values and beliefs. However, for protesters it is more likely for their politics to damage their personal legitimacy (as passive victims) than for their personal authenticity to authenticate their politics.

Whilst Occupy is part of a long tradition of anti-global capital or alter-globalisation movement, and connected to a countercultural identity that runs as a common thread through many contemporary social movements, that does not necessarily mean that we should understand it as a project identity that has arisen from a resistance identity (Castells 2010). Indeed you could argue that the political commitment came first, especially for those first time protesters who were not already part of a network of activism, and that the resistance identity emerged from the experience of the camp. However, for conservative critics such solidarity was portrayed as a lack of political seriousness, and any joy and camaraderie taken as evidence of protest motivated by its own social and (counter)cultural rewards.

The relationship between public and private is a complex and contradictory one. On the one hand, even Habermas (1996) argues that the motivations and authenticity of contributors to the public sphere must be scrutinised, so as to exclude powerful, manipulative and self-serving interests, but on the other hand this would seem to shift the focus from policy to personality and to assume that citizens' role is simply to choose representatives that reflect their own personal experience and qualities. Habermas' notion of civil society as an antenna for social problems, raising issues from experience in the lifeworld and translating them into publicly-acceptable reasons in the public sphere, creates a confusing situation whereby civil society actors are judged by the legitimating criteria of both the public and private spheres.

Judgements on authenticity are particularly problematic, with protesters judged to be authentically emotionally affected but politically passive, but also politically-motivated and therefore inauthentic and insincere. The dominant framing would seem to locate civil society within the private sphere, therefore regarding anger as bringing inappropriate feelings and attributes into the public sphere, but also the specific anger at injustice as bringing inappropriate politics into the personal realm. This is related to the notion, more common in the US, that political dispute among private individuals is impolite and *uncivil*. This is especially common in a context where political argumentation draws heavily on rights claims based on injured identity, with a focus on recognition and, especially, on offence, which can function to close down debate, or conversely to disrupt any notion of rights at all being meaningful.

Values as a problem for democracy

The discourse of conflicting rights – not least the exclusion of intolerance from civil society, painted as itself intolerant – seems designed to make the whole system collapse under the weight of its own contradictions. This is not helped by the tendency of those asserting rights to talk past each other, assuming either that a rights claim is a decisive trump card, or failing to recognise the different kinds of rights and their different logical bases, so that advocates of negative liberties on a utilitarian or ends-oriented basis can't see the value of positive freedoms of inclusion or empowerment, or misinterpret them in the frame of their own conceptual categories.

The absence of any political framework for discussing and debating the values of the good society, as opposed to asserting and counter-asserting them, has motivated a form of political communication that accepts the competitive model. One way of disrupting the dominance of neo-liberal values as common sense is to attempt to assert a counter-hegemony on the same rhetorical ground, using "wild public screens" (DeLuca et al. 2011). Whilst spectacular image events may to some extent be gaining acceptance as well as attention, it is difficult to see how this could resolve the value differences of a multicultural society. The challenges of negotiating social and political values in civil society, however, require that civil society itself remains a diverse space that is open to contestation.

Bibliography

Ackerman, Seth (2000). 'Prattle in Seattle: Media Coverage Misrepresented the Protest' in Kevin Danaher and Roger Burbach (eds.) *Globalize This!* Monroe, ME: Common Courage Press, pp. 59–63

Anderson, Benedict (1983). *Imagined Communities*. London: Verso

Badiou, Alain (2012). *The Rebirth of History: The Times of Riots and Uprisings*. London: Verso

Baynes, Kenneth (2002). 'Deliberative Democracy and the Limits of Liberalism' in Rene von Schomberg and Kenneth Baynes (eds.) *Discourse and Democracy: Essays on Habermas's Between Facts and Norms*. Albany, NY: State University Press, pp. 15–26

Becker, Howard (1967). 'Whose Side are We On?' in *Social Problems* 14(3): 234–47

Berezin, Mabel (2002). 'Secure States: Towards a Political Sociology of Emotion' in Jack Barbalet (ed.) *Sociology and Emotions*. London: Basil Blackwell: pp. 33–52

Berman, Marshall (1971). *The Politics of Authenticity: Radical Individualism and the Emergence of Modern Society*. London: George Allen & Unwin Ltd

Billig, Michael (1995). *Banal Nationalism*. London: Sage

Birks, Jen (2010). 'Press Protest and Publics: The Agency of Publics in Newspaper Campaigns' in *Discourse and Communication* 4(1): 51–67

Birks, Jen (2011). 'The Politics of Protest in Newspaper Campaigns: Dissent, Populism and the Rhetoric of Authenticity' in *British Politics* 6(2): 128–54

Bivens, Rena (2008) 'The Internet, Mobile Phones and Blogging: How New Media is Transforming Traditional Journalism' in *Journalism Practice* 2(1): 113–29

Bourdieu, Pierre (1979 [1972]). 'Public Opinion Does Not Exist' in Armand Mattelart and Seth Siegelaub (eds.) *Communication and Class Struggle*. New York: International General, pp. 124–9

Bringer, Joy D., Lynne H. Johnston, and Celia H. Brackenridge (2006). 'Using Computer-Assisted Qualitative Data Analysis Software to Develop a Grounded Theory Project' in *Field Methods* 18(3): 1–21

Bryant, Christopher G. A. (1995). 'Civic Nation, Civil Society, Civil Religion' in John A. Hall (ed.) *Civil Society*. Cambridge: Polity, pp. 136–54

Castells, Manuel (2010). *The Power of Identity: Economy, Society and Identity*. Chichester: Wiley-Blackwell

Castells, Manuel (2012). *Networks of Outrage and Hope: Social Movements in the Internet Age*. Cambridge: Polity

Cohen, Jean L. and Andrew Arato (1992). *Civil Society and Political Theory*. Cambridge, MA: MIT Press

Cohen, Joshua (2009). *Philosophy, Politics, Democracy*. Cambridge, MA: Harvard University Press

Cottle, Simon (2011). 'Transnational Protest and the Media: New Departures, Challenging Debates' in Simon Cottle and Libby Lester (eds.) *Transnational Protests and the Media*. Oxford: Peter Lang, pp. 17–102

Cottle, Simon and Libby Lester (2011a). 'Transnational Protests and the Media: An Introduction' in Simon Cottle and Libby Lester (eds.) *Transnational Protests and the Media*. Oxford: Peter Lang, pp. 3–16

Cottle, Simon and Libby Lester (2011b). 'Transnational Protests and the Media: Towards Global Civil Society' in Simon Cottle and Libby Lester (eds.) *Transnational Protests and the Media*. Oxford: Peter Lang, pp. 287–90

Crouch, David and Katarina Damjanov (2011). 'Piracy Up-linked: Sea Shepherd and the Spectacle of Protest on the High Seas' in Simon Cottle and Libby Lester (eds.) *Transnational Protests and the Media*. Oxford: Peter Lang, pp. 180–95

Curran, James (1993). 'Rethinking the Media as a Public Sphere' in Peter Dahlgren (ed.) *Communication and Citizenship: Journalism and the Public Sphere*. London: Routledge, pp. 27–56

della Porta, Donatella (1998). 'Police Knowledge and Protest Policing: Some Reflections of the Italian Case' in Donatella della Porta and Herbert Reiner (eds.) *Policing Protest: The Control of Mass Demonstrations in Western Democracies*. Minneapolis: University of Minneapolis Press, pp. 228–52

della Porta, Donatella and Herbert Reiter (1998). 'Introduction: The Policing of Protest in Western Democracies' in Donatella della Porta and Herbert Reiter (eds.) *Policing Protest: The Control of Mass Demonstrations in Western Democracies*. Minneapolis: University of Minneapolis Press, pp. 1–32

della Porta, Donatella and Mario Diani (2006). *Social Movements: An Introduction*. Malden MA, Oxford: Blackwell

DeLuca, Kevin Michael (1999). *Image Politics: The New Rhetoric of Environmental Activism*. Abingdon, Oxford: Taylor and Francis

DeLuca, Kevin Michael, Ye Sun, and Jennifer Peeples (2011). 'Wild Public Screens and Image Events from Seattle to China Using Social Media to Broadcast Activism' in Simon Cottle and Libby Lester (eds.) *Transnational Protests and the Media*. Oxford: Peter Lang, pp. 143–55

Dworkin, Ronald (1978). *Taking Rights Seriously*. London: Duckworth

Dworkin, Ronald (2011). *Justice for Hedgehogs*. Cambridge, MA: Harvard University Press

Edwards, Michael (2009). *Civil Society*. Cambridge: Polity

Eisenstadt, Shmuel (2007). 'The Resurgence of Religious Movements in the Processes of Globalisation – Beyond the End of History or the Clash of Civilisations' in Matthias Koenig and Paul de Guchteneire (eds.) *Democracy and Human Rights in Multicultural Societies*. Aldershot: Ashgate, pp. 239–50.

Elias, Norbert (1969). *The Civilizing Process*. Oxford: Blackwell

Elias, Norbert and John L. Scotson (1994 [1965]) *The Established and the Outsiders: A Sociological Enquiry into Community Problems*. London: Frank Cass & Co.

Elshtain, Jean Bethke (1997). 'The Displacement of Politics' in Jeff Weintraub and Krishnan Kumar (eds.) *Public and Private in Thought and Practice: Perspectives on a Grand Dichotomy*. Chicago, MA: University of Chicago Press, pp. 166–80

Etzioni, Amitai (2000). *The Third Way to a Good Society*. London: Demos. Available from: <http://www.demos.co.uk/publications/thethirdwaytoagood society> Accessed 18th February 2013

Etzioni, Amitai (2004). *The Common Good*. Cambridge: Polity

Feldstein, Richard (1997). *Political Correctness: A Response from the Cultural Left*. Minneapolis: University of Minnesota Press

Foucault, Michel (1980). 'Two Lectures' in Colin Gordon (ed.) *Power/Knowledge: Selected Interviews*. New York: Pantheon.

Fowler, Roger (1991). *Language in the News*. London: Routledge

Fraser, Nancy (2007). 'Transnationalising the Public Sphere: On the Legitimacy and Efficacy of Public Opinion in a Post-Westphalian World' in *Theory, Culture and Society* 24(7) DOI: 10.1177/0263276407080090

Galtung, Johan and Mari Holmboe Ruge (1965) 'The structure of foreign news: the presentation of the Congo, Cuba and Cyprus crises in four Norwegian newspapers' in *Journal of International Peace Research* 1: 64–91.

Gellner, Earnest (1995). 'The Importance of Being Modular' in John A. Hall (ed.) *Civil Society*. Cambridge: Polity, pp. 32–48.

Gitlin, Todd (1980). *The Whole World is Watching: The Making and Unmaking of the New Left*. Berkley and Los Angeles, CA: University of California Press

Glaser, B. G. and A. L. Strauss (1968) *The Discovery of Grounded Theory: Strategies for Qualitative Research*. London: Weidenfeld & Nicolson

Goffman, Erving (1959). *The Presentation of Self in Everyday Life*. Garden City, NY: Doubleday Anchor Books

Grant, Wyn (2000). *Pressure Groups and British Politics*. Basingstoke: Palgrave MacMillan

Habermas, Jurgen (1989). *The Structural Transformation of the Public Sphere*. Cambridge, MA: MIT Press

Habermas, Jurgen (1996). *Between Facts and Norms*. Cambridge: Polity / Blackwell

Habermas, Jurgen (2006). 'Pre-political Foundation of the Democratic Constitutional State?' in Florian Schuller (ed.) *Dialectics of Secularization: On Reason and Religion*. San Francisco: Ignatius Press, pp. 19–52

Hall, John A. (1995). 'In Search of Civil Society' in John A. Hall (ed.) *Civil Society*. Cambridge: Polity, pp. 1–34.

Hallin, Daniel (1989). *The Uncensored War: The Media and Vietnam*. California University Press: Los Angeles

Halloran, James D., Philip Elliot and Graham Murdock (1970). *Demonstrations and Communication: A Case Study*. Harmondsworth: Penguin

Hanisch, Carol (2006 [1969]). *The Personal is Political*. Available from: <http://www.carolhanisch.org/CHwritings/PIP.html> Accessed 1st August 2012

Hardt, Michael and Antonio Negri (2012). *Declaration*. Argo Navis

Held, David (2006). *Models of Democracy*. Cambridge: Polity

Herman, Edward S. and Noam Chomsky (1988). *Manufacturing Consent: The Political Economy of the Mass Media*. New York: Pantheon Books

HMIC (2009). *Adapting to Protest*. Available from: <http://www.hmic.gov.uk/publication/adapting-to-protest/> Accessed 4th August 2012

Joyce, Peter (2002). *The Politics of Protest*. Basingstoke: Palgrave MacMillan

Juris, Jeffrey S. (2011). 'Mediating and Embodying Transnational Protest: Internal and External Effects of Mass Global Justice Actions' in Simon Cottle and Libby Lester (eds.) *Transnational Protests and the Media*. Oxford: Peter Lang, pp. 98–108

Kaldor, Mary (2003). *Global Civil Society: An Answer to War*. Cambridge: Polity

Keane, John (1998). *Civil Society: Old Images, New Visions*. Cambridge: Polity

Kenny, Michael (2004). *The Politics of Identity: Liberal Political Theory and the Dilemmas of Difference*. Cambridge: Polity

Kiely, Ray (2005). 'Global Civil Society and Spaces of Resistance' in John Eade and Darren O'Byrne (eds.) *Global Ethics and Civil Society*. Aldershot: Ashgate, pp. 138–50.

Klein, Naomi (2001). 'The Vision Thing: Are the Protests Unfocused, Or Are Critics Missing the Point?' in Kevin Danaher (ed.) *The Battle Against the World Bank and the IMF*. Monroe, ME: Common Courage Press, pp. 145–55

Langer, Ana Ines (2010) 'The Politicization of Private Persona: Exceptional Leaders or the New Rule? The Case of the UK and the Blair Effect'. *International Journal of Press/Politics*, 15(1). pp. 60–76

Lewis and MacLeod (2005). 'Transnational Corporations: Power, Influence and Responsibility' in John Eade and Darren O'Byrne (eds.) *Global Ethics and Civil Society*. Aldershot: Ashgate, pp. 121–37

Lewis, Justin, Karin Wahl-Jorgensen, and Sanna Inthorn (2005). *Citizens or Consumers? What the Media Tell Us About Political Participation*. Maidenhead: Open University Press

Lewis, Justin, Andrew Williams and Bob Franklin (2008). 'Compromised Fourth Estate? UK News Journalism, Public Relations and News Sources' in *Journalism Studies* 9(1): 1–20

McAfee, Noelle (2000). *Habermas, Kristeva, and Citizenship*. Ithaca NY: Cornell University Press

McLeod, Douglas M. and James K. Hertog (1992). 'The Manufacture of 'Public Opinion' by Reporters: Informal Cues for Public Perception of Protest Groups' in *Discourse & Society* 3(3): 259–75

Malone, Noreen (2011). 'Why is Reuters Trying to Link George Soros to Occupy Wall Street?' in New York Magazine 13th October 2011. Available from: < http://nymag.com/daily/intelligencer/2011/10/why_is_reuters_trying_to_link.html> Accessed 23rd February 2013

Marx, Gary T. (1998). 'Afterword: Some Reflections on the Democratic Policing of Demonstrations' in Donatella della Porta and Herbert Reiner (eds.) *Policing Protest: The Control of Mass Demonstrations in Western Democracies*. Minneapolis: University of Minneapolis Press, pp. 253–69

Maus, Ingeborg (2002). 'Liberties and Popular Sovereignty: On Habermas's Reconstruction of the System of Rights' in Rene von Schomberg and Kenneth Baynes (eds.) *Discourse and Democracy: Essays on Habermas's Between Facts and Norms*. Albany, NY: State University Press, pp. 89–123

Mill, John Stuart (2003 [1869]). *On Liberty*. London: Yale University Press

Nash, Kate (2005). 'Cosmopolitan Political Community: Why Does It Feel So Right?' in John Eade and Darren O'Byrne (eds.) *Global Ethics and Civil Society*. Aldershot: Ashgate, pp. 34–43

Parekh, Bhikhu (2005). 'Principles of a Global Ethic' in John Eade and Darren O'Byrne (eds.) *Global Ethics and Civil Society*. Aldershot: Ashgate, pp. 15–31

Perez-Diaz, Victor (1995). 'The Possibility of Civil Society: Traditions, Character and Challenges' in John A. Hall (ed.) *Civil Society*. Cambridge: Polity, pp. 80–107

Philo, Greg (1990). *Seeing and Believing*. London: Routledge

Powell, Frederick (2007). *The Politics of Civil Society*. Cambridge: Polity

Price, Stuart (2007). *Discourse Power Address*. Aldershot: Ashgate

Price, Stuart (2011). *Worst Case Scenario*. London: Zed Books

Ratzinger, Joseph (2005). 'That Which Holds the World Together' in Florian Schuller (ed.) *Dialectics of Secularization: On Reason and Religion*. San Francisco: Ignatius Press, pp. 53–80

Rawls, John (1971). *A Theory of Justice*. Cambridge MA: Harvard University Press

Rawls, John (2001). *Justice as Fairness: A Restatement*. Cambridge, MA: Belknap Press

Rehg, William and James Bohman (2002). 'Discourse and Democracy: The Formal and Informal Bases of Legitimacy in between Facts and Norms' in Rene von Schomberg and Kenneth Baynes (eds.) *Discourse and Democracy: Essays on Habermas's Between Facts and Norms*. Albany, NY: State University Press, pp. 31–51

Reiner, Robert (1998). 'Policing, Protest, and Disorder in Britain' in Donatella della Porta and Herbert Reiter (eds.) *Policing Protest: The Control of Mass Demonstrations in Western Democracies*. Minneapolis: University of Minneapolis Press, pp. 35–48

Rheinfold, Howard (2002). *Smart Mobs: The Next Social Revolution*. New York: Basic Books

Riis, Ole (2007). 'Modes of Religious Pluralism under Conditions of Globalization' in Matthias Koenig and Paul de Guchteneire (eds.) *Democracy and Human Rights in Multicultural Societies*. London: Ashgate, pp. 251–66

Rojecki, Andrew (2011). 'Leaderless Crowds, Self-Organizing Publics, and Virtual Masses' in Simon Cottle and Libby Lester (eds.) *Transnational Protests and the Media*. Oxford: Peter Lang, pp. 87–97

Rowan, John R. (1999). *Conflicts of Rights: Moral Theory and Social Policy Implications*. Westminster, CO: Westfield Press

Sandel, Michael (2012). *What Money Can't Buy: The Moral Limits of Markets*. London: Penguin

Scarre, Geoffrey (1996). *Utilitarianism*. London: Routledge.

Schlesinger, Philip, David Miller, and William Dinan (2001). *Open Scotland? Lobbyists, Journalists and Spin Doctors*. Edinburgh: Edinburgh University Press

Seligman, Adam B. (1995). 'Animadversions upon Civil Society and Civic Virtue in the Last Decade of the Twentieth Century' in John A. Hall (ed.) *Civil Society*. Cambridge: Polity, pp. 201–17.

Silver, Allan (1997). '"Two Different Sorts of Commerce" – Friendship and Strangership in Civil Society' in Jeff Weintraub and Krishnan Kumar (eds.) *Public and Private in Thought and Practice: Perspectives on a Grand Dichotomy*. Chicago, MA: University of Chicago Press, pp. 43–69

Smith, Tara (1995). *Moral Rights and Political Freedom*. Lanham MD: Rowman and Littlefield.

Sokolon, Marlene (2006). *Political Emotions: Aristotle and the Symphony of Reason and Emotion*. Chicago: Northern Illinois University Press

Splichal, Slavko (2002) 'The Principle of Publicity, Public Use of Reason and Social Control' in *Media, Culture & Society* 24(1): 5–26

Taylor, Charles (1991). *The Ethics of Authenticity*. Cambridge MA: Harvard University Press

Ten, C. L. (2008). 'Mill's On Liberty: Introduction' in C. L. Ten (ed.) *Mill's On Liberty: A Critical Guide*. Cambridge: Cambridge University Press

Thorsen, Dag Einar, and Amund Lie (2010). 'What is Neoliberalism? University of Oslo' discussion paper. Available from: <folk.uio.no/daget/What%20is%20 Neo-Liberalism%20FINAL.pdf> Accessed 31st July 2012

Tocqueville, Alexis de (1835). *Democracy in America, Vol I*. New York: George Adlard

Wahl-Jorgensen, Karin (2001) 'Letters to the Editor as a Forum for Public Deliberation: Modes of Publicity and Democratic Debate' in *Critical Studies in Media Communication* 18(3): 303–20

Wahl-Jorgensen, Karin (2002a) 'The Construction of the Public in Letters to the Editor: Deliberative Democracy and the Idiom of Insanity' in *Journalism* 3(2): 183–204

Wahl-Jorgensen, Karin (2002b) 'Understanding the Conditions for Public Discourse: four rules for selecting letters to the editor.' *Journalism Studies* 3(1): 69

Weintraub, Jeff (1997). 'The Theory and Politics of the Public / Private Distinctions' in Jeff Weintraub, Jeff and Krishnan Kumar (eds.) *Public and Private in Thought and Practice: Perspectives on a Grand Dichotomy*. Chicago, MA: University of Chicago Press, pp. 1–38

Whitehouse, Lisa (2005). 'The Global Compact: Corporate Citizenship in Actions, But is it Enough?' in John Eade and Darren O'Byrne (eds.) *Global Ethics and Civil Society*. Aldershot: Ashgate, pp. 108–20

Widdows (2005). 'Global Ethics: Foundations and Methodologies' in John Eade and Darren O'Byrne (eds.) *Global Ethics and Civil Society*. Aldershot: Ashgate, pp. 74–86.

Wilson, John K. (1995). *The Myth of Political Correctness: The Conservative Attack on Higher Education*. Durham, NC: Duke University Press

Wolfe, Alan (1997). 'Public and Private in Theory and Practice: Some Implications' in Jeff Weintraub and Krishnan Kumar (eds.) *Public and Private in Thought and Practice: Perspectives on a Grand Dichotomy*. Chicago, MA: University of Chicago Press, pp. 182–99

Index

For Product Safety Concerns and Information please contact our EU
representative GPSR@taylorandfrancis.com Taylor & Francis Verlag GmbH,
Kaufingerstraße 24, 80331 München, Germany

Printed and bound by CPI Group (UK) Ltd, Croydon, CR0 4YY

01/05/2025

01858359-0004